Glorious Kingdom

A Handbook for Partial Preterist Eschatology

Stan Newton

Glorious Kingdom
A Handbook for Partial Preterist Eschatology
By Stan Newton

Copyright © 2012 by Dr. Stan Newton
ISBN 978-1-61529-047-5
Vision Publishing
1672 Main St. E 109
Ramona, CA 92065
1-800-9-VISION
www.booksbyvision.com

All rights reserved worldwide

All rights in this book are reserved worldwide. No part of this book may be reproduced in any manner whatsoever without the written permission of the author except brief quotations embodied in critical articles or reviews.

"Unless otherwise indicated, all Scripture quotations are from the Holy Bible, English Standard Version, copyright 2001 by Crossway Bibles, a publishing ministry of Good News Publishers. Used by permission."

Dedication

To my two sons, Chad and Joel; who grew up hearing the principles of God's Kingdom and now are putting them into practice.

Table of Contents

Introduction

Eschatology is the study of "the last things." Traditionally, eschatology studies only future events; but recent popular and scholarly studies are challenging this assumption. The first century is replacing the 21st as the most eschatological significant generation. When we view eschatology primarily in light of future events, it fails to account for the New Testament time texts where the coming of the Messiah is connected with "eschatological events." The incarnation of Jesus began a generation where the nation of Israel and the followers of Jesus experienced eschatology first hand. The first century is where the kingdom of God and eschatology meet; it is the "end of all things" and the dawn of a "new creation."

After decades of studying eschatology, I am convinced of two basic truths. First, the central message of eschatology is not the future Second Coming, coming famines or earthquakes, nor is it the antichrist or any future event. The main theme of eschatology is the kingdom of God. This should adjust our thinking from "going to heaven when we die" to fervently praying the Lord's Prayer, *"your kingdom come, your will be done, on earth as it is in heaven* (Matt. 6:10)." Second, the contour of eschatology comes not from the events in our time but events in the first-century. The events of two-thousand years ago are the context of many eschatological passages found in the New Testament. I believe the Scripture supports these two propositions, which is the premise of this book.

Glorious Kingdom is written with the conviction that a partial preterist hermeneutic is necessary to understand eschatology. Partial preterists take seriously the time issues as presented throughout the pages of our New Testament. By properly locating the timing issues of prophecy, partial preterism opens the door to a victorious view of the future. Our first step toward victorious eschatology is placing the inauguration of God's kingdom at Jesus' first advent. Jesus said the kingdom is "at hand" and it was.This kingdom movement of Jesus is the same kingdom prophesied by the Hebrew prophets. It should not surprise us that the kingdom language used in the New Testament comes from the background of Hebrew expectations. All the prophets spoke of it; and now it is here. Centering eschatology on the incarnation and first century events differs from many popular books on "end times" which sees the kingdom as being future and dependent upon the second coming of Christ. The kingdom of God came on earth with Jesus' first coming, not some future coming.

The word eschatology means the last of something (literally the study of the eschaton), therefore we must ask, "What is ending?" Over the previous generation many evangelicals have told us, "The world is ending" or "The church age is ending." Was this the position of the early apostles? No! The apostles understood that the old covenant and its temple worship were ending. The physical world was not ending; the old covenant entered its last days. Our world is not ending! The church is not coming to its end! This fits with how Peter saw things when he wrote the *"end of all things is at hand"* (I Peter 4:7). Peter and other New Testament authors use end of the world language to show that the old covenant and its worship practices were marked for destruction. The first generation of Christians witnessed the old covenant fading away and some lived long enough to see its abrupt end with the destruction of Jerusalem and the Temple.

Jewish eschatology, at the time of Jesus, foresaw a time of great trials and tribulation that would precede the ushering in of God's kingdom. Therefore, any kingdom-centered eschatology must consider the place of "tribulation" as seen in the New Testament. Using a partial-preterists[1] interpretation connects these elements. A partial preterists hermeneutic clarifies the role of Jesus as the eschatological prophet who not only ushers in the kingdom, but also ignites the flames of tribulation that precede it. Jesus said that some listening to his voice would not die before the *"Son of Man comes in kingdom (Matt. 16:28)."* What was he referring to in this passage? When Jesus spoke these words, he alluded to a

---

[1] See Appendix 1

future manifestation of the kingdom that would come within a generation. These words of Jesus are often ignored because it presents exegetical nightmares for those teaching a future kingdom that has not arrived even after waiting 2,000 years.

The goal of this book is to examine Scriptural passages dealing with eschatology and show how this re-centering is both necessary and biblical. It is necessary because the church needs a biblical foundation for its goal of transformation. If this "kingdom-centered" eschatology is found to be biblical, then a theology that reflects it must be affirmed. At the end of the day, the reader must choose for themselves, does the Bible place the center of eschatology in the first century or a future one. The student of the Bible must apply solid hermeneutical rules and allow the Holy Spirit to lead them.

As a handbook for partial-preterism, my hope is that students of the word of God are challenged to pursue further studies. We are only beginning the development of this important eschatological view. Over time, much will be added (or subtracted) from what is written here. Future students of the biblical text will advance these meager first steps and create an eschatological environment where the present kingdom of God and the events of 70 A.D. are no longer ignored, but accepted as a mainstream theological position.

This book aims at students with previous foundational teaching in eschatology, accomplished either through formal classroom instruction or through self-study. If this is not the case, first read Appendix 1 to become familiar with the basic terms.

Chapter 1

Challenging Evangelical Tradition

Evangelical doctrines of the end times have been suspect for decades. The foundation of these "end time" teachings is dispensationalism, and it is quickly breaking apart. For over a century, pastors and Bible teachers told faithful believers that Jesus is coming soon. Life as we know it is quickly ending. World conditions will progressively get worse. Finally, a man will manipulate the political and religious systems and gain power in the word; he is the antichrist. Yet, despite these dire predictions, Christians should not fear. Jesus will rapture the saints before the real trouble, the great tribulation. If this scenario sounds familiar, it is because this "dispensational eschatology" has been the most prominent teaching in our generation.

The kingdom of God is the missing link for understanding biblical eschatology. Many Evangelicals endorse dispensational eschatology. It derives not from the "great tradition" based on the Protestant Reformation-16th century- but the Evangelical tradition from the 19th century. The dispensational view of eschatology postpones God's kingdom to a future time. Postponing the kingdom fractures the relationship between the kingdom that arrived with Jesus and eschatology.

Dispensational eschatology teaches the "rapture." The "rapture" is not the second coming of Christ, but a secret coming that precedes it. Christians are taken to heaven for a period of seven years and then they return to earth. During these seven years, the earth endures the "great tribulation" where a possible four billion people or more are killed in the judgment of God. The "rapture" mentality has frozen the church. We retreated from long-term goals because the clock of eschatology is ticking; and it is almost midnight. Most dispensational plans for the future build around a five to ten year period. It creates an escapist theology, which devastates the church's desire for cultural transformation.

Nevertheless, things are changing. Even though the rapture still captures the attention of many, it is losing ground, practically and biblically.

Jay Rogers provides some historical perspective on the modern day "rapture" teaching.

> "Are you pre-trib, mid-trib or post-trib?" This is too often the entire scope of eschatological debate among today's Christians. Dispensational premillennialism is the view of most 21st century evangelical Christians. Indeed, most would be surprised to discover that the great figures of the Christian faith, such as Athanasius, Augustine, Luther, Calvin, Wesley, wrote absolutely nothing on the "rapture" nor the "seven year tribulation." Such ideas were foreign to them. Dispensational eschatology, with its elaborate prophecy charts and theories on the "mark of the Beast," appeared on the scene as recently as 1830. Yet it did not become a prevailing view until the beginning of the 20th century."[2]

As we move through the Bible, it is necessary to keep in mind how the kingdom of God is linked with a future Messiah (from the Old Testament perspective), and how a "coming of the son of man" is linked to the full realization of the kingdom (a New Testament perspective). Dispensationalism is correct in connecting a coming of Jesus with the coming of the kingdom, what they miss is the time element; which is, the arrival of the kingdom of God was in the first century based upon the ministry of Jesus. This relationship between Jesus and the kingdom is significant for building a biblical and practical eschatology.

The eschatology presented here centers around Jesus and his kingdom. Instead of being rapture centered, it is kingdom centered. Instead of focusing on the 21st century, it centers on the first

---

[2] Jay Rogers, Rebuttal to Dispensational Premillennialism, WWW.forerunner.com/eschatology/X004-4, 2008

century. Instead of being defeatist and escapist, it is victorious and transformational. At the current stage of development, this view of eschatology has various names. Since the debate continues, its final terminology is yet to be determined. Christians in traditional Protestant churches refer to this view as postmillennialism, optimistic amillennialism or realized eschatology. Those in Pentecostal/charismatic churches call it dominion theology, optimistic ends times or victorious eschatology. In addition, the term "partial-preterist" is catching on and may be the one term that unites us. "Victorious Kingdom" or "Glorious Kingdom" can be added to the list, since advancing the kingdom is a primary consideration. A single term may be allusive, but a fresh emphasis upon the present and growing kingdom is catching the attention of many.

Although there are differences within these various terms, they share two important elements of eschatology. First, the kingdom of God was established with the first coming of Christ; and second, the kingdom of God will advance and grow in the earth until the knowledge of the glory of God covers the earth (Habakkuk 2:14). Our task is to review the pertinent biblical literature pertaining to eschatology and draw conclusions from biblical exegesis, not from our tradition or presuppositions.

A common mistake in studying eschatology is beginning with the book of Revelation. Dispensationalists teach John's book is a prophecy about our future; therefore, it seems to be the logical place to start; but it is not. Eschatology appears in every book of the Bible; therefore, Revelation must fit with the rest of Scripture. It cannot stand as a single voice. Since the Bible has one divine author, the entire Word of God will be in harmony.[3] Eschatology is not just a study of how "everything ends" but concerns the overall purpose of why God sent his Son to earth. The book of Revelation is important; nevertheless, its content must be seen in light of the entire Scripture.

---

[3] Keith A. Mathison, From Age to Age, P&R Publishing, 2009, Phillipsburg, New Jersey, p.4

Another mistake of dispensationalists is thinking their view is the exclusive position of Evangelicals. When presenting a seminar on eschatology, I often get the same question, "Why have I not heard this before?" After inquiring about their church background, the answer is easy; people from a Pentecostal/charismatic, Baptist, or other conservative evangelical churches have a common history. This common history links them to a common eschatology, which is dispensationalism. What is not well known is that there are many conservative Christians holding other views. Another assumption dispensationalists make is claiming that differences in eschatology derive from a liberal or conservative view of Scripture. They claim a literal interpretation of the Bible leads to dispensationalism, while other views use allegory to interpret eschatology. This argument fails under investigation. Both dispensationalists and non-dispensationalists use the, "grammatical-historical" method of biblical interpretation. Differences come from the application, not the method of hermeneutics.

A Brief History of Dispensationalism

In the first few decades of the 19th century, many Christians in England were separating from the national church. They felt the Church of England had become cold and excessively formal. Among these separatists was a group known as the Plymouth Brethren. One of its leaders was a man named John Nelson Darby.

John Darby was born in 1800 in London. He studied law and received his B.A. degree from Trinity College of Dublin. Darby then changed his plans and began ministerial studies, and in 1826, he was ordained to the Anglican priesthood. While serving a parish in Ireland, he became dissatisfied with the formality of the Anglican Church. Darby left Ireland and traveled to Oxford. During his stay, he attended home meetings hosted by the wealthy Lady Powerscourt. In these meetings, Darby found answers to what was troubling him. After his stay in Oxford, he moved to Plymouth and joined the Plymouth Brethren.

While living in Plymouth, Darby received a large inheritance from his uncle. With significant financial resources, Darby began publishing his new teaching. His teaching spread across England, Europe, and then to the United States, where his new doctrine would find rich soil.

Among historians, there is disagreement as to exactly who first spoke of a "secret rapture." Was it Darby, at the home meetings of Lady Powerscourt? Dave Macpherson, in writing the history of dispensationalism believes that it was Margaret McDonald. She was an Irvingite who first mentioned the rapture during a vision that she had. We may never know the exact beginning of the "rapture teaching."

What is beyond dispute is the influence of John Darby in carrying the dispensational message around the world. Darby died in England in 1882, by this time there were over 700 Plymouth Brethren congregations following his teachings.

The father of American dispensationalism is James H. Brookes. Born in 1830, he went on to attend Princeton Seminary. In 1858, Brookes arrived in St. Louis, Missouri. During his stay in St. Louis, he met John Darby, although there is little knowledge of the extent of their relationship. While Brookes began writing and teaching "Darby's dispensationalism," he never mentioned or gave any credit to Darby. With this new understanding of the Bible, Brookes began to gather young men to his home for Bible study. One of the young men studying under Brookes was Cyrus Ingerson Scofield. In today's Christian circles, few know the name of James H. Brookes, but nobody has forgotten C.I. Scofield.

C.I. Scofield was born in 1843 in the state of Tennessee. He served in the confederate army in the Civil War. After the war, he went to Law School and became a lawyer in Kansas. While in Kansas, he served in the State House of Representatives. After a few years, he moved to St. Louis to start a private law practice. In St. Louis, he became a Christian and began to study the Bible. In 1879, he began attending the home meetings conducted by Brookes. After many months of study with Brookes, Scofield moved to Dallas, Texas and became the Pastor of a Congregational

Church. By 1885, he published his first book describing dispensational teaching, <u>Rightly Dividing the Word of Truth</u>. The book was a great success and Scofield became a popular Bible Conference speaker across the United States.

In 1902, Scofield began his most ambitious project, publishing a Bible with his personal notes. This project proved to be very costly, and Scofield looked to men of the Plymouth Brethren to assist with the publication of his Bible. Four men are responsible for the financing of the Scofield Reference Bible, they were Alwyn Ball Jr., John Pirie, John B. Buss, and Francis B. Fitch, and all were Plymouth Brethren.[4]

Most current dispensational writers trace their history to C.I. Scofield, not wanting to credit Darby. Charles Ryrie, in his book, "<u>Dispensationalism Today</u>"[5] admits to the influence of John Darby, "There is no question that the Plymouth Brethren, of which John Nelson Darby (1800-1882) was a leader, had much to do with the systematizing and promoting of Dispensationalism." Ryrie makes a statement that I agree with wholeheartedly, "After all, the ultimate question is not, is dispensationalism- or any other teaching- historic? But, is it Scriptural?"[6] Since there is little that I agree with in Ryrie's book, I will give him credit on this statement. History, good or bad, is not our final authority. History helps us understand the biblical context, but determining Christian doctrine and truth is exclusively the domain of Holy Scripture.

What is dispensationalism? Now that we have a slice of its history, what are the main tenets of their teachings? The term "dispensational" comes from their divisions of history. Their insistence is that God deals with His people for a season (a dispensation) and after man has failed, God judges and begins a new dispensation. C.I. Scofield divides biblical history into seven dispensations, although others have six or eight ages, Scofield is

---

4 Macpherson, Dave, The Incredible Cover-Up: The True Story on the Pre-Trib Rapture, Plainfield, New Jersey, Logos International, 1975.

5 Charles Caldwell Ryrie, Dispensationalism Today, 1965, Moody Press, Chicago, Illinois, page 7

6 Ibid, page 67

the standard. You have probably seen his chart of dispensations in various books and Bibles. His seven time periods are, the age of Innocence, Conscience, Human Government, Promise, Law, Grace (called the church age), and the Kingdom (called the millennium).

Dispensational theology builds upon two basic tenants, the separation of Israel and the Church, (which is the reason for the two-second comings of Christ) and their teachings of the Kingdom (which does not begin until after the second of the two comings of Christ). With the first teaching, we receive the popular belief of the "rapture." Ryrie says, "The essence of dispensationalism then is the distinction between Israel and the Church."[7] He then explains why this distinction is important to the dispensational teaching of the "rapture," "The distinction between Israel and the church leads to the belief that the Church will be taken from the earth before the beginning of the tribulation (which in one major sense concerns Israel)."[8] For the dispensationalists, there must be a "rapture" of Christians so the tribulation can then begin. The rapture teaching did not grow naturally out of the Scripture, but came after theological assumptions were already in place. The assumption that the Bible always keeps Israel and the church as separate people is the primary reason for the doctrine of the rapture.

The second major tenet of dispensationalism claims the postponement of the Kingdom of God. God's kingdom now awaits the Second Coming for its entrance into the earth. When Jesus preached the "kingdom of God is at hand" it was a genuine offer; but it was rejected. Jesus' kingdom offer was rescinded when Jesus ascended back to heaven. Instead of bringing about the kingdom on earth, God established "the church." This strict separation of the church from the kingdom is the foundation of dispensationalism and is the reason for many of the problems we have in eschatology.

---

[7] Charles Caldwell Ryrie, Dispensationalism Today, 1965, Moody Press, Chicago, Illinois, page 47

[8] Ibid, page 159

When the second revision of the "Scofield Study Bible" was published in 1917 (first release in 1909), the time was ripe for a new view of God's purposes. Since then, it has essentially become the exclusive eschatology of fundamentalism. Synonymous with dispensational theology, the Scofield Bible has probably done more to spread the cause of dispensationalism than any other entity.[9] By 1917, the optimism of previous generations had eroded with World War I. The mood of the world was darker, and Christians interpreted this as a sign of God's impending judgment. Scofield taught the world is facing judgment by a soon coming tribulation, but added a new feature; the "rapture" of the church. This "rapture" would remove Christians from the earth before the start of the tribulation. During this time, numerous Bible Schools were established and most adopted this new dispensational view of eschatology. Soon multitudes of new preachers were teaching the doctrines of Darby and Scofield. Conferences with "prophetic themes" became popular as places where believers would go and hear the latest news about "end times" revelations. In addition, many Christian publishing houses filled the need of these Christians by printing books by dispensational teachers.

Major Points of Dispensational Eschatology

1. The church and Israel are distinct people-Israel is God's earthly people and the church is God's heavenly people. They have separate callings and promises.

2. The age of the church is between the first and second coming of Christ, whereas the kingdom age begins after the Second Coming. They are different ages. The kingdom is future, not present in this age.

3. We presently live in the final generation before Jesus returns, called in Scripture the "last days." The last days

---

[9] Peter Laitres, Scofield Reference Bible, www.megalink.net

are approximately 40 years, and they began in 1948 or 1967.10

4. Seven years before the Second Coming, the "rapture" takes place. The rapture is when Christians meet the Lord in the air and return to heaven.

5. After the "rapture" and before the Second Coming the "great tribulation" occurs on earth, with as many as four billion people being killed.

6. No Old Testament Scripture or prophecy is being fulfilled in or by the church. The Old Testament promises are for Israel; not the church. Even the new covenant prophesied by Jeremiah is not fulfilled by the church, but is exclusively for the nation of Israel.

7. Following the great tribulation, Jesus sets up his 1,000-year millennial kingdom in Jerusalem and rules the world from a newly built temple. At this time, the promises and covenant of the Old Testament are fulfilled. Millennial worship will include the sacrifice of animals.

The dispensational argument claims a consistent literal interpretation. Advocates stress this literal approach separates them from other eschatological systems. Nevertheless, is this true? What does it mean to interpret the Bible literally; is that even possible? Is Jesus a real door? On the other hand, is the door a symbol for entering salvation?" Is Jesus the literal "light of the world?" Or is he a moral and spiritual light? Does Jesus really have seven stars in his hands? Words in Scripture have the same meaning as in normal literature; therefore, the style of writing needs to be determined.

---

[10] 1948 is when Israel became a nation. Since a biblical generation is forty years, 1967 has replaced the original date. In 1967, Israel captured the old city. The problem with this method of interpretation is time has ran out on both dates. Dispensational eschatology now must stretch the meaning of 'generation' or find a new starting point for the beginning of the 'last days."

Study Questions

1. What is the missing element in many eschatological studies? Why should it be included?

2. According to "Dispensational Eschatology," explain the difference between the rapture and the second coming of Christ?

3. What are the different names given to a kingdom centered eschatology and the two important points in which they agree?

4. Who was John Darby and what new doctrine did he add to historic eschatology?

5. The essence of dispensationalism is the separation of Israel and the church. Explain this view and provide three Scriptures that help prove or disprove it.

Chapter 2

A Kingdom Centered Eschatology

The view of eschatology endorsed and presented here begins not in the 19th century, but with the apostles and early church fathers. Kingdom eschatology is not new. Dispensational Premillennialism also claims an early beginning. A few church fathers taught a premillennial[11] view of eschatology but beyond that, there is no trace of dispensationalism. Early support for a victorious kingdom view does exist and some evidence points to a preterists interpretation. We begin by listing the major points of the victorious kingdom view.

Major Points of Victorious Kingdom View

1. The church is the new people of God, made up of Jews and Gentiles, by the cross of Jesus the two groups become one new man.

2. The church and the kingdom occupy the same time. Both begin with the first coming of Jesus and continue without end. The Bible never teaches a "church age." We are the church and we live in the age of the kingdom. In the future, at the resurrection and general judgment the Father receives kingdom from Christ. Even though this brings about certain changes in the kingdom, the majority of Scriptures talk about the "everlasting kingdom."

3. The "last days" were the ending days of the old covenant era. All the events of the last days occurred in the first century.

---

[11] Premillennial eschatology teaches a single Second Coming followed by a 1,000-year millennium kingdom. All Dispensationalists are premillennial but not all premillennialists are dispensational.

4. There is no "secret rapture" seven years before the second coming of Christ.

5. The "great tribulation" prophesied by Jesus occurred in the first century. It was the final covenantal judgment against unbelieving Israel. The major component was the destruction of Jerusalem and the temple.

6. The church presently fulfills promises made in the Old Testament, including prophesies concerning the kingdom of God and the new covenant.

7. The church lives in the kingdom now. The kingdom of God will be victorious in time and space, in the earth. There is no need for a new temple in Jerusalem neither will animal sacrifices ever be accepted by God. Nations become followers of Jesus, his enemies made a footstool, and the knowledge of the glory of God will cover the earth. The purposes of God include the renewal and transformation of the earth, not its destruction.

The differences between these two systems of eschatology are sharp. There is little ground in the middle. It is similar to those that believe speaking in tongues is of the devil and those who believe it is of the Holy Spirit; choose one or the other. People must decide for themselves what they believe. Likewise, with eschatology we must study the word of God and take our stand. As with all doctrines, we maintain our beliefs with conviction but without arrogance. Our journey in the word of God is a humble process of diligent study, prayer, and help from the Spirit. There will be occasions where we admit we were wrong, and make corrections. This is not defeat; but shows integrity of mind and heart to follow what we currently believe to be the teachings of the word.

With these points in mind, we began our study of Scripture. Throughout various chapters, points of both views are considered. As an example, point number one is considered under the subject of the Abrahamic covenant; since the main point speaks to the issue of who are the inheritors of the promises made to Abraham.

Biblical doctrine depends upon sound exegesis and hermeneutics. Currently there is too much speculation in the study of eschatology; Christians must return to basic principles of biblical interpretation. Exegesis is determining the meaning of the original text. Hermeneutics is how we apply the meaning to our current times. When the Apostle John says, *"Children, it is the last hour"* (I John 2:18), "What does John mean? Moreover, what did it mean to those reading John's letter? According to biblical scholar Gordon Fee, "a text cannot mean what it never could have meant to its author or his or her readers."[12] Therefore, John does not refer to some distance future, but was using the term, "last hour" in speaking of the day he and his readers were living.

Everyone studying the Bible has doctrinal bias and assumptions. More often, instead of exegesis we engage in eisegesis (reading into the Scripture). Our goal must be to allow each passage to flow in its natural path and refrain from forcing it into a text in a foreign direction. Doctrines must come out from the Scriptures, not forced into them. Good exegetes follow basic rules.

Victorious Kingdom

1. Scripture interprets Scripture

   This is a standard rule for good exegesis and proper hermeneutics. Our first step in understanding and applying a text is to allow the whole of Scripture to help shed light on the text we are reading.

2. Context and literary style are necessary to interpret Scripture.

   The Bible is literature inspired by God. Accordingly, our interpretation of Scripture follows common principles as

---

[12] Gordon D. Fee, Douglas Stuart, How to Read the Bible for All Its Worth, Zondervan, Grand Rapids, Michigan, 2003, page 74

in other literature. Knowing the difference between doctrinal prose, poetic psalms, Hebrew parallelism and apocalyptic writings is critical for understanding and applying the biblical text.

3. The author's original intent is primary, not our theology.

This is not easy, as everyone tends to bring their own preconceived doctrines into the text instead of letting their doctrines come out of the text. Nevertheless, we must be diligent and discipline ourselves as we study God's word.

4. The church fulfills Old Testament prophecies.

The church by type, shadow and direct prophecy are prominent throughout the pages of the Old Testament. The church is not a mystery; it is not God's second plan; but his purpose before the foundation of the earth.

The Messianic kingdom and the age of the church are the same. Jesus established the kingdom of God in the first century by his death and resurrection. The people of faith, joined to the body of Christ receive the kingdom promises. There is no separation by time or covenant.

Study Questions

1. Explain why exegesis and hermeneutics are necessary in establishing Bible doctrine. What is eisegesis and explain if you think it is a problem in the church?

2. Explain why a passage of Scripture cannot mean what it was never meant to be by the author or the readers. Give two examples where people explain a verse in a way that violates this principle.

3. According to the Victorious Kingdom view of eschatology, how did Israel and the Gentiles become one people?

Chapter 3

Preterism

Reading the Scriptures from a preterist perspective is a great asset in centering eschatology on the kingdom of God. What is preterism? It simply means "past fulfillment." An Old Testament passage taken from Isaiah is a good example.

Isaiah 9:6

For to us a child is born,to us a son is given; and the government shall be upon his shoulder ,and his name shall be called Wonderful Counselor, Mighty God, Everlasting Father, Prince of Peace.

Isaiah prophesies the birth of the Messiah over 700 years in advance. Jesus was born, fulfilling the prophecy. All scholars agree that the birth of Jesus (the incarnation) will not happen again. Our understanding of this prophecy looks back to its fulfillment; therefore, a preterist interpretation is applied. In the current eschatological debate, preterism interprets numerous New Testament passages that dispensationalism applies to the future, our future. These future events include the kingdom of God, the last days, the rise of antichrist and the Great Tribulation.

Preterism gained notoriety through its interpretation of the book of Revelation. Instead of interpreting the images as events in our future, preterism sees the timing of these events occurring in the first century. John's prophecy found its fulfillment with events happening during the Jewish wars with Rome, and ending with the destruction of Jerusalem and the temple. Preterism as a system of interpretation has benefited by the failed prophecies of dispensational teachers. A book by Richard Kyle entitled, The Last Days Are Here Again, gives a detailed history of those teachers and movements that preached a contemporary "last days."

"My studies in Christian history introduced me to the considerable diversity in the way God's people have viewed the last days. While the belief in Christ's return has persisted through two thousand years of Christian history, it has taken many shapes, largely because apocalyptic thinking is often conditioned by contemporary events."[13]

These contemporary events fuel the fire for continuous publications of prophetic books. Interpreting Bible prophecy using current events has grown immensely in the last few generations. Many Christian bestsellers come from the ranks of prophecy books predicting the soon coming of Christ and the end of the world. When authors claim new revelations dealing with apocalyptic themes, book sales increase. Christians who chase after the sensational constantly look for keys to unlock the mysteries of the apocalypse.

A past-fulfillment method of interpretation helps to understand the time the Bible calls the "last days." There are numerous books about preterism. This book is not a defense of the complete preterist system and there are areas of preterism that I disagree with.[14] I would align my teaching around partial preterism. Partial preterism interprets many New Testament prophecies as fulfilled, but not all of them. Advocates of full preterism deny any future coming of Christ and any future resurrection of the dead. All prophecy is fulfilled for the full preterist. I believe the partial preterist interpretation of the New Testament is beneficial in understanding the kingdom of God. Without the use of preterism, the kingdom is out of reach and forced into the future.

Do any early church fathers use preterism to understand New Testament eschatological passages? Many are surprised by the answer, because while preterism is often overlooked in modern

---

[13] Richard Kyle, The Last Days Are Here Again, Baker Books, Grand Rapids, Michigan, 1998, page 9-10

[14] Many full preterists deny the present day work of the Holy Spirit, no gifts of the Spirit after 70A.D.

studies, it was not centuries earlier. Even though eschatology was overshadowed by other doctrines during the first three-four hundred years of the church[15], we do have writings from this period endorsing a biblical optimism and a preterist view of the last day's events.

Did early church fathers teach that Jesus established his kingdom during his first coming? Did they believe the kingdom would advance and be victorious? Dispensationalists attempt to use statements from the early church in discounting preterist interpretation. The lack of preterist commentary (they say) proves it is a recent development in biblical theology. The trouble with this logic is that there is also a lack of dispensational commentary from the early church fathers. Studying the evidence (early church writings), shows the basic premise of preterism is more prevalent than dispensational teachings.

We have four primary documents that constitute the earliest of the church fathers, The Didache, I Clement, The Epistle of Barnabas, and the Shepherd of Hermas. Of the four documents, only I Clement and the Didache allude to Matthew 24.[16] Matthew 24 is the pivotal passage that separates futurists from preterists. If Jesus is teaching concerning the distance future (our time) in his Olivet Discourse, then numerous other New Testament texts must be interpreted in like manner. Yet, if Jesus is speaking about the events that will occur within one literal generation from when he spoke them, then it opens the door for other passages to have a similar meaning.

The Didache

The Didache is the oldest document of extra-biblical writings. Although no one knows for certain, the twelve apostles may have

---

[15] Christology was the most important subject for the church during this time. Was Christ God? What is the nature of Christ? Once Christology was settled, the most important debates were centered on the Holy Spirit and the doctrine of the Trinity. Little time was given to matters of Eschatology.

[16] Gary DeMar, Francis X. Gumerlock, The Early Church And the End of the World, American Vision, Powder Springs, GA., 2006, p. 27

written it. The Didache does refer to events in Matthew 24-25 and places these events in their future. Is this proof that a futurist interpretation is correct? It may seem so, but it all depends on its date. If written before the destruction of Jerusalem and the Temple in 70 A.D., then it would be future for them, but past for us. The Didache, like many of the old manuscripts, opinions about dating vary.

In The Apostolic Fathers by Michael W. Holmes we read.

> "The Didache may have been put into its present form as late as 150, though a date considerably closer to the end of the first century seems more plausible. The materials from which it was composed, however, reflect the state of an even earlier time…reflect a time closer to that of Paul and James (who died in the 60's) than Ignatius (who died sometime after 110)."[17]

The form we see today comes from the second century, but the source materials used according to Holmes, are documents from the time of Paul and James. In their book, The Early Church and the End of the World, authors Gary DeMar and Francis X. Gumerlock quote the definitive work of Jean-Paul Audet on the dating of the Didache, "that it was composed, almost certainly in Antioch, between 50 and 70."[18] DeMar and Gumerlock state their conclusion on the dating of the Didache, and therefore its usefulness in defending the preterists interpretation.

> "So then, if the Didache was written prior to the destruction of Jerusalem in A.D. 70, as many scholars suggest, then its use of prophetic passages later found in Matthew 24-25 to describe events that were yet to take place, including "the Lord coming

---

[17] Michael W. Holmes, ed., The Apostolic Fathers: Greek Texts and English Translations, rev. ed., Baker Books, Grand Rapids, MI, 1992, p.247-248

[18] Gary DeMar, Francis X. Gumerlock, The Early Church And The End Of the World, American Vision, Powder Springs, GA., 2006, p. 30

on the clouds of heaven" (Matt. 24:30), makes perfect sense given a preterists interpretation of the Olivet discourse."[19]

I Clement

Like The Didache, many Dispensationalists use the writing of I Clement to show their system has early church support. Yet, once again, the dating of I Clement is important. Dispensationalists place the date around 95-96, primarily due to the testimony of church historian Eusebius, yet many scholars see evidence of an earlier date. Biblical scholars George Edmundson and T. J. Herron give I Clement a date before the destruction of Jerusalem.[20] In I Clement, it states that Paul and Peter were martyred in "our generation." Yet, the strongest support for a date prior to the destruction of Jerusalem comes from Clements's own description that the sacrifices in the temple are ongoing.

> "Not in every place, brethren, are the continual daily sacrifices offered, or the freewill offerings, or the sin offerings, but in Jerusalem alone. And even there the offering is not made in every place, but before the sanctuary in the court of the altar; and this too through the high-priest and the aforesaid ministers."[21]

With the destruction of the temple, sacrifice of animals ceased. Therefore, if this practice was continuing in his day, he wrote before such worship had ended. Therefore, instead of affirming dispensational history, it only tells us that the fulfillment of Matthew 24 was still in their future, not ours.

---

[19] ibid

[20] Ibid,p.32

[21] I Clement as quoted by Gary DeMar, Francis X. Gumerlock, The Early Church And The End Of the World, American Vision, Powder Springs, GA., 2006, p. 32

Of the four early church writings, the two that mention Matthew 24-25 fail to support the dispensational system of eschatology. In fact, the opposite may be true, it seems more likely to support a preterist interpretation. Early church documents are not proof for futurism or preterism. They help in establishing doctrinal history but Scripture is our final authority.

Preterism as a tool in interpreting the Bible is gaining influence within the Evangelical community. Although overlooked for many years, it now occupies a place in biblical hermeneutics. Its value in understanding eschatology is vital because it takes the biblical statements on the "timing issue" serious. When Jesus states that people standing and listening to him speak will live to see the *"son of man coming in his kingdom,"* only the preterists take the language literally. Likewise, when the Apostle John states that the antichrists in his day are proof that the church was living in the *"last days,"* it is again the preterist understanding that fits the history and language of the text.

Moving past the oldest of documents, we must determine if the early church fathers saw the future with optimism, and if they believed the "last days" were over. Early Church Father Cyprian (200-258 A.D.) believed the prophecies concerning the "last days" were contemporary with the New Testament authors. Commenting on II Timothy 3 he says, "the Holy Spirit foretells and forewarns us by the apostle," saying, "In the last days," says he, (quotes the passage) and then concludes, "Whatever things were predicted are fulfilled."[22]

Many scholars of history accepted the importance of interpreting the New Testament in light of a preterist hermeneutic. C. Jonathan Seraiah writes.

> "It is true that the "eschatology" of the New Testament is predominantly preterist. For those unfamiliar with the preterist perspective, it is the ancient view that many of the eschatological passages of the New Testament were fulfilled

---

[22] Treatises of Cyprian Treatise I, sec. 16

(completely) in the destruction of Jerusalem in AD 70. This view may sound novel, but in reality, there have been orthodox adherents to it throughout church history (e.g., Clement of Alexandria, Eusebius, John Lightfoot, John Owen, Milton Terry, and Jay Adams). This interpretation does not deny the Final Coming of Christ; it merely finds that not all "coming" passages refer to that event. The preterist interpretation is actually the most faithful to the biblical text because it recognizes that Old Testament prophetic terminology was used by the New Testament authors."[23]

The partial preterists view of eschatology begins by clearing away many false assumptions about the future. Many pastors and current Christian authors claim everything is getting worse, believers will fall away in great numbers and finally the antichrist will assume power. In contrast, when Matthew 24 and passages dealing with the 'last days' are viewed through a preterist lens, a new view of the future comes into focus. Then, an eschatology embracing victory emerges. When these first century events receive a 21st century interpretation, there is little room for advancing the kingdom. Faulty exegesis drains away our hope. Today, the theological tide has turned; hope is returning to the church.

Study Questions

1. Why is it important that Victorious eschatology use preterism as a New Testament hermeneutic?

2. Explain the difference between full and partial preterism.

3. What is the Didache and explain why an early date is plausible.

---

[23] C. Jonathan Seraiah, The End of All Things: A Defense of the Future, Canon Press, Moscow, Idaho, 1999

4. Do you think I Clement was written before the destruction of the Temple in 70 A.D.? Why?

Chapter 4

Hermeneutics

Hermeneutics is the science and art of interpretation. It is science because there are common laws and rules that we follow. It is art because even with proper rules, it takes ability. Our desire to understand the Scripture and eschatology in particular, must begin with a review of basic principles of hermeneutics.

When it comes to eschatology, our hermeneutics becomes very personal. We have firm convictions, and have a sense that we already "know" what the Bible teaches. These presuppositions can be roadblocks to a proper understanding. Vern S. Poythress addressed the need for honest interpretation even if it means changing directions.

> "The growth of technique and of technical detail in interpretation may snare us into idolatry. We want interpretation without crucifixion. We trust in technical expertise and in method, in order to free ourselves from the fear of the agony of hermeneutical crucifixion. That is, we do not want to crucify what we think we already know and have achieved. We want painless, straightforward progress toward understanding, rather than having to abandon a whole route already constructed."[24]

I love Poythress' term "hermeneutical crucifixion." I know what that feels like. Studying eschatology will likely bring crucifixion. Being honest with the word of God often leads to changes in old patterns of thinking. Letting go of traditions is difficult. Keep in mind, resurrection follows crucifixion.

---

[24] Vern S. Poythress, God-Centered Biblical Interpretation, P&P Publishing, Phillipsburg, New Jersey, 1999, page 191

This chapter covers hermeneutics as it primarily relates to eschatology. David Chilton writes on reading prophecy without forcing our thoughts into the text. "We must allow the Bible's own structure to arise from the text itself, to impose itself upon our own understanding. We must become accustomed to the biblical vocabulary and modes of expression, seeking to shape our own thinking in terms of Scriptural categories."[25] Learning the Bible's vocabulary and style is important in reading the text and especially in the area of eschatology where many have strong preconceived conclusions. Our goal is allowing the word of God to transform our minds; not just confirming our own thoughts.

John Piper and D.A. Carson provide a practical approach to hermeneutics.

1. **Textual** – A Christian reading of the Bible pays attention to the words, sentences, paragraphs and books of the Bible in detail.

2. **Pneumatological** – A Christian reading of the Bible is rooted in recognition of the Spirit's inspiration of the text and in a reliance on the Spirit for understanding (illumination).

3. **Christotelic** – A Christian reading of the Bible understands that the purpose of the Scriptures is not only to reveal Christ but also to transform his church into his image through the Spirit.

4. **Communal** – A Christian reading of the Bible takes place in the context of the community of the faithful, the church.

5. **Transformational** – A Christian reading of the Bible is not only concerned with information but with transformation, namely into the image of Christ.

6. **Holistic** – A Christian reading of the Bible regards both the Old and New Testaments as the true, complimentary, and

---

[25] David Chilton, Paradise Restored, Reconstruction Press, Tyler, Texas, 1985, page 15

complete revelation of God through Christ that are to be read in the above ways.[26]

These six points show the practical side of hermeneutics, which is the transformation of believers by the word of God. The role of the Holy Spirit is important. The role of the church is important. Keeping Christ at the center of biblical discovery is important.

We now discuss additional principles to interpret biblical prophecy.

1. Focus on the 'timing issues'

Close attention to the Scriptures that restrict prophecy to a particular period is critical in the understanding of biblical eschatology. The problem with the dispensational view is that it forces a future fulfillment for passages that demand a first century interpretation. Getting the 'timing" issues right is extremely important in understanding the message of God's kingdom. "The coming of Christ led the apostles to practice new patterns of exegesis, centered on their conviction that the eschatological age had been inaugurated. It is foolish to think we can get our doctrine from the apostles without also employing their hermeneutic."27

2. Intertextuality

What is intertextuality and why is it important? Rick Lusk provides the answer.

> "As we've seen Biblical Theology reads the Bible as a unified narrative. One aspect of Biblical Theology, then, is looking at how texts within the Scriptures interface with one another. The technical name for this is "intertextuality." Understanding how intertextuality works gives the biblical theologian an important hermeneutical tool. Here, we are looking for more than conceptual and

---

[26] John Piper, D.A. Carson, Scriptural Hermeneutics, http://www.intertextual interpretation.com, 2011

doctrinal coherence in the Scriptures; we are actually looking for fragments of earlier texts buried in later ones. Intertextuality uses Scripture to interpret Scripture by listening for quotations, echoes, and allusions to other inter-canonical texts. It is a form of inner-biblical exegesis. Intertextuality includes explicit quotations (e.g., quotations of the OT in the NT), as well as more subtle uses of texts."[27]

We need the Bible to interpret the Bible. Its sounds easy but takes skill and training to use "intertextuality" properly. When reading Paul or Peter, we find their letters immersed in the background of Old Testament texts. At times, these texts are clear, often they are not. Reading the Bible is more than what we see on a page, it is seeing what is not on the page. Often the missing elements are the most imperative to proper interpretation.

Peter J. Leithart says interpreting Scripture is similar to understanding a joke. In his book, Deep Exegesis, he gives an example. A priest, a rabbi, a nun, a doctor, and a lawyer enter a bar. As the group approach the bartender he looks at the five and says, "What, is this a joke."[28] Not everyone gets this joke. The words are simple, the key people and their professions are well known. Anyone with basic language skills can determine the literal meaning of the story. The problem is that a literal interpretation leads to a blank stare. What is funny? Those old enough to hear hundreds of jokes with these same characters (or similar) get the joke immediately. Those with little experience, because of age or from different cultures, find little meaning. Interpreting the Bible can create a similar problem. To "get" the Bible it is often necessary to know more than the actual words of a single verse or passage. This is especially true with New

---

[27] Rich Lusk, The Art of Biblical Theology: Intertextuality, http://.homes.org/ theologia/rich-lusk-art.com

[28] Peter J. Leithart, Deep Exegesis, Baylor University Press, Waco, Texas, 2009, page 113

Testament eschatology where the approaching "day of the Lord" influences many texts; even when nothing specific is mentioned.

The written words of the Bible are not always to be interpreted just by the literal words we see on the page. Some previous experience is required. Some Christians are better at interpretation than others are; they get it. This is why Jesus gives the church "Teachers" as one of his ascension gifts (Eph. 4:11). With few exceptions, authors of the New Testament wrote from a rich background of Jewish history. A lot of information is left out. Serious Bible students must familiarize themselves with the background of the passage. Like the Apostle Peter bringing up the *"new heavens and a new earth* (II Peter 3:13)."* Peter relies on his knowledge of Isaiah who first introduced the subject. When Jesus speaks of the *"abomination of desolation"* (Matthew 24:15) he is building upon Daniel the prophet. Reading the book of Hebrews is impossible without some knowledge of the numerous Old Testament passages the author refers to in the text.

3. Prophecy and Apocalyptic

One problem we have in interpreting particular sections of Scripture is failing to discern between prophecy and apocalyptic literature. Many overlook this vital tool of hermeneutics.

From 200 BC to 200 AD there were many "apocalypses" written and distributed. It was a common form of writing and people understood what they were reading. The only book of the Bible written in this style is the book of Revelation. There are however, portions of this style that make their way into other biblical passages.

Apocalyptic writing from the Christian era used the Old Testament as the source for their writings. We can find several common denominators of apocalyptic writings. The bulk of these points come from Gordon D. Fee and Douglas Stuart in their excellent book, How to Read the Bible for All its worth.[29]

---

[29] Gordon D. Fee, Douglas Stuart, How to Read the Bible for All Its Worth, Zondervan, Grand Rapids, Michigan, 2003, pages 250-251

1. The main theme is the coming judgment and salvation. Apocalyptic literature is born in times of persecution or oppression.

2. Most of the prophetic books were oral, prophets spoke from God and a scribe wrote it down. Apocalypse is a form of literature. It has a form and style of its own. The prophets were told to speak, John was told to write.

3. Apocalyptic literature contains visions, dreams, and cryptic language with hidden meanings.

4. The images often take the form of fantasy rather than reality.

The prophets also used symbolic language, but their symbols involved real images- like birds, known animals, cakes, mountains, rivers, and other physical items. On the other hand, the symbols of apocalyptic literature come from fantasy; like a beast with seven heads, a woman clothed with the sun, and insects with human heads. Attempting to use these apocalyptic symbols and find their 21st century counterpart is missing the point entirely. John is telling a story for the people of his own day to read and understand.

5. Because these types of writing were literary, they had a formalized style. Time and events are divided into neat packages. The use of numbers as symbols is common in apocalyptic writings.

4. Symbolism

Symbolism in the Bible can be tricky. Some love it, take it to extreme, and create interpretations that are wildly speculative. Others attempt to deny symbolism. When the dispensational teachers claim a pure literal interpretation, they are being disingenuous because it is impossible to interpret the whole of Scripture in a strictly literal fashion without missing the meaning entirely.There are portions that are straight prose and a literal interpretation is necessary. The book of Romans is literal. The book of Revelation is not. The Bible has different forms of literature. Poetry uses symbols and metaphors so a literal reading would miss the point. Chilton comments on the use of biblical symbolism.

> "The symbolism of the Bible is not structured in a flat, this-means-that style. Instead, it is meant to be read visually. We are to see the images rise before us in succession, layer upon layer, allowing them to evoke a response in our minds and hearts. The prophets did not write in order to create stimulating intellectual exercises. They wrote to teach. They wrote in visual, dramatic symbols; and if we would fully understand their message, we must appreciate their vocabulary. We must read the Bible visually."[30]

Interpreting passages pertinent to eschatology, the use of symbolism is even more prevalent. "Eschatological language by its very nature is often metaphorical. Sometimes these metaphors express poetically the language of the final events but are not necessarily intended to be predictions of those events per se."[31]

Study Questions

1. Explain "hermeneutical crucifixion?" Give a personal example.

2. What is the difference between prophetic and apocalyptic writings?

3. Explain this sentence; "the apostles believed that the eschatological age had been inaugurated."

---

[30] David Chilton, Paradise Restored, Reconstruction Press, Tyler, Texas, 1985, page 19

[31] Gordon D. Fee, Douglas Stuart, How to Read the Bible for All Its Worth, Zondervan, Grand Rapids, Michigan, 2003, page 201

4. Give four scriptural examples where a strict literal interpretation makes little sense.

5. What are the rules for interpreting biblical symbolism?

Chapter 5

The Sons of Abraham

God's first step in bringing his kingdom to earth is creating a people for his name and purposes. Abraham is God's choice; he will be the father of Israel, and of us all. Abraham has significant eschatological overtones. The big question is, "Do we possess the promises of Abraham?" Advocates of dispensationalism say no. They deny the church has any role in fulfilling these promises (also promises made to David and Jeremiah). Charles C. Ryrie said, "If the yet unfulfilled prophecies of the Old Testament made in the Abrahamic, Davidic, and new covenants are to be literally fulfilled, there must be a future period, the millennium, in which they can be fulfilled, for the church, is not now fulfilling them."[32] Advocates of victorious eschatology disagree with the dispensational approach and see no need for a future kingdom age. Christ fulfills the promises to Abraham; therefore, the church (in Christ) is heir of the promises.

Are we heirs of Old Testament promises or not? One system of theology says, "Absolutely not" (dispensational), and another says, "yes" (partial preterist). The Apostle Paul knew the importance of this issue and he is our primary source.

GALATIANS 3:6-9

"Just as Abraham "believed God, and it was counted to him as righteousness"? 7 Know then that it is those of faith who are the sons of Abraham. 8 And the Scripture, foreseeing that God would justify the Gentiles by faith, preached the gospel beforehand to Abraham, saying, "In you shall all the nations be blessed." 9 So then, those who are of faith are blessed along with Abraham, the man of faith.

---

[32] Charles C. Ryrie, Dispensationalism, Moody Press, Chicago, Illinois, 1966, page 147

Who are the sons of Abraham? This important question received lots of first century attention. Moreover, it continues today, with no less intensity. Jews looked to their father Abraham in an attempt to diffuse Jesus' judgment upon them (John 8:33). Jesus tells the Jews, *"You are of Abraham's children, do the deeds of Abraham"* (John 8:39). He tells them their father was the Devil (John 8:44). Jesus followed up with saying, *"But because I speak the truth, you do not believe me"* (John 8:45). Jesus then claims to speak in the authority of Yahweh. *"Truly, Truly, I say to you, before Abraham was born, I Am"* (John 8:58). At this point, the Jews gathered stones to kill the man who claimed to be greater than Abraham. Jesus says that Abraham looked forward to this day and saw it (John 8:56). By the Holy Spirit, Abraham saw into the future and saw the day of Christ and rejoiced. What was the basis of his rejoicing? Abraham rejoiced because prophetically he knew the Messiah would fulfill all the covenant promises.

The failure of the old covenant was not being able to fulfill the promises given to Abraham. Dispensationalism agrees and therefore insists we must revert to the covenant of death (II Corinthians 3:7) in order to fulfill the kingdom promises contained in the Abrahamic covenant. Turning back the pages to the old covenant has no place in the New Testament, yet according to dispensational eschatology; God's people must go back and live under the law in order to partake of the promises.

Paul in the book to the Romans builds upon his teaching in Galatians. Paul now identifies those who are the *"sons of Abraham"* (Gal. 3:7). True sons are those who are *"of faith."* In the book of Romans, Paul expounds on this same theme.

Romans 4:13-14 & 16

For the promise to Abraham and his offspring that he would be heir of the world did not come through the law but through the righteousness of faith. 14 For if it is the adherents of the law who are to be the heirs, faith is null and the promise is void. 16 That is why it depends on faith, in order that the promise may rest on grace and be guaranteed to all his offspring—not only to the adherent of the law but also to the one who shares the faith of Abraham, who is the father of us all.

Paul makes it clear; those who receive the promises are those who have experienced grace through faith. Those who are *"of faith"* are the redeemed in Christ. Believers in the Messiah will be the beneficiaries of the promises made in the Old Testament.

Paul, in Galatians, uses a New Testament term in referring to the Abrahamic covenant. He writes, *And the Scripture, foreseeing that God would justify the Gentiles by faith, preached the gospel beforehand to Abraham, saying, "In you shall all the nations be blessed"* (Gal.3:8). It is new covenant Christians who are the heirs of the Abrahamic covenant. Dispensationalism teaches that only national Israel can fulfill these promises. Dispensationalism is wrong because the New Testament uses the Old Testament terms and concepts in referring to New Testament believers.

Galatians 3:14

So that in Christ Jesus the blessing of Abraham might come to the Gentiles, so that we might receive the promised Spirit through faith.

Paul makes it clear; Gentiles can partake of the blessing given to Abraham. All peoples, including Jews, are freely welcomed into this newly formed body of people. The people of Israel have the same opportunity as anyone. They may come to Christ and receive the blessings of Abraham. Some dispensationalists argue that this is "replacement theology," where the Gentiles replace Israel. This is an attempt to ignore the fact that Israel is reorganized around the Messiah. Yes, old Israel is gone, but the newly formed people of God made up of both Jew and Gentile continue under a new covenant and constitute a new Israel. As a people, Jews will come to Christ in large numbers as God's Kingdom grows. Israel as a nation (like all nations) has a bright future.

Galatians 3:16

Now the promises were made to Abraham and to his offspring. It does not say, "And to offsprings," referring to many, but referring to one, "And to your offspring," who is Christ.

Paul wants no one confused on this matter. There is one way to receive the blessings of Abraham, in Christ. There is no alternative. Paul closes the door to any dispensational thinking.Jews cannot come to God apart from Christ. There are not two paths to Abraham. Christ is the only way. God has one people, one body of Christ, one wife, the people of the new covenant. The dispensational error is creating two separate peoples of God. L.S. Chafer, a prominent dispensational theologian writes.

> "The dispensationalist believes that throughout the ages God is pursuing two distinct purposes: one related to the earth with earthly people and earthly objectives involved, which is Judaism; while the other is related to heaven with a heavenly people and heavenly objectives involved, which is Christianity."[33]

Unpacking this statement is somewhat frightening. With this type of rhetoric, it is amazing that dispensationalism has any advocates. Dispensational Evangelicals go around the world proclaiming Christ as the only way to God. Yet, a key element of their theology is the belief that there are two paths to God. One path is Christianity; the other is Judaism. Pick one or the other. At this point, any serious Bible student should recognize that dispensational theology has made a turn away from historical Christianity. For two thousand years, the church has preached Christ as the only source for salvation. One door leads to God. In Christ alone is there forgiveness of sins.In Christ, alone we inherit eternal life.

The New Testament includes both Jew and Gentile in the offer of salvation. The blessings of Abraham include all nations. This echoes the words of Christ "*Go and make disciples of all nations*" (Matthew 28:18). The church will not end in defeat. The church's calling is simple; take the blessings of the Abrahamic covenant to

---

[33] L.S. Chafer, Dispensationalism, Dallas Seminary Press, 1936, page 107.

the entire world. The fact that the new covenant is open to both Jew and Gentile alike is widely acknowledged. What now needs acknowledging is how this simple fact runs counter to dispensational doctrine. Andrew Sandlin writes about the barriers of race and religion.

> "Ethnic Israel traces its racial and religious lineage to Abraham; but, according to Christ and Paul, Abraham is father only to those who by faith belong to Christ, whether ethnic Jew or Gentile. Christians are the true seed of Abraham. The Abrahamic covenant cuts across all racial barriers...if this be the case, then the dispensationalist notion of a fundamental distinction between Israel and the church cannot be true."[34]

In Galatians, Paul makes a case that believers in Christ are included in the Abrahamic covenant. How does Paul approach this same subject in his letter to the Romans? Paul calls saved Gentiles Jews. If we understand Paul correctly on this point-and he is straightforward on the matter- then the wall of separation between Israel and Christians is an artificial one and not a biblical one. With this wall erased, the key element of dispensationalism begins to unravel. When this happens, their whole scheme of eschatology breaks apart.

Romans 2:28-29

For no one is a Jew who is merely one outwardly, nor is circumcision outward and physical. [29] But a Jew is one inwardly, and circumcision is a matter of the heart, by the Spirit, not by the letter. His praise is not from man but from God.

Paul declares that being Jewish and part of Israel no longer comes through circumcision. The New Testament changes the meaning of Old Testament rituals. Under the Law, circumcision was a physical event. It was not some mystical or spiritual experience. The cutting of flesh was real. Yet, Paul confronts the

---

[34] Andrew Sandlin, A Postmillennial Primer, Chalcedon Foundation, 1997, page 11

old system and offers a new understanding of circumcision for those under the new covenant. Circumcision is now a work of the Spirit. This circumcision of the heart is what brings believers into a new covenant. Paul in writing the epistle of Philippians states Christians are the ones who, *"Glory in Christ Jesus, and put no confidence in the flesh"* (Philippians 3:3). Now, true Jews receive the true circumcision; it is a matter of grace and Spirit.

The events of the New Testament create a new Israel. Jesus began his ministry choosing twelve men. He chose twelve not fifteen or six. Jesus at the start of his ministry was constituting a new Israel. Racial Jews were the first chosen but this new way of Israel soon included Gentiles as well. We must begin by seeing the Old Testament through the lens of the New Testament.

When the New Testament becomes our primary resource for understanding the Old Testament, we have a very different outcome than what the dispensationalists would have us to believe. A major doctrine of dispensationalism is the "secret rapture" of believers. The reason this "rapture" is vital is that it is the conviction that the New Testament does not alter the promises made to racial Israel in the Old Testament. God intends (according to the theory) to go back and work with natural Israel on the conditions set forth in the Old Testament. This being the case, the church is in the way. The church's removal is necessary. Because of the prophecies in Daniel are about *"a time of distress"* (interpreted as the Great Tribulation that Christ predicted in Matthew 24) God must bring judgment to Israel in the future. The removal of the church of Jesus Christ is theologically necessary; hence, the secret rapture. The doctrine of the rapture does not come out of a deductive study of the Bible, rather is a necessary element to maintain the dispensational scheme.

I have not found a single New Testament Scripture where God intends to re-establish the old covenant with racial Israel. Nor is there any promise that affirms the physical land of Palestine belongs to them as an ongoing covenant promise. God does indeed have a people, it the church of Jesus Christ, made of Jew and Gentile alike. Since the blessings of Abraham belong to the people of the new circumcision, the church has a commission to bring these blessings to the nations of the world. Concerning the promise of the land, that also is renewed, from a small piece of the earth to the entire earth (Rom. 4:13).

Romans 9:6-8

But it is not as though the word of God has failed. For not all who are descended from Israel belong to Israel, [7] and not all are children of Abraham because they are his offspring, but "Through Isaac shall your offspring be named." [8] This means that it is not the children of the flesh who are the children of God, but the children of the promise are counted as offspring.

Paul addresses the subject of who is truly a Jew. He tells us that just because one is a physical descendant of Israel; it is no longer valid in the eyes of God. A major shift occurred with the coming of the new covenant. It is not enough to prove your inclusion in the covenant of the past. Access to God now comes through the new covenant. It is the only access offered; then and forever. Christ is our only path into a relationship with the Father. This is true for both Jews and Gentiles. God is moving forwards, not backwards.

Paul makes his case clear. God accepts the children of promise, not children of the law. To rely on a relationship based upon the old covenant would be a major mistake. Paul makes it very clear; His Jewish countrymen must come to Christ and be part of this new and living way. What is interesting is that Paul does not tell the Jews that everything in the Old Testament is invalid. No, Paul teaches a new way of fulfillment. Jesus fulfills the hope of Israel. The prophets predicted this eschatological time. The Messiah is here, the kingdom of Yahweh is at hand!

It is here where a victorious kingdom view rises above other forms of eschatology. It uses Paul's argument for a new way to identify God's people. The people of God are now New Testament Christians.Christians possess the glorious promises of the Old Testament. Dispensationalism gives these wonderful promises to the racial Israel. Amillennialism assign these promises to heaven, whereas the victorious kingdom view agrees with Paul, it is the spiritual people of promise, the believers in Christ, the church, who are the beneficiaries of the multitudes of promises that are made in the Old Testament. These promises are for a people living on the earth.

Romans 9:23-24

In order to make known the riches of his glory for vessels of mercy, which he has prepared beforehand for glory— [24] *even us whom he has called, not from the Jews only but also from the Gentiles?*

Paul reminds his reader that even in the Old Testament, the plan was to include Gentiles as the people of God. Dispensationalism teaches the church is absent in the Old Testament. Paul firmly disagrees. Hosea prophesied about a new people of God (Hosea 2:23). This confirms that the church is not a new concept; it was the plan of God from the beginning.

Paul continues to expound on these prophecies in the Old Testament. *What shall we say, then? That Gentiles who did not pursue righteousness have attained it, that is, a righteousness that is by faith; (Rom. 9:30).* " The dispensational plan excluding any reference to the church in the Old Testament does not come from Paul. In fact, the opposite is true. We agree that the term "church" is absent. However, in what group would we place these believing righteous Gentiles? Should we place them among the old covenant adherents? Paul is talking about the current people of faith who were the subject of Old Testament prophecy. Surely, the evidence shows the intent of the old prophets was to include the Gentiles into a newly formed people of God.

Ryrie states the dispensational case clearly on this point.

> "The main point in question is whether or not the Church is a distinct body in this present age. If the Church is not a subject of Old Testament prophecy, then the Church is not fulfilling Israel's promises, but instead Israel herself must fulfill them and that in the future. In brief, premillennialism with a dispensational view recognizes the Church as a distinct entity, distinct from Israel in her

beginning, in her relation to this age, and in her promises. If the Church is not a distinct body, then the door is open wide for amillennialism (and also postmillennialism) to enter with its ideas that the Church is some sort of full-bloomed development of Judaism and the fulfiller of Israel's promises of blessing."[35]

The church, as dispensationalists proclaim, has been a distinct body of people since the first coming of Christ. Since the church is a new and very distinct body of people from Israel, it cannot fulfill any prophecy from the Old Testament. Paul in the book of Romans seems to disagree with dispensational logic. For Paul, there is a new people of God, not Jewish nor Gentile, but a newly formed spiritual people. He states his view in Ephesians 2:*14* *"For he himself is our peace, who has made us both one and has broken down in his flesh the dividing wall of hostility."*

Galatians 6:15-16

For neither circumcision counts for anything, nor uncircumcision, but a new creation. [16] *And as for all who walk by this rule, peace and mercy be upon them, and upon the Israel of God.*

Our final scripture supporting "Israel" to include Gentiles as well as Jews is very convincing. Dispensationalists say Paul makes a clear distinction between the church (those of the new creation) and Israel. They teach that the term "them" refers to Christians whereas the term "Israel of God" refers to those of Judaism. This interpretation creates enormous problems. In verse 15, Paul declares that circumcision and uncircumcision are no longer valid before God. Paul includes those called "Israel of God" with those who are members of the "new creation." Did the nation of Israel automatically become included in the church? No, the opposite happened. A majority of the nation rejected Christ (John 1:12).

---

[35] Charles C. Ryrie, The Basis of the Premillennial Faith, Loizeaux Brothers, page 126.

The kingdom was taken away and assigned to the newly formed people of God (Matthew 21:43). Those that Paul includes in this "Israel of God" are those who are born again and placed among those in the "new creation." This term "Israel of God" is the same people who are a part of the new people of God, the church.

The victorious kingdom builds upon the truth that the church has become the new people of God. The church does not eliminate Israel from God's promises but fulfills them. Every person is welcome to be a part of God's new people; those who receive the blessing foretold in the Old Testament. The new covenant includes all nations, including Israel. Dispensationalists claim the old covenant still exists and comes back to life during the millennium. Those advocating a victorious kingdom believe the new covenant is God's fulfillment of the old. The old has passed away, never to return. The work of Christ affirms our future.

The church as the new people of God now fulfill the promises made to Abraham. People around the world are receiving the promises of Abraham. Abraham is our father of faith, and through the ministry of Christ, we are heirs of the world (Romans 4:13). This is kingdom-centered eschatology. It begins with a new people of God, connected in Jesus, and recipients of the great promises of the Old Testament.

Study Questions

1. Explain why Abraham is important to the study of eschatology.

2. Explain the meaning of Galatians 6:15-16.

3. Who are the sons of Abraham? Explain the connection.

4. How does the Abrahamic covenant find fulfillment within dispensational eschatology?

5. How was it that Abraham preached the gospel 2,000 years before Jesus was born?

Chapter 6

The Kingdom of King David

The greatest period of Israel's history began with David. Along with his son Solomon, they created an empire that was the envy of the world. Kings and Queens traveled to Israel to pay homage and witness the achievements of this small nation. In the midst of this glorious time, God delivers a prophecy that affects us 3,000 years later. In the book of II Samuel, God promises David that his house (family) and his kingdom (reign) shall be established forever.

II Samuel 7:16

And your house and your kingdom shall be made sure forever before me. Your throne shall be established forever.'

The book of Psalms repeats the promise.

Psalms 89:3-4

You have said, "I have made a covenant with my chosen one;I have sworn to David my servant:[4] 'I will establish your offspring forever,and build your throne for all generations."

The problem is that after Solomon died the kingdom split and eventually ended. Has the Scripture failed? How can this prophecy be true when the sons of David failed to maintain his reign? The apostles of the New Testament solve this mystery.

In the book of Acts, Luke retells the events of Pentecost. In the sermon following the outpouring of the Holy Spirit, Peter provides historical and prophetic insight.

Acts 2:29-36

"Brothers, I may say to you with confidence about the patriarch David that he both died and was buried, and his tomb is with us to this day. Being therefore a prophet, and knowing that God had sworn with an oath to him that he would set one of his descendants on his throne, he foresaw and spoke about the resurrection of the Christ, that he was not abandoned to Hades, nor did his flesh see corruption. This Jesus God raised up, and of

that we all are witnesses. Being therefore exalted at the right hand of God, and having received from the Father the promise of the Holy Spirit, he has poured out this that you yourselves are seeing and hearing. For David did not ascend into the heavens, but he himself says, "'The Lord said to my Lord, Sit at my right hand, until I make your enemies your footstool.' Let all the house of Israel therefore know for certain that God has made him both Lord and Christ, this Jesus whom you crucified."

How does Peter understand David? David was as a great king, but Peter calls him a prophet. He looked ahead and saw Christ. Jesus (the Messiah) is the legitimate heir to David's throne. Jesus is now reigning from the throne of David in the heavens over all creation. Scripture points to a spiritual fulfillment, not a natural one. Jesus does not reign from a physical seat in Jerusalem. For Peter the resurrection is proof that Jesus is at the right hand of God. Therefore, his kingdom reign has begun. The throne of David represents the authority Jesus received at the ascension. Peter understands the promises to King David as now fulfilled in the resurrection of Jesus. This is a fatal blow to any postponement theory and the creation of a millennial kingdom in the future. If Jesus is now (from the time of the ascension) reigning as king from the throne of David, then the kingdom of God is in session. Chilton explains the throne of Christ.

> "It is crucial to understand the bible's own interpretation of the throne of Christ. According to the inspired Apostle Peter, David's prophecy of Christ being seated on a throne was not a prophecy of some earthly throne in Jerusalem...David was prophesying about Christ's throne in heaven."[36]

The dispensational scheme claims Jesus offered the kingdom to Israel but later (upon Israel's rejection) postponed that offer. The kingdom now waits in heaven until the second coming of Jesus. When Jesus returns to earth then the kingdom age begins.

---

[36] David Chilton, Paradise Restored, Reconstruction Press, Tyler, Texas, 1985, page 71

This "postponement theory" is vital in maintaining their premillennial eschatology. The Bible is clear, Jesus sits on David's throne and the age of the kingdom has begun. Therefore, the theory of a literal 1,000-year kingdom crumbles beneath Peter's words.

This position of a postponed kingdom assumes too much. It assumes Jesus must be physically on earth before his reign can commence. It also assumes a rebuilt temple and a physical throne from which Jesus reigns. When the Scriptural evidence is in, the truth is clear, Jesus receive his authority to reign as king at the resurrection and ascension.

Ephesians 1:20-21

"That he worked in Christ when he raised him from the dead and seated him at his right hand in the heavenly places, far above all rule and authority and power and dominion, and above every name that is named, not only in this age but also in the one to come."

Paul agrees with Peter, Jesus is seated at the right hand of God. This is the same thing as sitting on a throne. Whoever sits on the throne has *"all rule and authority and power and dominion."*

Hebrews 1:3

"He is the radiance of the glory of God and the exact imprint of his nature, and he upholds the universe by the word of his power. After making purification for sins he sat down at the right hand of the Majesty on high."

Psalm 110:1

"The Lord says to my Lord, Sit at my right hand until I make your enemies a footstool for your feet."

Psalms 110 is the most quoted Old Testament passage in the New Testament. It speaks directly about Christ's fulfilling the role of King based on the Davidic covenant. Some Christians insist Christ is not presently fulfilling the promise of a ruling king. Only in the future 1,000-year millennium will Christ fulfill this covenant. Despite their theory, the ascension of Christ insures us He possesses all authority. Christ presently is seated at the right hand of the Father, and ruling over his kingdom through his church. The enemies of Christ are now being subdued. One by one, they are falling before the king.

Will the throne of David endure forever? Yes, it will! Yet, this can only be true if King David is but a representative of the true David, Jesus Christ.

Psalm 89:27-29 &35-36

"And I will make him the firstborn, the highest of the kings of the earth. My steadfast love I will keep for him forever, and my covenant will stand firm for him. I will establish his offspring forever and his throne as the days of the heavens .[35]*Once for all I have sworn by my holiness; I will not lie to David. His offspring shall endure forever, his throne as long as the sun before me. "*

The throne of David, which Jesus now occupies, is forever. The increase of Christ's reign is a promise to all generations. Forgot about the "good old days," thinking we will never again see God move as in the past. Believe for increase! Believe the Kingdom of God will increase in your life. Every local Church should be praying that the "throne" (which is the seat of Godly government) would increase in their communities. The generation to come must expect greater things. We must adjust our attitude to the Bible's or else we will quickly fall towards some pessimistic worldview not supported by God.

Acts 15:14-16

Simeon has related how God first visited the Gentiles, to take from them a people for his name. [15] *And with this the words of the prophets agree, just as it is written,*[16] *" 'After this I will return, and I will rebuild the tent of David that has fallen; I will rebuild its ruins ,and I will restore it. "*

This section in Acts is pivotal by showing how we interpret promises made in the Old Testament. I will introduce its major contribution to hermeneutics. James is summarizing the argument about the status of Gentiles in the new Christian church. He quotes a passage out of Amos speaking about rebuilding the Tabernacle of David. It is vital to see what Amos prophesies and then how James applies the prophecy in light of the new covenant.

Amos 9:11- 15

In that day I will raise up the booth of David that is fallen and repair its breaches, and raise up its ruins and rebuild it as in the days of old, [12] that they may possess the remnant of Edom and all the nations who are called by my name," declares the LORD who does this. [13] "Behold, the days are coming," declares the LORD, "when the plowman shall overtake the reaper and the treader of grapes him who sows the seed; the mountains shall drip sweet wine, and all the hills shall flow with it. [14] I will restore the fortunes of my people Israel, and they shall rebuild the ruined cities and inhabit them; they shall plant vineyards and drink their wine, and they shall make gardens and eat their fruit. [15] I will plant them on their land, and they shall never again be uprooted out of the land that I have given them," says the LORD your God.

Amos prophesies the restoration of David's tabernacle. This restoration includes Israel coming back into their land with great blessing upon it. The passage seems clear, Israel as a nation restored back to their land. There is only one problem; James interprets the passage entirely different. James does not tell us to expect Israel to regain sovereignty and rebuild her temple. He uses Amos as a proof text for God's intention to save Gentiles. The rebuilding of David's tabernacle is not a temple of stone but of people, Jews and Gentiles alike. The revival prophesied in natural terms finds its fulfillment in a harvest of souls among the Gentiles. The hills (representing human kingdoms) will give way to the one mountain of God, Mount Zion. This passage is one of the clearest in teaching how the church fulfills Old Testament prophecy.

Author Oswald T. Allis wrote <u>Prophecy and the Church</u> and it presents a devastating blow to dispensational eschatology. Allis exegetes numerous New Treatment texts and shows that the church does indeed fulfill the promises made in the Old Testament. Here are his comments concerning James in Acts 15.

> "It is hard to believe that James would have beclouded the issue by quoting a passage from the Old Testament which had no bearing upon the question under consideration. If James was a good

dispensationalist, he should have said something like this: "Brethren, what you say may be perfectly true. I believe it is true, since the Holy Spirit has blessed and owned our labors among the gentiles. But you must remember that the prophets have nothing to say about the church. So we cannot appeal directly to them."[37]

Obviously, James was not a dispensationalist. We use the word promise more often than covenant, but the term covenant better illustrates what is taking place here. Covenant establishes a binding agreement that God backs by His own person and character. God establishes a covenant with David that contains promises. God is a covenant keeping God and using the word covenant further strengthens God's resolve to bring complete fulfillment of the "Davidic covenant" in His Son Jesus. We can be assured, as followers of Jesus that every word given to David will happen in and through the church.

Study Questions

1. Explain the meaning of "house" and "kingdom" in view of the Davidic Covenant.

2. How does James (in Acts 15) interpret the Tabernacle of David?

3. What is one of the most quoted Old Testament passages in the New Testament? Why do you think it is important?

4. Where is the throne of David? When does Jesus receive the authority to reign from this throne? What does this mean for eschatology?

---

[37] Oswald T. Allis, Prophecy and the Church, Presbyterian and Reformed, 1972, page 148

Chapter 7

Daniel's Fifth Kingdom

Reviewing the Old Testament prophets concerning the kingdom of God, two primary questions must drive our inquiry. First, we must take notice of any descriptions of the kingdom; what will this kingdom be like? Second, we must look for any timetable for the kingdom. With these questions in mind, we move to the prophet Daniel.

Daniel was kidnapped as a teenager. From his home in Jerusalem to Babylon, he entered a training program to serve king Nebuchadnezzar. When the king had a puzzling dream, he called for his wise men to interpret it, which they could not. The angry king then sent out execution orders for all the wise men, this included Daniel and his Jewish friends. He quickly looked to God for help and received the interpretation. The dream centered on a great statue that represented four great empires, starting with Babylon, and finishing with Rome. The Roman Empire becomes the pivot point of all history because in the days of those kings, God takes action and sets up his very own kingdom.

The first significant kingdom was Nebuchadnezzar's Babylon, which was in power at that time. The second kingdom was the Medo-Persia Empire, and the third was Greece. The fourth kingdom is clearly Rome. This brings us to verse 44 that tell us *"in the days of those kings"* there would be a fifth and final world power.

Daniel 2:44

And in the days of those kings the God of heaven will set up a kingdom that shall never be destroyed, nor shall the kingdom be left to another people. It shall break in pieces all these kingdoms and bring them to an end, and it shall stand forever.

This fifth kingdom is the kingdom of God. Most biblical scholars agree that the Messianic kingdom begins with Christ, in the days of the Roman Empire. Once this fifth kingdom begins, it will endure forever. It has no rivals; the power of the cross and the resurrection of Christ crush the basic elements of the previous evil kingdoms. There is no mention of an additional coming of Christ to set up this fifth kingdom. This occurred during the first century with the first coming of Christ. Once this kingdom is "set up," it continues forever. The people of God can now experience the full blessing of all that the prophets foretold. Daniel supports a kingdom-centered eschatology beginning in the first-century.

Daniel saw four empires created by man and then God entering in a dramatic way to begin his kingdom. This is Daniel's fifth kingdom. The establishment of God's kingdom is during the same period as the fourth kingdom. Rome portrayed as iron, used its strength to crush its enemies—but it has a soft spot (represented by the mixture of clay); it can be defeated. Even though Rome was not defeated in history for several centuries, Jesus defeated it at the cross. Not only Rome, but also Jesus defeated all attempts by power driven people for world domination. The only world domination in our future will be under the Lordship of Jesus. If there are 10,000 evil conspiracies against the Messiah's reign, then over time and history all 10,000 are defeated. Jesus will have no rivals.

Mark 1:15 (The Message)

"Times up! God's Kingdom is here. Change your life and believe the message."

What time was Jesus referring to in this passage? I believe Jesus was referring back to Daniel, as Daniel was the prophet that prophesied the exact timing of the arrival of the kingdom. What are we to believe? We are to believe the message of God's kingdom! From this point forward, the primary message of Jesus was the kingdom of God.

Daniel has a second dream where he sees four great beasts (Dan. 7:1-8). These four beasts represent the same four kingdoms as in his first vision. The first was *"like a lion and had eagles wings"* the second, *"like a bear, it was raised up on one side"* and had *"three ribs between its mouth between its teeth."* The third was *"a leopard, with four wings of a bird on its back"* and had *"four heads."* The forth beast Daniel saw in his vision was *"terrifying and dreadful and exceedingly strong. It had great iron teeth; it devoured and broke in pieces and stamped what was left with its feet. It was different from all the beasts that were before it, and it had ten horns."* These four great beasts symbolized the same great empires as the previous vision, that of Babylon, Medo-Persian, Greece and Rome. What is different from the first vision is the use of "apocalyptic" language. The animals are not normal animals but are 'other worldly' and in our day considered cartoonish.

After describing the Roman Empire (fourth beast), Daniel unveils a scene from heaven.

Daniel 7:9-10 &13

As I looked, thrones were placed, and the Ancient of Days took his seat; his clothing was white as snow, and the hair of his head like pure wool; his throne was fiery flames; its wheels were burning fire. A stream of fire issued and came out from before him; a thousand thousands served him, and ten thousand times ten thousand stood before him; the court sat in judgment, and the books were opened. I saw in the night visions, and behold, with the clouds of heaven there came one like a son of man, and he came to the Ancient of Days and was presented before him.

When Jesus ascended into heaven, (Acts 1:9) the disciples wondered what happened and probably somewhat confused. Heaven was out of their sight. They were unaware of the amazing events about to take place. We are not confused about what happened when Jesus ascended into heaven, because we can now examine the ascension in light of Daniel's vision (Ch. 7). He saw the future and recorded the coronation of Jesus.

Allow your imagination to create the scene. Jesus enters heaven after accomplishing redemption through his death and resurrection. Now back in heaven, there is a grand celebration planned on his behalf. This event changed all of history. This is the coronation of Jesus as King of Kings.

This grand celebration in heaven starts with the seating of the Ancient of Days. This is Yahweh, the one and only God of the universe. He is the God of creation and therefore the God of the entire world. In the gospel of John it says, *"For God so loved the world, that he gave his only Son* (John 3:16)." God's gift to the world was his Son, who gave his life for the redemption of mankind. Now, back in his Father's heaven, he is officially presented. This is no casual presentation because it has all the markings of a royal and majestic event. Jesus now receives rewards for his mission on earth. Daniel sees, *"A stream of fire issued and came out from before him; a thousand thousands served him, and ten thousand times ten thousand stood before him."*

Can you image a long luxurious carpet leading up to the throne or maybe a walkway of gold. Along each side were thousands upon thousands, singing, bowing, and honoring Jesus as he approaches the throne. Daniel does not tell us, but perhaps as he reaches the throne, a high-ranking angel, or John the Baptist, gives the official announcement. "Now presenting Jesus, who humbled himself and went to earth. He died a cruel death upon a cross of wood as a sacrifice for sin. By the power of God, he rose from the grave; he defeated Satan and death for all who believe. He taught followers the new ways of the kingdom and he left them to proclaim the message to the ends of the earth. Now, this Jesus has returned to heaven and now crowned King of kings and Lord of lords. Here he is, Jesus, the son of Abraham, the son of David, the Son of God."

Even if we use our imagination to re-create the scene, no imagination is necessary to understand what took place. Daniel records the event.

Daniel 7:14

And to him was given dominion and glory and a kingdom, that all peoples, nations, and languages should serve him; his dominion is an everlasting dominion.

In verse thirteen, Daniel sees one like the *"son of man"* coming with the clouds (just as he left the earth) and presented before the Father. This is not a picture of the "rapture." Jesus is coming up to heaven not down to earth. Jesus is ascending into heaven. This happened historically at his ascension. He comes with the clouds just as the disciples saw Him leave (Acts 1:9). The disciples' perspective was from earth while Daniel's was from heaven. Daniel sees the son of man come before the Father and presented before the courts of heaven. The son of man receives *"Dominion, Glory and a Kingdom"* in which all men of the nations will serve him. The ascension is another vital aspect of Jesus establishing the kingdom during the first century.

Combining chapter two with chapter seven, a picture of the promised messianic kingdom is set forth. We now know the general timing when God takes action and brings his kingdom to earth. God will send the Messiah in the days of the Roman Empire. When his work on earth is complete, he will return to heaven and receive all authority to reign as King over His kingdom, the kingdom given to him by the Father. There is no need to create a revised Roman Empire in order to see this scripture fulfilled. The European Union is not now, nor will it ever be, the new Roman Empire.

In Daniel chapter nine, we go from a general time to a specific time. Daniel has an angelic visitation and records the number of years before the Messiah arrives.

Daniel 9:24-27

Seventy weeks are decreed about your people and your holy city, to finish the transgression, to put an end to sin, and to atone for iniquity, to bring in everlasting righteousness, to seal both vision and prophet, and to anoint a most holy place. ²⁵ Know therefore and understand that from the going out of the word to restore and build Jerusalem to the coming of an anointed one, a prince, there shall be seven weeks. Then for sixty-two weeks it shall be built again with squares and moat, but in a troubled time. ²⁶And after the sixty-two weeks, an anointed one shall be cut off and shall have nothing. And the people of the prince who is to come shall destroy the city and the sanctuary. Its end shall come with a flood, and to the end there shall be war. Desolations are decreed. ²⁷And he shall make a strong covenant with many for one week, and for half of the week he shall put an end to sacrifice and offering. And on the wing of abominations shall come one who *makes desolate, until the decreed end is poured out on the desolator.*

Verses 24-27 contain the message from the angel sent in response to Daniel's prayer. Daniel was reading the prophecy of Jeremiah and realized the end to the present exile was almost completed. The 70 years were ending. Daniel prays and repents in earnest. He repents for his own sins and for the sins of his people. He wanted to be sure that he and the people were prepared for the end of exile.

The message from the angel Gabriel was not exactly what Daniel desired. Yes, God would allow a few Jews to return and rebuild the city and the temple after the 70 years were complete. However, a new timetable with greater significance takes precedent. Most biblical scholars interpret the 70 weeks to mean 70 periods of seven years or 490 years in total. The true exile from bondage for the Jews would not be in the original 70 years, but would come in 490 years. The 490 years were to begin *"from the going out of the word to restore and build Jerusalem* (vs. 25)." There were three such declarations to restore Jerusalem.

1. Cyrus in 538 B.C. (Ezra 1:2-4)
2. Darius in 520 B.C. (Ezra 6:3-12)
3. Artaxerxes in 457 B.C. (Ezra 7:11-26).

Cyrus is a favorite because there are numerous passages connecting him and a decree that the Jews return to Jerusalem. Yet, the decree from Artaxerxes better fits the time frame. This decree takes us to the first century during the time of Jesus (Jesus may have been born around 4 BC). Daniel's prophecy was a favorite in the first century. The "Qumran Jews" made more copies of Daniel than any other Old Testament book.[38]

Our purpose here is to show how Daniel moves from the general time line to a specific time when the kingdom and Messiah will come. Those reading Daniel now have a specific time, in 490 years the Messiah will come. At this time, the kingdom will be

---

[38] John Noe, Beyond The End Times, Preterists Resources, 1999, Bradford, PA., p. 284

established and everlasting righteousness be brought in. The end of the animal sacrifices would come and a final atonement for sin accomplished. This provides the answer why there were so many "false messiahs" in the first century; they knew the prophecy of Daniel.

Before leaving Daniel 9, it is good to know that dispensational eschatology uses this prophecy to predict a seven year Great Tribulation in the future. They divide the prophecy into two parts, the first 69 weeks occurred in the ministry of Jesus during his first coming, but the final 70th week takes place after the "rapture" and therefore is in our future. This final week is the Great seven-year Tribulation. Dispensationalists force interpretation because there is not a single reference in Scripture that speaks of a seven-year tribulation. We have numerous references to a period of three and a half years (42 months) but never seven years. This gap theory is forced into the text. It is poor application of rules of exegesis and normal biblical interpretation. The 70 weeks runs consecutively and there is no gap separating the weeks.

Study Questions

1. What is the fifth kingdom and when does it begin?

2. How does dispensational eschatology arrive at a seven-year tribulation? List every biblical reference to a seven-year period of tribulation.

3. What event does Daniel describe in chapter seven? How do we know that it is Jesus and not another person presented before the courts of heaven?

4. Daniel writes that the time of the Messiah is calculated *"from the going out of the word to restore and build Jerusalem."* Who gave this word to rebuild Jerusalem?

5. Explain the gap theory of dispensational doctrine. Do you think this huge gap of time is justified by the text? If so, then why?

Chapter 8

Isaiah's World of Peace

Isaiah 2:2-4

It shall come to pass in the latter days that the mountain of the house of the LORD shall be established as the highest of the mountains, and shall be lifted up above the hills; and all the nations shall flow to it, ³ and many peoples shall come, and say: "Come, let us go up to the mountain of the LORD, to the house of the God of Jacob, that he may teach us his ways and that we may walk in his paths." For out of Zion shall go the law, and the word of the LORD from Jerusalem. ⁴ He shall judge between the nations, and shall decide disputes for many peoples; and they shall beat their swords into plowshares, and their spears into pruning hooks; nation shall not lift up sword against nation, neither shall they learn war anymore.

Isaiah speaks of a time when the kingdom of God comes to earth. The mountain of the house of the Lord speaks of the kingdom. In Scripture, mountains represent mighty acts of God. In the vision by Daniel, he sees a small stone that becomes a mountain and fills the entire earth (Daniel 2). This stone is Jesus and his kingdom. Isaiah writes that the kingdom of God will start in the latter day (or last days). The writer of Hebrews explains when these *"last days"* came into reality. *"In these last days has spoken to us in His Son"* (Hebrews 1:2). With the first coming of Christ, we saw the start of the period called the *"last days."* All these events described in Isaiah's prophecy happen progressively throughout the present age.

Isaiah 9:6-7

For to us a child is born, to us a son is given; and the government shall be upon his shoulder, and his name shall be called Wonderful Counselor, Mighty God, Everlasting Father, Prince of Peace. ⁷ Of the increase of his government and of peace there will be no end, on the throne of David and over his kingdom,

*to establish it and to uphold it with justice and with righteousness
from this time forth and forevermore. The zeal of the LORD of hosts
will do this.*

Isaiah goes beyond predicting the birth of the coming
Messiah. He ties many great Old Testament prophecies into one
beautiful portrayal of Jesus Christ and His future kingdom. He
tells of the government that God will rest upon the Messiah. In the
New Testament, Christ reassigns this authority to his disciples and
apostles, and later to all those who make up his church. The New
Testament makes it clear that upon the basis of the death,
resurrection, and ascension of Christ, the father has given him *"all
authority"* (Matthew 28:18).

A key component for kingdom-centered eschatology is that
there shall be no end to the increase of his government. Once the
kingdom is established (beginning with the incarnation) there is no
break in the continuity of the Messianic Kingdom; it continues to
increase. Premillennialists place the kingdom between the church
age and eternity. For them, the kingdom of God becomes the
1,000-year millennium after the second coming of Christ. Isaiah
portrays a different starting point; he shows a continual advance of
the kingdom beginning with Christ's birth. The meaning is clear.
We are in the kingdom and have been for over 2,000 years, and we
will continue to be there for a long time.

Isaiah 11:1-2

*There shall come forth a shoot from the stump of Jesse, and a
branch from his roots shall bear fruit. ² And the Spirit of the LORD
shall rest upon him, the Spirit of wisdom and understanding, the
Spirit of counsel and might, the Spirit of knowledge and the fear of
the LORD*

Isaiah writes about a future kingdom of David. King David is
no longer alive, having been dead for 300 years by the time
Isaiah's prophecy. The words *"shall bear fruit"* strike a familiar
New Testament association with the lack of fruit by the first
century nation of Israel. Christ proclaimed to Israel *"the kingdom
of God will be taken away from you and given to a people (nation),
producing the fruit of it"* (Matthew 21:43). Who will possess the

kingdom? Peter says to the new covenant believers in Christ "*but you are a chosen race, a royal priesthood, a holy nation,*" (I Peter 2:9). New covenant people now possess the Messianic kingdom. Through this people, the entire blessing and promises made by the Old Testament prophets will come true. Through the ministry of God's new people, the church, the earth will realize its full potential.

Isaiah 35:10

And the ransomed of the LORD *shall return and come to Zion with singing; everlasting joy shall be upon their heads; they shall obtain gladness and joy, and sorrow and sighing shall flee away.*

Isaiah 40:3-5

A voice cries: "In the wilderness prepare the way of the LORD; *make straight in the desert a highway for our God. [4] Every valley shall be lifted up, and every mountain and hill be made low; the uneven ground shall become level, and the rough places a plain. [5] And the glory of the* LORD *shall be revealed, and all flesh shall see it together, for the mouth of the* LORD *has spoken."*

Isaiah 44:3

For I will pour water on the thirsty land, and streams on the dry ground; I will pour my Spirit upon your offspring, and my blessing on your descendants.

Isaiah 61:6

But you shall be called the priests of the LORD; *they shall speak of you as the ministers of our God; you shall eat the wealth of the nations, and in their glory you shall boast.*

Isaiah 61:11

For as the earth brings forth its sprouts, and as a garden causes what is sown in it to sprout up, so the Lord GOD *will cause righteousness and praise to sprout up before all the nations.*

Isaiah 62:1-2

For Zion's sake I will not keep silent, and for Jerusalem's sake I will not be quiet, until her righteousness goes forth as brightness, and her salvation as a burning torch. [2] The nations shall see your righteousness, and all the kings your glory, and you shall be called by a new name that the mouth of the LORD *will give.*

These prophecies by Isaiah need no additional comment to bolster the concept of the coming glorious Kingdom. Among the prophets, Isaiah speaks more to the coming Messiah and his kingdom than the other Hebrew prophets do. He uses many images and metaphors in describing the glorious day of the kingdom. From pictures of bountiful farms, to peaceful cities, the kingdom of God is the glorious age upon the earth that every person longs for.

Isaiah 65:17-22 &25

"For behold, I create new heavens and a new earth, and the former things shall not be remembered or come into mind. [18] But be glad and rejoice forever in that which I create; for behold, I create Jerusalem to be a joy, and her people to be a gladness. [19] I will rejoice in Jerusalem and be glad in my people; no more shall be heard in it the sound of weeping and the cry of distress. [20] No more shall there be in it an infant who lives but a few days, or an old man who does not fill out his days, for the young man shall die a hundred years old, and the sinner a hundred years old shall be accursed. [21] They shall build houses and inhabit them; they shall plant vineyards and eat their fruit. [22] They shall not build and another inhabit; they shall not plant and another eat; for like the days of a tree shall the days of my people be, and my chosen shall long enjoy the work of their hands. [25] The wolf and the lamb shall graze together; the lion shall eat straw like the ox, and dust shall be the serpent's food. They shall not hurt or destroy in all my holy mountain," says the LORD.

In Isaiah 65, we have a passage that centers on the debate of various eschatological positions. What the prophet saw is certainly beyond his historical or contemporary setting. When these conditions become part of our lives, this is where eschatology divides. For the amillennialists, the prophet's vision comes true in heaven. There are no earthly expectations. Within the premillennial camp, this passage is about the 1,000-year millennium that begins with the second coming of Christ. They strongly oppose the concept that these conditions prevail before Christ returns. For those holding this view, there is no hope for this present age. Evangelism and waiting for Christ to return is their main priority. Advocates of a progressive eschatology of victory believe Isaiah sees a time on earth not heaven, and that it is in the same age in which we live, the age of the kingdom. Neither amillennialism nor premillennialism supports a growing kingdom like the one we see in Isaiah.

Even though the passage speaks about new heavens and a new earth, we should not immediately think everything is for the future. The kingdom begins small (as a mustard seed) and grows to the conditions set forth by Isaiah. This passage is set in time and history because people grow old and die (this cannot be heaven). Even though life spans are long, people still die. This is not the 1,000-year millennium either. In the premillennial theory, believers return to earth after being in heaven and after receiving their resurrection bodies, hence no death.

Isaiah reveals a picture of a peaceful, glorious time upon earth, everyone being productive and fruitful. This is not describing heaven, but the blessings of heaven on earth. This is not describing a time post-resurrection either, because death still occurs. The events described here are part of our age and show the direction the world is heading.

Isaiah 66:12, 18, 22-23

For thus says the LORD: "Behold, I will extend peace to her like a river, and the glory of the nations like an overflowing stream; and you shall nurse, you shall be carried upon her hip, and bounced upon her knees. [18] "For I know their works and their thoughts, and the time is coming[c] (AB) to gather all nations and tongues. And they shall come and shall see my glory, [22] "For as the new heavens and the new earth that I make shall remain before me, says the LORD, so shall your offspring and your name remain. [23] From new moon to new moon, and from Sabbath to Sabbath, all flesh shall come to worship before me, declares the LORD.

For those embracing a kingdom-centered eschatology, Isaiah portrays the age of the kingdom in its fullness. This passage, filled with metaphors and poetry, paints a picture of the earth during our age. We are not there yet. It may take generations. This is God's dream for the earth and it should be ours. Exactly how literally or symbolically this passage should be interpreted remains uncertain. Nevertheless, we must acknowledge that symbolic language and metaphors have meaning; and the clear meaning is a time of unparalleled blessings upon God's people on the earth.

The universal worship that shall cover the earth is a common theme in eschatological passages. Worship is the proper response to God because of his blessings upon the earth.

Study Questions

1. What can we learn about the kingdom of God from Isaiah 9:6-7?

2. How should we interpret Isaiah 65? Is this a time after the general resurrection or will these conditions occur before it?

3. Explain how "the stem of Jesse" is part of understanding eschatology.

4. According to the prophet Isaiah, should we expect (over time) that the world conditions would get worse or get better? Give verses from Isaiah to prove your position.

5. What can we expect from the prophecy in Isaiah 2? In what ways will the church and the world change in fulfillment of this passage?

Chapter 9

Jeremiah's New Covenant

Jeremiah 31:31-34

"Behold, the days are coming, declares the LORD, when I will make a new covenant with the house of Israel and the house of Judah, [32] not like the covenant that I made with their fathers on the day when I took them by the hand to bring them out of the land of Egypt, my covenant that they broke, though I was their husband, declares the LORD. [33] For this is the covenant that I will make with the house of Israel after those days, declares the LORD: I will put my law within them, and I will write it on their hearts. And I will be their God, and they shall be my people. [34] And no longer shall each one teach his neighbor and each his brother, saying, 'Know the LORD,' for they shall all know me, from the least of them to the greatest, declares the LORD. For I will forgive their iniquity, and I will remember their sin no more."

Considering the abundance of Old Testament Messianic passages, Jeremiah's prophecy is one of the best, as far as pointing us in the direction of eschatological victory. Jeremiah foretells major changes God has in store for his people. He prophesies a new covenant will succeed the old covenant. Dispensationalists, because of their radical separation of Israel and the church deny this new covenant is for Christians. They see natural Israel as the only group that can fulfill this prophecy, and only in the future millennium. The book of Hebrews makes it clear that we have come to this new and better covenant (Hebrews 8-10). Hebrews primary readers are Jewish Christians, showing the superiority of Christ over the old temple worship. The book of Hebrews shows clearly that Christians are the recipients of the new covenant and receive the messianic promises.

Jeremiah's promise says God will actually write his laws in people's hearts. The key question that dispensationalists ask is, "Who receives the new covenant?" What group of people has the legal authority to receive benefits of this new covenant?" Because of their radical separation of Israel and the church, they teach no prophecy or promise found in the Old Testament applies to the church. Therefore, since Jeremiah says the new covenant is for the house of Judah and the house of Israel, it is theirs exclusively. According to dispensational doctrine, only Jews receive the new covenant.[39] Christians have no part of Jeremiah's promise.

Charles C. Ryrie is a well-known dispensational scholar. In His book, <u>The Basis of the Premillennial Faith,</u> Ryrie states three reasons why Jeremiah's prophecy of a new covenant, are exclusively for the natural Israel.

> "The teaching of the Old Testament is that the new covenant therein given is for the Jewish people. This is seen for several reasons. First, it is seen by the fact of the words of establishment of the covenant...Secondly, that the Old Testament teaches that the new covenant is for Israel is also seen by the fact of its very name. In the central passage in Jeremiah 31:31-34 it is contrasted with the Mosaic covenant. Since, then, the new covenant is made with the same people as the Mosaic was, the important question is, with whom was the Mosaic covenant made? We believe that the Scripture clearly teaches that the Mosaic covenant of the law was made with the nation Israel only...Thirdly, that the old Testament teaches that the new covenant is for Israel is also seen by the fact that in its establishment the perpetuity of the nation Israel and her restoration to the land is vitally linked with it...The Church is never called a nation, and the national aspect of this covenant concerns an

---

[39] Because Jesus says the New Covenant "is in my blood", some dispensationalists separate the New Covenant spoken of by Jesus (for Christians) from the promised New Covenant spoken by Jeremiah (for Israel). This creates two New Covenants.

earthly people... Thus we conclude that for these three incontrovertible reasons, the very words of the text, the name itself, and the linking with the perpetuity of the nation, the new covenant according to the teaching of the Old Testament is for the people of Israel."[40]

If the new covenant is for the nation Israel, when is its fulfillment? Ryrie says, "The new covenant is not only future but millennial."[41] The new covenant will finally come to fulfillment in the future 1,000- year millennium kingdom and be established exclusively with the nation Israel; all this according to dispensational doctrine. Is this the teaching of the New Testament? We begin in chapter eight of Hebrews.

HEBREWS 8:6-8

But as it is, Christ has obtained a ministry that is as much more excellent than the old as the covenant he mediates is better, since it is enacted on better promises. [7] For if that first covenant had been faultless, there would have been no occasion to look for a second. [8] For he finds fault with them when he says: "Behold, the days are coming, declares the Lord, when I will establish a new covenant with the house of Israel and with the house of Judah,

Our passage links the ministry of Christ with creating a better covenant than the former one. The old covenant was not without fault. It was a temporary covenant used as a gateway into the new. Since Christ is the one who mediates the covenant, those in him, receive the benefits. Just because Jeremiah uses old covenant language (house of Judah and Israel) it does eliminate Christians from partaking of it rich benefits.

Paul wrote that he and other believers were benefactors of the new covenant (II Cor. 3:16). Even though Paul was a Jew, he included all who were following Jesus. Jesus taught his disciples that the new covenant was in his blood; therefore, all cleansed from sin by his blood were included in the new covenant. *"And*

---

[40] Charles C. Ryrie, The Basis of the Premillennial Faith,
[41] Ibid

likewise the cup after they had eaten, saying, "This cup that is poured out for you is the new covenant in my blood" (Luke 22:20).

The covenant prophesied by Jeremiah is not exclusively a Jewish covenant but is the new arrangement brought about by the death and resurrection of Jesus.

The book of Hebrews makes it clear that we have come to this new and better covenant (Hebrews 8-10). The author writes repeatedly how Jesus is better than "anything" from the old. Since Christians are the recipients of the new covenant, they are also the ones that receive the messianic promises. The dispensational teaching that Jeremiah's new covenant is for only natural Israel departs from historic Christian doctrine and must be rejected.

Study Questions

1. According to dispensationalist Ryrie, when does the new covenant begin? Why?

2. Do you think the book of Hebrews agrees with Ryrie? Why?

3. Give a New Testament verse that links the church with being a nation.

4. Explain the relationship between the new covenant and the cross.

Chapter 10

Worldwide Blessings of the Kingdom

The kingdom of God is present with us. That being the case, what is the nature of this kingdom? The nature of the kingdom determines how we see the blessings of the kingdom. If the kingdom is a different word for heaven and the spiritual blessings that await Christians when they die, then we miss the focus of Scripture, which is bringing the blessings of God to earth.

Over the years, many have attempted a definition of the kingdom of God and realized later its inadequacy. Why is defining God's kingdom so difficult? It is because the Bible has no comprehensive definition. There are numerous ways to describe it. The kingdom is the "reign of Christ in the hearts of believers." The kingdom is the sovereign reign of God. The kingdom of God is a realm of authority. The kingdom is the life of God within each believer. Some describe the kingdom in terms of Christian civilization, and others indentify it with supernatural gifts. Is the kingdom purely spiritual or is it only the visible aspects of the church (Christian institutions)? Is the kingdom of God a return to the old covenant practices where Jesus sets on a physical throne and reigns from a rebuilt temple in Jerusalem? There are many ways people have defined the kingdom of God.

Defining the Kingdom

Victorious eschatology teaches the continual growth of the Messianic Kingdom until all the nations of the world have been discipled. It stands alone, as the one-eschatological theology that believes this present world experiences the knowledge of God's glory like the Old Testament promises. Jesus receives the kingdom at his coronation (an aspect of the ascension) and now reigns as king over all. There is no waiting. He is both Savior and King. His kingdom is destined to grow. We have an abundance of prophetic literature that speaks directly to this issue.

Genesis 3:15

I will put enmity between you and the woman, and between your offspring and her offspring; he shall bruise your head, and you shall bruise his heel."

After Adam sinned, he lost the glory of God for a covering. He then received a prophetic word that brought hope. Dominion was not lost. Sin did not destroy God's dream. The enemy shall receive a mortal blow, while the redeemer receives a painful wound, but it is not a fatal one. Regaining authority over the earth begins with an encounter with our redeemer, Jesus Christ. We have no hope of personal or corporate transformation apart from the supernatural act of spiritual rebirth. No human effort, no matter how talented or well financed, can accomplish this. As evangelicals, we must affirm that the born again experience is the first step in any return to biblical dominion and kingdom growth.

There are a plethora of eschatological significant passages in the Old Testament, including, Ezekiel 47:1-5, Zechariah 9:9-10, Zechariah 14:8-9, Joel 2:28-29, Amos 9:11-13, Malachi 1:11, and Malachi 4:1-6. However, we now look to the book of Psalms for passages showing worldwide blessings and growth of God's kingdom.

Psalms 2:8

Ask of me, and I will make the nations your heritage, and the ends of the earth your possession.

The cross and the resurrection of Christ have ramifications beyond what most Christians ascribe to it. The church is not on some rescue mission trying to win a few souls before Jesus comes. We should be on a mission to win the world for Christ. Transformation of the world, not escaping it, is our assignment. The promise of God the Father to his Son is that the world would be His (the Son's) inheritance. What kind of gift would the world in its present condition be? Our task is bringing all opposition forces under Christ's authority. We are to make the nations a suitable gift for the Son. This kind of thinking elevates the glory of God as our highest priority (if meeting all the needs of fallen humanity becomes our priority it can become extremely wearisome). Kingdom centered eschatology acknowledges the glory of God as man's highest achievement.

Evangelism is out of concern for the lost, and out of a desire to see the world as a gift that Jesus deserves. As we preach the gospel and see the nations converted, we will return to a new Garden of Eden. The world then will be a gift worthy of our Lord and savior Jesus Christ.

Psalms 22:27

All the ends of the earth shall remember and turn to the Lord, and all the families of the nations shall worship before you.

God promises that all families of the world shall turn and worship the Lord. This begins with Abraham and finally fulfilled in Christ. Our hope encompasses the entire world. Victorious eschatology is not some whimsical dream, but builds upon a solid biblical foundation. Christ did not die to end up with a world filled with sin and corruption. He will have a world where obedience and worship fill the land.

What is our place in the promise? When Jesus departed for heaven, the ministry to the nations was only beginning. The command was to go into the entire world and "disciple the nations" (Matthew 28:18-19). This is not dropping into a country for several weeks and converting a handful of pagans. Jesus' command is that each nation is destined to become a people that follow his ways. Salvation is the start not the ending. We must learn obedience to the commands of Jesus.

Psalms 47:2

For the LORD, the Most High, is to be feared, a great king over all the earth.

The concept of Christ as the King has not prevailed in many Evangelical Churches. The reason lies in the dividing of Christ's act of saving from his role as Lord and King. I have heard many times that Christ came the first time as the Savior, but when He returns he will come as a King. The teachings of the New Testament make it very clear that Christ is seated at the right hand of God and has been given all authority in heaven as well as on the earth. Christians are portrayed as "reigning in life" with Christ.

There is no division of the office of Savior and King in the present role of Christ. He is both, Savior and King; now and forever.

Psalms 72:8

May he have dominion from sea to sea, and from the River to the ends of the earth!

The Bible teaches Christ's rule is comprehensive and full. Nations presently resisting the gospel, over time, will bow before the King of kings. The kingdom of God will reign over the entire earth. As the good news of the kingdom goes forth and disciples arise in every nation, the world will witness country after country experiencing transformation. Things are not getting worse; they are and will continue to get better. This may seem overly optimistic considering the present state of things, but our faith is in the Word of God not the current display of sinful humanity. In addition, a study in history will show that we do live in better times than many previous generations. Ask yourself one simple question; "Would you rather go to a dentist today or in the 16th century?" How many are killed in present wars when compared to wars of previous generations? Are there more believers today than ever before? Are more people coming to Christ today than ever before? The answer is yes. Today we have the highest percent of Christians to the population than ever before. The light of God's kingdom shines brighter from generation to generation.

Psalms 72:17

May his name endure forever, his fame continue as long as the sun! May people be blessed in him, all nations call him blessed!

As long as the sun shines, God's name will be blessed in the earth. We know that even if the sun would fail, God will be praised. We should expect the church to grow. We should expect the kingdom to expand. In the New Testament, these promises come together in the advent of Christ.

Psalms 72:19

Blessed be his glorious name forever; may the whole earth be filled with his glory! Amen and Amen!

Psalms 86:9

All the nations you have made shall come and worship before you, O Lord, and shall glorify your name.

These two passages are prophetic evidence to the great days that lay ahead. Eschatology of victory sees these promises coming to pass through the preaching of the gospel. As the power of Christ begins to convert masses of people in any given nation, we will see these prophecies come to fulfillment.

We only defined one aspect of the kingdom, the reign of Christ over all nations. Yet, without this basic revelation, we tend to define the kingdom in terms of heaven or push it into the future. Any biblical concept of God's kingdom must begin with this comprehensive view of Christ's reign.

Study Questions

1. Explain the meaning of Genesis 3:15 in light of Jesus' ministry.
2. Will the Great Commission be fulfilled? How?
3. Explain the role of Jesus as both Savior and King.
4. How can believers teach progressive improvement in the world when there are so many problems?
5. Give a definition of the kingdom of God.

Chapter 11

Jesus and the Kingdom

Jesus remains the subject of scholarly studies both by liberal and evangelical scholars. Liberal scholars are taken up with the 'historic Jesus' and attempt to discover who this "Jesus" person was. Evangelicals accept the Bible as inspired of God and base their arguments primarily on exegesis. Lately, scholars like N.T. Wright are bringing to light how Jesus, the Son of God, must be studied as the son of man within history. This is stirring up renewed interest in Christian origins, and with that fresh study on the relationship between Jesus and the kingdom of God.

Who was Jesus, and what was his mission? As Evangelicals, we accept Jesus as the promised Messiah. In his incarnation, he brought together humanity and God. Consider another question, was Jesus primarily a sacrificial lamb who came to take away our sins, or was he an eschatological prophet bringing forth a new age? Scholars debate whether Jesus came primarily as a teacher in the Greek tradition or as a prophet in the Jewish tradition. John J. Collins in, The Apocalyptic Imagination, reviews this discussion.

> "Schweitzer's view of Jesus as an apocalyptic prophet was not without basis. One of the best-attested facts about Jesus is that he preached that the kingdom of God was at hand. While the symbol of "kingdom" was used in various ways in antiquity, it lent itself to an eschatological interpretation in the context of Jewish literature from around the turn of the era, especially in literature deriving from the land of Israel that was originally composed in a Semitic language."[42]

---

[42] John J. Collins, The Apocalyptic Imagination, William B. Eerdmans Publishing Company, Grand Rapids, Michigan, 1988, page 258

My conclusion is that Jesus came as Savior and prophet. He came to Israel as their Messiah, as the one who brings deliverance, yet he also came announcing the "kingdom of God" in prophetic fashion. Yes, he "announced" the kingdom, but he went much further. He brought into the world the events of the eschatological kingdom. He lit the fire that set ablaze the events prophesied for hundreds of years by the ancient prophets.

The testimony of the gospels and the rest of the New Testament writings point clearly to Jesus as the Messiah, who came and gave his life on a cross, rose from the dead and is now seated at the right hand of God. These same documents also picture Jesus as the eschatological prophet who came to bring in the kingdom. It is this message of the kingdom that we take up now.

Luke 4:43

"But he said to them, "I must preach the good news of the kingdom of God to the other towns as well; for I was sent for this purpose."

Ask a group of Christians, why did Jesus come? How many answers will match what Jesus said? Most likely, there will not be many. God the father sends Jesus to earth to preach and establish the kingdom of God. The Christian church would transform over night if this one truth were embraced. This "kingdom aspect" is as important as his coming to take away our sin. One leads to the other. Removal of sin is necessary so people can live in the kingdom. Without the death and resurrection of Jesus, the kingdom of God would not be accessible. Jesus saw himself as commissioned to preach God's kingdom, and that is exactly what he did.

Matthew 1:1

"The book of the genealogy of Jesus Christ, the son of David, the son of Abraham.

The first verse of the New Testament provides credentials for connecting Jesus with the promises from the Old Testament. Matthew wants his readers to know that this Jesus is of the direct line of Abraham and David. He is the one who will fulfill all of the prophecies for Israel. Truly, Jesus is the new Israel. The church is included in this newly constructed Israel because of their relationship with Christ.

Matthew 3:1-3

In those days John the Baptist came preaching in the wilderness of Judea, [2] *"Repent, for the kingdom of heaven is at hand."* [3] *For this is he who was spoken of by the prophet Isaiah when he said,*

"The voice of one crying in the wilderness: 'Prepare the way of the Lord; make his paths straight.'"

The arrival of the Messiah meant that the long awaited kingdom was at hand, it was within reach. John's message started with repentance and intended to prepare people for the more radical teaching of Jesus. The preaching of Jesus caught most people off guard. They thought the Messiah would free them from the bonds of Rome and reintroduce the glorious times of the nation Israel. When Jesus came preaching a spiritual kingdom that needed a supernatural experience to even see it, trouble began to spread.

Matthew 4:23

And he went throughout all Galilee, teaching in their synagogues and proclaiming the gospel of the kingdom and healing every disease and every affliction among the people.

When Jesus began his public ministry, his message was exactly what John the Baptist told us. He preached the kingdom of God. This kingdom was not something new. This was the same kingdom prophesied by Isaiah and Daniel. Jesus was bringing about the kingdom prophesied for hundreds of years by the ancient prophets. Because of its spiritual nature, it did not mean that it was a different kingdom. This is the argument of dispensationalism, that Christ started a new and different kingdom called a "mystery kingdom." There is no evidence in the New Testament that the kingdom inaugurated by Jesus was anything other than the kingdom foreseen throughout the Old Testament.

Jesus preached the kingdom of God, and signs and wonders followed. The connection between miracles and the preaching of the kingdom is important. As we preach a present kingdom, confirming signs should be expected.

Jesus saw his role as Messianic and eschatological. With Daniel seven in the background, he brings both roles into view. By using the Old Testament imagery where one like the "son of man" is presented before the "Ancient of Days," Jesus connects the ascension with the promise of the kingdom. We now turn to an amazing promise (although bewildering to some) where Jesus promises to return before the present generation ended.

Matthew 16:28

Truly, I say to you, there are some standing here who will not taste death until they see the Son of Man coming in his kingdom.

This verse stands in opposition to the teaching that the kingdom of God was postponed for generations to come. Jesus tells his followers that some of them would live to see his "*coming in his kingdom.*" There is no way around the impact of this verse. We must allow the clear implications of this Scripture to form our theological foundations, not force this verse into our traditional doctrines.

In the book of Daniel, we saw the Son of Man come up to God the Father and receive a kingdom. This event is the ascension of Christ. Even though Jesus receives the kingdom at this time, it would be another forty years before the old covenant fades away-making way for the fullness of God's kingdom on earth. This progressive growth of the kingdom helps us to understand the "now" part of the kingdom and the "yet to come" part that Jesus speaks about. We are not to place this "yet to come" aspect into our future but exactly where Jesus places it, within the first century.

The language of Jesus points to the destruction of Jerusalem in 70 A.D. The final judgment upon Jerusalem during this time separated any confusion between Jews and the church. Once the temple burned and Jerusalem destroyed, the church possessed the kingdom of God. Either way one looks at this verse, we cannot overlook its impact that demands a first century fulfillment.

Mark 1:14-15

Now after John was arrested, Jesus came into Galilee, proclaiming the gospel of God, [15] *and saying, "The time is fulfilled, and the kingdom of God is at hand; repent and believe in the gospel."*

Mark states the message of Jesus. Here all of the elements come together in one thought. We have the passing of John's ministry and the beginning of the Messiah's ministry. We see the connection between the prophecies of the Old Testament with the arrival of Jesus. We see the role of repentance and then the message concerning the kingdom of God. Mark links this "preaching of the kingdom" with believing the gospel. This is another blow to dispensational eschatology, which, according to them, the gospel and the kingdom are two different ages. They see the gospel as belonging exclusively for the age of the church whereas the message of the kingdom is for the 1,000-year Millennium. The gospel of Mark links these two concepts into one unified thought. Preaching the kingdom of God is preaching the gospel.

Luke 16:16

The Law and the Prophets were until John; since then the good news of the kingdom of God is preached, and everyone forces his way into it.

Luke informs us when the transition between the old and the new takes place. Dispensationalists would have us believe that the transition into the age of the kingdom is still in the future. Luke clears up any confusion on the matter. Since John the Baptist, we preach the gospel of the kingdom. Luke affirms a first century establishment of the kingdom of God. The strength of this one passage should alone be enough to eliminate dispensational thinking about the timing of the kingdom.

Acts 1:3

He presented himself alive to them after his suffering by many proofs, appearing to them during forty days and speaking about the kingdom of God.

The book of Acts records how Jesus spent much of his time between the resurrection and the ascension. His appearance over a 40-day period was primarily to teach his disciples about the kingdom of God. Our theological debates would disappear if we knew the content of his teaching. For Jesus, understanding the kingdom was of the upmost importance. It is enlightening that even with the master teaching them directly, their comprehension remained clouded until the day of Pentecost.

Acts 14:22

Strengthening the souls of the disciples, encouraging them to continue in the faith, and saying that through many tribulations we must enter the kingdom of God.

Attempts to defend the postponement theory go like this, once Jesus ascends to heaven, kingdom-preaching stops (postponed until his return). A few passages from the book of Acts should be enough to prove this incorrect. In this particular Scripture, dispensationalists point out that the kingdom is future. It is true that the tense is future, but that reveals an aspect of the kingdom that the disciples are yet to experience. The kingdom is more than just a rule; it is also a realm of the Spirit. Christians face affliction, persecution, and endure suffering. Victorious eschatology does not mean a life free from pain. These difficulties produce character. Spiritual growth in the midst of suffering was common in the first century and modern day believers find this true as well. An attempt to force this passage into some future millennial kingdom does the passage injustice and undervalues what the early Christians went through.

The gospels tell us the story of Jesus and his teachings. It is unfortunate that many evangelicals skip Jesus' teaching and focus almost exclusively on his death. We have reduced the gospel message to "Jesus died for my sins so I can go to heaven when I die." Having our sins forgiven is great, more than great; it restores us back to God and we are eternally grateful. However, there is more to it; lots more.

Too many Christians race pass the gospels in favor of doctrines presented in the epistles. Dispensational eschatology has removed much of the gospels from any practical application because for them large sections are exclusively millennial. Since according to dispensationalists, the kingdom is a future age, therefore the gospels are less useful.

As we approach the gospels, we must not cloud our understanding with a poor hermeneutic that reduces their value. What we have in the gospels is the teachings of Jesus, which connect the promise of the kingdom from the Old Testament to the Christian church. We must not eliminate Jesus as a source of invaluable kingdom teaching.

As the Old Testament ends, it appears that all hope is lost. Where are the promises of the kingdom? Will the Messiah ever come? Four hundred long years have elapsed since the last prophets spoke. A lot can happen in that amount of time. Things change. Promises of God are lost over time. When will God send another prophet? We need to hear from God!

Israel had an elaborate system of religion built upon the foundations of the old covenant laws, yet much changed during the four hundred years without a prophet. During the intertestament period, Pharisees and Sadducees got their start along with a host of traditions. Israel had the Law of Moses but now generations later; these traditions have eclipsed the Scriptures. Even today, our traditions often trump the word. The long silence was about over and the hope was about to reignite. His name is John the Baptist.

When word spread that a man, maybe even a prophet was preaching in the wilderness; crowds flocked to hear him. If this were a true prophet of Yahweh, what would he say to Israel after all these years? The message of John was simple and clear; "the kingdom of God is at hand."

The gospels, Matthew, Mark, Luke and John tell the events of Jesus from their perspective. Why would we need four versions from four authors, especially, when they repeat large sections of the story? A closer look reveals how each author tells the story slightly different, either by adding or by simplifying it. We are blessed to have the life of Jesus presented in such fashion. One reason for four gospels is that each addresses a different group of people who needed to hear about Jesus from their perspective. We can never be certain as to why we need four versions, but having them provides a comprehensive retelling of Jesus' life and teaching.

As to John the Baptist and his message of the kingdom, we must ask, "How did the people understand John's proclamation?" After centuries of hearing the prophets talk about a coming reign of Yahweh, the exact wording John uses is, "the kingdom of God." The exact phrase "the kingdom of God" never appears in the Old Testament. One thing is for certain, even though the wording is slightly different; the knowledge of God's coming kingdom was prevalent in the first century.

The stimulus for kingdom expectations came from Daniel's 70-week prophecy located in Daniel 9. The Jews went into exile because of sin; therefore, repentance was the key for its end. John the Baptist added one small word to his kingdom announcement we often overlooked. His announcement was, "*Repent, for the kingdom of heaven is at hand* (Matt. 3:2)." Verses five and six explain how people responded. *"Then Jerusalem and all Judea and all the region about the Jordan were going out to him, and they were baptized by him in the river Jordan, confessing their sins."* Why were they confessing their sins? Were they under personal conviction of wrongdoing? No one knows the hearts of people when they repent, but the connection between the coming kingdom and repentance was not lost on these perceptive first century Jews. Their thinking may have been, "Now that the kingdom is at hand, we must reverse what put us in this bondage to Rome." "Sin put us in exile; therefore repentance will get us out." It might have been their desire to end the long exile and rid themselves of the yoke of Rome, and not their personal guilt, that brought about the frenzy of repentance. We learn later that their repentance was somewhat shallow. John the Baptist went to the heart of the issue and urged them to *"bear fruits in keeping with repentance* (Luke 3:8)."

John's message that God's kingdom is at hand touched off waves of excitement. Yet, he is not the main attraction. He came to introduce Jesus, *"he who is coming after me is mightier than I, whose sandals I am not worthy to carry. He will baptize you with the Holy Spirit and fire* (Matt. 3:11)." It is common in Pentecostal/charismatic groups to pray to receive the "fire" of the Holy Spirit, yet is quite clear in this context it is not the empowering of the Spirit that John had in mind, but of judgment.

Jesus follows John and announces the kingdom. Mark's gospel says it like this, *"Now after John was arrested, Jesus came into Galilee, proclaiming the gospel of God, and saying, "The time is fulfilled, and the kingdom of God is at hand; repent and believe in the gospel* (Mk. 1:14-15)."

Jesus adds to John's statement *"the time is fulfilled."* The connection to Daniel's prophecy would not have escaped Jewish eschatological expectations. For Jesus, the gospel of God is the good news of the coming kingdom. The long awaited arrival of Yahweh and his reign has dawned. His coming will bring to pass all that the prophets spoke. A new era is here.

The gospel of Matthew and Luke include a passage where Jesus provides a timeframe separating the old and new covenant.

Matthew 11:11-13

Truly, I say to you, among those born of women there has arisen no one greater than John the Baptist. Yet the one who is least in the kingdom of heaven is greater than he. From the days of John the Baptist until now the kingdom of heaven has suffered violence, and the violent take it by force. For all the Prophets and the Law prophesied until John.

This saying has confused many, including biblical scholars.[43] Why is John the one who begins the new age instead of Jesus? Then, possibly the most difficult part is when Jesus says the kingdom is suffering violence and men of violence take it by force. What is this all about? Careful exegesis must precede any conclusions or we can drift from the meaning. This is not an easy passage. Too many sermons highlight how Christians must take

---

[43] John P. Meier, Matthew NTM 3, Liturgical Press, Collegeville, Minnesota, 1980, p. 122

the kingdom with "violence," without considering the context and culture of the text.

The best exegesis I have found on this passage is by Dr. Brant Pitre. First, we begin with his summary of both passages.

> "In sum, while the versions lack consistent word for word correlation, they appear to be making the same two basic points in similar forms. (1) First, the law and the prophets somehow lasted up until the time of John, with his appearance marking the in breaking of the kingdom of God. (2) The kingdom of God currently suffers some kind of violence."[44]

The old covenant coming to its end with John is not difficult to harmonize with the rest of the New Testament. He introduces the Messiah, who is the one ushering in the new covenant. What seems difficult to interpret is how the kingdom suffers violence. Many in Pentecostal/charismatic groups preach this as our intense enthusiasm and determination to see the kingdom grow. Something seems wrong with the fact that in one place Jesus says it was his Fathers good pleasure to give the kingdom *"Fear not, little flock, for it is your Father's good pleasure to give you the kingdom"* (Luke 12:32), and here we have to take it by force. If we must fight our way into the kingdom and fight for its increase, what kind of fight is necessary? Pitre offers a better interpretation. He first traces the history where he sees a connection between the eschatological tribulation (Matt. 24: 21) and end-time violence.[45] He sees this violence not in some odd Christian behavior but fitting into the overall circumstances of the time. Jesus has come, and his intention is to usher in God's kingdom, yet preceding the kingdom is a time of distress and tribulation. With the death of John the Baptist begins a time of afflictions, difficult days and false

---

[44] Brant Pitre, Jesus, The Tribulation, And the end of Exile, Baker Academic, Grand Rapids, Michigan, 2005, p. 165-166

[45] Pitre, p. 167

Messiahs, all leading towards the final destruction of Jerusalem and its temple. Pitre concludes his exegesis with this summary.

> "It appears that Jesus saw in the sufferings undergone in the person of John, not only the dawn of the kingdom of God, but also the onset of the final time of lawlessness and false prophecy-in short, the eschatological tribulation…not only is the kingdom beginning to be realized in the ministry of John, but the tribulation that precedes the kingdom has also begun in the violence done against him. Hence, the eschatological tribulation not only provides a better understanding of a difficult logion, it also potentially furnishes us with a deeper grasp of Jesus' understanding of John's role in salvation history and a glimpse of the origins of realized eschatology."[46]

John links the coming kingdom with the necessary trials and tribulations preceding it. Have you wished to live in the days of the early church? It would have been wonderful, yet it also was a season of intense troubles and trails. Paul says the last days are *"times of difficulty"* (II Tim. 3:1). Peter explains to his readers that yes, the last days are days of salvation, but first be prepared because, *"for a little while, if necessary, you have been grieved by various trails* (I Peter 1:6)." John the beloved, warns his readers not to be deceived during these days, *"For many deceivers have gone out into the world, those who do not confess the coming of Jesus Christ in the flesh. Such a one is the deceiver and antichrist* (III John 7)." In John's first letter, he explained how believers would confirm they were living in the "last days." He told them, *"Children, it is the last hour, and as you have heard that antichrist is coming, so now many antichrists have come. Therefore we know that it is the last hour* (I John 2:18)."

---

[46] Pitre, p.177

Realized Eschatological of Jesus

How did Jesus view the kingdom? Was it just an announcement and then quickly postponed for numerous generations (dispensational view)? On the other hand, was Jesus the one bringing Yahweh's kingdom to earth? The words and works of Jesus favor a realized eschatology. He began his ministry by preaching the kingdom was at hand. He told the Jewish leaders the kingdom was in their midst. He taught the binding of the strongman was a sign of the kingdom. There is little doubt that Jesus saw in his actions and words, the arrival of the kingdom.

Jesus also spoke of a coming kingdom, a future kingdom. Does this future kingdom negate the reality of the present one? Bringing these two concepts together should not be difficult. The kingdom began with his public ministry, then spiritually established by his death, resurrection and ascension. Nevertheless, the "coming of the kingdom" was not complete until something else happened. The future aspect of the kingdom is the "*coming of the son of man.*" This was his spiritual return in judgment and the final days of the old age. This occurred 40 years later when the temple and Jerusalem burned with fire.

If we view the New Testament period as a season of overlapping ages, the realized kingdom and future kingdom comes into focus. The new people of God, those of the new creation, had their official start at Pentecost. Nevertheless, it was not until the temple came down in a blaze of fire that the age of the old covenant stopped. Therefore, the first century church lived in a transition period, 40 years when the old covenant stood alongside the new. This explains the realized and future kingdom of Jesus. It was very real during his life, yet had one final event to bring its fullness to the earth.

The church has a commission to "make disciples of all nations." We accomplish this by preaching Jesus and the kingdom. We obey Jesus by teaching; baptizing, training, and seeing every believer find their place in the grand project of God. The kingdom of God has already come in its fullness, yet may still be in its infancy as to its final goal, the renewal of the earth.

Parables

Jesus uses parables to teach the kingdom of God. Parables were common in the first century, being used by rabbis and frequently appearing in the Talmud and other Jewish books.[47] Our word "parable" comes from the Greek and means to "place by the side of."[48] It teaches a moral truth by placing one thing aside another. Parables make use of everyday items; you never see singing dogs, flying horses, or other cartoonish type creatures. They keep close to normal human experiences. At the start of Jesus' ministry parables were absent from his teaching. One day as the crowds gathered he taught them *"many things in parables."*

Matthew 13:1-3

That same day Jesus went out of the house and sat beside the sea. And great crowds gathered about him, so that he got into a boat and sat down. And the whole crowd stood on the beach. And he told them many things in parables.

It is on the shores of the Sea of Galilee that Jesus began teaching in parables. His disciples took notice and later asked him *"Why do you speak to them in parables?"* His answer was a parable itself, a blend of proverb, metaphor, enigma and a prophecy from Isaiah.[49]

Matthew 13:11-12

And he answered them, "To you it has been given to know the secrets of the kingdom of heaven, but to them it has not been given. For to the one who has, more will be given, and he will have an abundance, but from the one who has not, even what he has will be taken away. This is why I speak to them in parables, because seeing they do not see, and hearing they do not hear, nor do they understand."

Most ministers teach so their hearers understand. We study carefully and work hard to communicate God's word so people

---

[47] Milton S. Terry, Biblical Hermeneutics, Academic Books, Zondervan Publishing house, Grand Rapids, Michigan, page 276

[48] Ibid.

[49] Ibid.

will understand. Yet, Jesus operated with a different philosophy. He taught using a method where those with hungry hearts would pursue the truth whereas the rebellious walked away unaffected by the parable. Parables did not test the intellect of people but their character.

Studying Jesus' parables is worth our effort, as in them we find our hearts exposed. Nevertheless, for time sake and keeping on topic, only two parables need reviewing. Both show the growth of God's kingdom.

Matthew 13:31-33

"He presented another parable to them, saying, 'The kingdom of heaven is like a mustard seed, which a man took and sowed in the field; and this is smaller than all other seeds, but when it is full grown, it is larger than the garden plants and becomes a tree, so that the birds of the air come and nest in its branches.' He spoke another parable to them, 'The kingdom of heaven is like leaven, which a woman took and hid in three pecks of flour until it was all leavened."

Both parables teach the growth and advancement of the kingdom. God's kingdom is destined to grow and make incredible advances in the earth. Parable number one uses the example of a simple mustard seed. The mustard seed starts small, just like the kingdom in the first century. From its small beginning, its growth has been continual. In the first century, the percentage of Christians to that of the world was very small, less than one percent. If we drew a chart, showing the growth of the church for the last two thousand years it would go steadily upward. Every 100 years shows an increase of the number of Christians to the population of the world. This trend will continue, and in time, God's glory will cover the earth. The parable of the mustard seed is the external growth of God's kingdom. Building Christian institutions that bring blessing to people for hundreds of years is part of this external kingdom growth.

The second parable uses leaven as its example. Leaven transforms from within. It transforms people as well as cultures, changing it from the inside out. The leaven of God is in the earth.

It will keep working and working until the entire world is full of God's glory. Christians are the good leaven that causes increase for God's kingdom. Our problem is that we over spiritualize this and place a large amount of guilt on ourselves if we are not "witnessing" and winning people to the Lord. We must win all we can, but the leaven in us represents our kingdom calling, our God given gifts. Our callings are different. If a Christian has a call as a medical research scientist then their primary task is to find cures for diseases, not just "be there" to witness. Yes, share your faith when the door is open, but the kingdom of God is growing in a multitude of ways. The kingdom grows internally and externally.

Study Questions

1. Explain the theological implications in the parable of the mustard seed and the leaven.

2. Why did Jesus use parables as a teaching tool?

3. Should Christians today "force" the kingdom in the manner spoken of by John the Baptist?

4. Explain how the Victorious kingdom view and dispensationalism disagree on how to use and interpret much of the gospels.

5. In Mark 4:43 Jesus gives the reason he came to earth. Explain in your view why there is so little preaching on this subject.

Chapter 12

The Apostles and the King__ _

Once Jesus ascended into heaven, the apostles were responsible for continuing the message. Did they preach the kingdom of God? Do we see evidence they stopped preaching the kingdom, thinking it was postponed? Dispensationalists claim the kingdom preached by Jesus was exclusively a Jewish kingdom. Once rejected, our only hope for God's kingdom on earth is the Second Coming. Therefore, all promises and prophecies of the kingdom wait for a 1,000-year millennium. Liberal scholars claim Paul and his partners created the message of modern Christianity. They view Jesus as a prophet of the kingdom whereas the apostles preached the cross. Both scenarios find little support in Scripture. The apostles preached the kingdom and preached the cross, because they are aspects of one gospel.

Acts 19:8

And he entered the synagogue and for three months spoke boldly, reasoning and persuading them about the kingdom of God.

Luke provides us with the message preached by the early church. During his stay in Ephesus, Paul used his time teaching the kingdom. There is absolutely no hint that the early Christians stopped preaching the kingdom of God after Christ ascended back to heaven. We also learn that a twenty-minute sermon cannot cover the subject; it took Paul three months.

Those called to teach the kingdom must not succumb to shallow feel good sermons. Most people are under challenged from the pulpit. Like small children, believers are treated as if cannot follow biblical doctrine. We do this especially with our teens. We expect them to study advanced mathematics, biology, history, languages, and literature; yet in the church, "They cannot learn doctrine." Young people want a challenge. They want a solid foundation that gives hope for their future. The church has a responsibility to provide this. Before graduating high school, young people should have a solid grasp of biblical eschatology. If the local church does not teach a clear vision for God's kingdom people, they will "learn" their eschatology outside their church, which most likely will be dispensationalism.

Acts 20:25

And now, behold, I know that none of you among whom I have gone about proclaiming the kingdom will see my face again.

Acts 28:23&30-31

When they had appointed a day for him, they came to him at his lodging in greater numbers. From morning till evening he expounded to them, testifying to the kingdom of God and trying to convince them about Jesus both from the Law of Moses and from the Prophets.

30He lived there two whole years at his own expense, and welcomed all who came to him, 31proclaiming the kingdom of God and teaching about the Lord Jesus Christ with all boldness and without hindrance.

Paul used his final years to preach the kingdom of God. In verse twenty-three, Paul used the Law and the Prophets to teach about Jesus and his kingdom. The dispensational position of a future millennium reign of Christ on earth is absent in the New Testament. The theory of the 1,000-year of Christ is created only by forcing a wooden literalism onto Revelation 20. The early church did not stop preaching the kingdom after the ascension. This was no mistake in misunderstanding the timing of the kingdom. To them the kingdom was a present reality, and it is today as well.

Colossians 1:13

13He has delivered us from the domain of darkness and transferred us to the kingdom of his beloved Son,

Paul teaches how the Kingdom of God relates to conversion. When we believe that Jesus is God's son, and that he rose from the dead, we receive deliverance from the kingdom of darkness and into the kingdom of light. The kingdom is a present reality, not an event waiting for the Second Coming. This change of "domains" from darkness to the kingdom of Jesus brings about a rescue.

People are in need of rescue; they need the message of Jesus and his kingdom.

I Corinthians 15:22-28

For as in Adam all die, so also in Christ shall all be made alive. [23] But each in his own order: Christ the firstfruits, then at his coming those who belong to Christ. [24] Then comes the end, when he delivers the kingdom to God the Father after destroying every rule and every authority and power. [25] For he must reign until he has put all his enemies under his feet. [26] The last enemy to be destroyed is death. [27] For "God has put all things in subjection under his feet." But when it says, "all things are put in subjection," it is plain that he is excepted who put all things in subjection under him. [28] When all things are subjected to him, then the Son himself will also be subjected to him who put all things in subjection under him, that God may be all in all.

Having established that God's kingdom arrived with the first coming of Christ, we must now learn about the extent of this kingdom. For the premillennialists the kingdom begins with the second coming of Christ and continues for exactly 1,000-years. Since the Messianic kingdom began over 2,000 years ago, we know the literal 1,000-years cannot correct. The 1,000-year statement in the book of Revelation is a symbolical number meaning a large round number. This is how the Bible uses this phrase.

First Corinthians 15 portrays the kingdom as continually growing and defeating the enemies of Christ. Why it is that many Christians believe evil must prevail over righteousness? Paul was convinced Christ the King will succeed. This passage presents some mystery, as we really are not sure why Christ gives up the kingdom to the Father. Does this mark a change within the function of the Godhead? Some have suggested that there is a change from the kingdom of Christ (Messianic Kingdom) to the eternal kingdom of God, yet this presents problems in that the kingdom of the Messiah is to endure forever. Whatever this refers to, it does not alter the plethora of passages that speak about the kingdom of God having no end of its increase.

Note once again, that the 1,000-year millennium kingdom is absent in this passage. This would have been the perfect place for Paul to introduce it if he had any premillennial leanings. Paul's eschatology is straightforward; the kingdom begins with the incarnation, it advances throughout the age and finalizes with the Father receiving it back.

Our Message

What is our message today? John the Baptist preached the kingdom, Jesus preached the kingdom, and the Apostles preached the kingdom, so why do we not preach the kingdom? The answer is simple, bad doctrine. If it were not for the rise of dispensational eschatology in the nineteenth century, the church would hopefully still be preaching the kingdom of God as a present and advancing reality. The apostles provide details on how they perceived their purpose.

Acts 13: 44-47

The next Sabbath almost the whole city gathered to hear the word of the Lord. But when the Jews saw the crowds, they were filled with jealousy and began to contradict what was spoken by Paul, reviling him. And Paul and Barnabas spoke out boldly, saying, "It was necessary that the word of God be spoken first to you. Since you thrust it aside and judge yourselves unworthy of eternal life, behold, we are turning to the Gentiles. For so the Lord has commanded us, saying, "'I have made you a light for the Gentiles, that you may bring salvation to the ends of the earth.

When the Jews rejected the word of Paul, he quotes a passage from Isaiah (49:6). The text is about the "Servant of the Lord" which is clearly a prophecy of Jesus as the Messiah. The apostles saw the ministry of Jesus as being theirs. They were the ones who would be "*a light to the Gentiles.*" They were the ones who would bring "*salvation to the ends of the earth.*" The message of the apostles and our message is the same; we proclaim salvation to the entire earth. We do not have a commission to evangelize only a few nations, only to provide a witness, but we are told to go and preach the gospel to all creation (Mark 16:15) and to make disciples of all nations (Matthew 28:18-19).

The apostles knew their gospel. There was no division between preaching the kingdom and preaching the cross and resurrection. Defining the gospel is not easy. On one hand, we have those who simply say the gospel is the message of Jesus death on a cross. Others point to the statements of Jesus and ascribe to a definition centering on the kingdom of God. Both are overly simplistic. The "good news" **is** the message that the kingdom of God is now here. Yet, this statement alone misses a key important ingredient; how do we enter the kingdom? Any attempt to define the gospel without both concepts of the cross and resurrection of Jesus and the good news of God's kingdom fall short of the biblical understanding of the gospel.

Study Questions

1. When Israel refused her Messiah, did this postpone the kingdom? Provide biblical support for your answer.

2. How does the Apostle Paul connect the kingdom with the return of Christ in I Corinthians 15:22-28? Do we find any rapture or 1,000-year kingdom in this statement of Paul's eschatology?

3. Did the apostles continue preaching the kingdom of God after Jesus ascended to heaven? Why?

4. What should our message be today? Give a definition of the gospel.

Chapter 13

The Last Days

It is imperative to understand the time element of the *"last days."* Knowing the "when" of these *"last days"* is certain to bring doctrinal sanity back into the discussion. A system of biblical hermeneutics that pays close attention to the time frames of New Testament prophecy is the preterist view. This view offers an alternative from modern eschatology that interprets the prophetic passages dealing with the last days as future (our future). It is my conviction that the preterist method of interpreting biblical statements dealing with the *"last days"* will bring us closer to the apostles understanding and will help curb the appetite of prophetic speculation so prevalent today.

What are our options when it comes to the timing issue? I see three available choices. First is the widely held view that the final generation before the second coming of Christ is the *"last days"* This is primarily the dispensational/premillennial view. Many premillennial authors connect the return of Israel in 1948 or 1967 as the beginning of the *"last days."* Once the *"last days"* begin, progressive fulfillment of the signs of the times is to be expected. This has been a popular view for several generations, and many Evangelicals grew up thinking they were living at the end of the age in these *"last days."*

The second option sees the *"last days"* beginning in the first century and continuing until the return of Christ. In this view, held mostly by amillennialists, the period of the *"last days"* are the same as the entire age of the church, strung out over hundreds and hundreds of years. Paul lived in the *"last days,"* Martin Luther lived in the *"last days"* and we live in the *"last days."* This position is weak because the very term "last" is lost in this definition. The birth of the church, the establishment of the kingdom and coming of the Holy Spirit all speak of something that is beginning, not ending. What is ending in this view? I understand why they begin the period in the first century (to agree with many New Testament passages) but fail to see where the Bible portrays this time period lasting thousands of years. The *"last days"* must mean the soon ending of "something" or it loses all meaning.

Our third option and the one taken here, is that the *"last days"* is a term New Testament writers used to describe the days in which they were living. This unique time in biblical history connects both covenants like a hinge. It closes a door to one age and opens it for another one. The *"last days"* were the end of the old and the ushering in of a completely new thing, Jeremiah called this new thing the new covenant, and Paul calls it a *"new creation."*

The missing key in understanding the timing of the kingdom is how the New Testament uses the words, *"last days," "latter days," "latter times,"* and *"last hour."* When the *"last days"* and first century events are disconnected, we lose sight of its theological significance.

For the church of Jesus Christ to influence our society, and make a difference, we need a biblical based theology that generates a long-term view of progress. Adopting a preterist interpretation of some New Testament prophetic sections clears away many confusing aspects of modern prophetic teaching. It also gives the church a foundation of hope for the coming generations. The church must build a biblical foundation for its optimism and goals of transformation. Otherwise, over time we end up returning to newspaper eisegesis.

In much of modern preaching, the *"last days"* are the final generation before Jesus returns. Many Christians grew up hearing Jesus is coming soon and the world is ending. Over the years of teaching on the kingdom, challenging this assumption has upset and angered people more than any other area. Many cling to their view of the *"last days"* as if their salvation depended on it. Accusations of deceiving people when I teach are not the norm, yet, I have been called an antichrist when teaching the *"last days."* This subject stirs up raw emotions like few others (especially in connection to taking away their rapture and great tribulation). If this is your first time hearing that we missed the *"last days,"* please consider the Scriptures and not allow feelings or tradition to dictate your conclusions.

Many believers know only the dispensational view of the *"last days"* (final generation before the return of Christ). There are historical reasons why this view is prominent among many Evangelical/Charismatic believers. Growing up in an evangelical local church and later in Bible School, the *"last days"* were always the final generation before the rapture. We were the "terminal generation." Evil is growing, the antichrist would come to power, and Christians would fall from their faith. We expected increases in earthquakes, wars, and church apostasy as signs of the end. Our role as Christians was winning the lost before it was too late. We had color charts, films and a host of scary stories proving everything. Our biggest fear is being "left behind."

After years of teaching I arrived at one fundamental conclusion, the Kingdom message will never grip our hearts and minds until we make a proper connection with the *"last days."* A future filled with apostasy and antichrists cannot fit with an ever-increasing kingdom. We are headed in one direction or the other, not both at the same time. Either evil is overtaking righteousness (hang on to the end mentality) or righteousness is overcoming evil (kingdom mentality). There will always be some unbelief in our midst; nevertheless, I believe the Bible teaches victory and dominion is our future, not defeat and escapism.

II TIMOTHY 3:1-5

But understand this, that in the last days there will come times of difficulty. [2] For people will be lovers of self, lovers of money, proud, arrogant, abusive, disobedient to their parents, ungrateful, unholy, [3] heartless, unappeasable, slanderous, without self-control, brutal, not loving good, [4] treacherous, reckless, swollen with conceit, lovers of pleasure rather than lovers of God, [5] having the appearance of godliness, but denying its power. Avoid such people.

II Timothy 3 may rank as the favorite for dispensational preachers. I remember many sermons starting with these verses. Even if the subject was on faith, the sermon began, "In these last days we need faith." If the sermon was love, it began, "In these last days we need love." No matter what the sermon, we were to hold on to the end. Time is short.

What was Paul telling Timothy? When Timothy read Paul's remarks about the "*last days*," how would he understand the warning? Would Timothy and first century readers assume Paul was talking about the far distance future? That is not likely. On the other hand, would they read Paul as addressing events and circumstances they were facing?

Our first step is locating clues or direct statements that identify the "timing" of the "*last days.*" Too often Christians read a passage like this and go directly to contemporary application without allowing the passage to speak for itself. When Paul warns about people being "*lovers of money, proud*" and "*disobedient to partners*" and "*without self-control*" it seems he is speaking directly to our generation. Yet, a closer look reveals that most generations would also match these conditions.

In II Timothy 3, I can find no direct reference to "when" these last days will come, yet, there is a hint that Paul refers to his own generation not ours. After describing various sins of the last days and about the people that succumb to these sins, Paul says, "*Avoid such men as these.*" How could Timothy avoid these "*last days*" men if they were not going to be born for 2,000 years? There are other New Testament Scriptures providing hints on the timing factor, yet, for the sake of space, we will limit our study to those passages that give us direct statements.

HEBREWS 1: 1-2

Long ago, at many times and in many ways, God spoke to our fathers by the prophets, [2] but in these last days he has spoken to us by his Son, whom he appointed the heir of all things, through whom also he created the world.

What we have in this verse is one of the clearest in settling the timing issue around the "*last days.*" The God who spoke in the Prophets now speaks in His Son. "*In these last days*" refers to the generation of the author, when Jesus was alive on the earth. The "*last days*" was in the first century not the 21st Century. The dispensational teaching that the time period of the *"last days"* begins approximately four years before the second coming of Jesus cannot be found here, or any other passage using *"last days"* terminology. With the coming of Jesus, the *"last days"* arrived. It was the last days of the old covenant, the temple worship and animal sacrifices. We have made a mistake placing the *"last days"* at the end of the church age, when the Scriptures teach it was the end of the Jewish age.

I PETER 1:19-20

But with the precious blood of Christ, like that of a lamb without blemish or spot. ²⁰ He was foreknown before the foundation of the world but was made manifest in the last times for the sake of you.

When did Jesus appear as a lamb? Your answer will be the same answer as to the timing of the *"last days."* Peter says Jesus appeared *"in these last times"* for our sake. The Bible is clear; there should be no confusion on the timing of the last days. This special generation lived in a unique season of history and perhaps was the most significant in human history. During the *"last days"* Jesus came to earth and provided a way of salvation, the Kingdom of God was established, and we became part of an eternal plan through the new covenant. All of these events took place in the *"last days."* Although there was plenty of good news during the first century, the time was also filled with persecution, tribulation, false prophets and false Messiahs, people falling away from their faith, and constant apprehensive about wars and the rumors of war. The *"last days"* were the best and the worst of times.

I John 2:18

Children, it is the last hour, and as you have heard that antichrist is coming, so now many antichrists have come. Therefore we know that it is the last hour.

Apostle John writes to ensure his readers understand that the circumstances of the *"last days"* are intensifying. John was not confused, he was not speculating, he knew the *"last days"* were upon them. It is bewildering to see how many books there are on the subject of the antichrist. In many churches, there is more conversation about the antichrist than about Jesus Christ. Where does the fuel for this apocalyptic fire come from? It is not from the Bible! At least it is not from passages in the Bible that mention the antichrist. John tells his readers that it is the *"last hour."* Whereas, Paul and other New Testament writers use the term, *"last days,"* or *"latter times,"* John writing a few years later, shortens the time to the *"last hour."* When we read John's letter, it is vital that we understand the times in which he lived. Many antichrists were crisscrossing the land, attempting to deceive even the elect. John makes an important point, because of the presence of these many antichrists; he knew the *"last hour"* had arrived.

The coming of the kingdom and the "last days" are biblically connected. Our mistake is taking the warning for these days and applying it to our generation when it really belongs to the people in the first century. In the Old Testament, the term "latter days" or "the time of the end" refers to the day of the Messiah. The last days and the arrival of the Messiah must be kept in one generation, the first century.

I Tim. 4:1-5

Now the Spirit expressly says that in later times some will depart from the faith by devoting themselves to deceitful spirits and teachings of demons, [2]through the insincerity of liars whose consciences are seared, [3] who forbid marriage and require abstinence from foods that God created to be received with thanksgiving by those who believe and know the truth. [4]For everything created by God is good, and nothing is to be rejected if it is received with thanksgiving, [5]for it is made holy by the word of God and prayer. If you put these things before the brothers, you will be a good servant of Christ Jesus.

Paul felt it important to remind Timothy of the times in which he lived. In our times, we see little of the practice of forbidding marriage or requiring abstinence of certain foods. There are religions that have certain foods that are off limits for its followers, but in the first century these issues were much more significant than today. Why is it important that Timothy remind *"the brothers"* of these things if the *"last days"* were many generations in the future? These circumstances can occur within any generation, but they were special to the first century because they were signs of the coming destruction of Jerusalem, which would have practical as well as theological consequences.

Hebrews 9:26

For then he would have had to suffer repeatedly since the foundation of the world. But as it is, he has appeared once for all at the end of the ages to put away sin by the sacrifice of himself.

Jesus appeared "*at the end of the ages.*" The first generation of believers lived in a special time, the old was fading away and the new had already began.

I Peter 1:20

He was foreknown before the foundation of the world but was made manifest in the last times for the sake of you.

Jesus was destined for earth before the creation of the world. Sometime in ancient eternity, there must have been some agreement on the division of labor and responsibility within the triune God. The Son would take upon himself a human body. He would come to earth, take on a human body and pay for the sins of humanity. When did Jesus come to earth? He came during the "*last times.*" He came because old Israel was ending; it was Israel's "*last days.*" The temple and the old worship practices were ending and all things would become new. Jesus came during the "end times" for our sakes. Once the old way was gone there had to be another way to worship God. Jesus came and accomplished this through the cross. He came during the ending of one age so a new age could be born. What is this "new age?" It is the kingdom of God!

James 5:3

"Your gold and silver have corroded, and their corrosion will be evidence against you and will eat your flesh like fire. You have laid up treasure in the last days."

James is the presiding elder and apostle of the Jerusalem church. He warns people not to "*heap up*" their treasure because it will be evidence against them in the coming days. With the burning of the temple only 20 years away, any treasure in the temple area or hidden in homes would be lost. James continues in verse five, "*You have fattened your hearts in a day of slaughter.*" This must refer to the destruction of Jerusalem where 1.1 million Jews lost their lives. Later in the letter, he tells his readers, "*Be patient, therefore brothers until the coming of the Lord....establish your hearts, for the coming of the Lord is at hand...behold the judge is at the door* (James 5:7-8)."

Jude 17-20

But you must remember, beloved, the predictions of the apostles of our Lord Jesus Christ. [18] They[f] said to you, "In the last time there will be scoffers, following their own ungodly passions." [19] It is these who cause divisions, worldly people, devoid of the Spirit. [20] But you, beloved, building yourselves up in your most holy faith and praying in the Holy Spirit.

The Apostle Peter warns believers about the "*mockers,*" here Jude calls them "*scoffers.*" The first century church lived in the last days; we do not. Even if Jesus returned today, it does not make our time the "*last days.*" The New Testament marks out this period as the special time when the Messiah came, the old covenant came to its end and the new day of Christ arrived. The period of the "*last days*" was from the birth of Christ to the destruction of Jerusalem. The early church lived at the end of one age and saw the birth of a new age.

Here is a list of verses where the "timing" of the "last days" cannot be determined (with certainly) by the text (although they are small hints pointing towards first century events).

1. I Timothy 4:1-3
2. II Timothy 3:1-5
3. James 5:3, 7-8
4. Jude 18-19

Verses where the "timing" of the "last days" specifically points to the first century

1. I Peter 1:20
2. I John 2:18
3. Hebrews 1:1-2
4. Hebrews 9:26

Verses where the "timing" of the "last days" specifically points to a far distance future (our time)

1. There are no verses

The biblical evidence is clear, the *"great tribulation"* and *"last days"* are over. It is time to embrace these events as part of Christian history, not in our future. Seen from a preterists hermeneutic, the *"last days"* provide a path to a kingdom centered eschatology. The preterist view answers a multitude of questions concerning the time elements of prophecy. The position that the "kingdom age" is the present age fits the biblical record. The kingdom of God, the Messianic kingdom and the millennial kingdom are different biblical terms for the one and only kingdom, established by Jesus at his first coming.

Current New Testament studies are setting forth a view that preceding the arrival of the kingdom age there is a time of great persecution. This leads to the "eschatological tribulation." In my view, the preterist position of the *"last days"* is the clear teaching of Scripture and thus compliments kingdom centered eschatology.

The first century is the hinge generation. Hinges connect things. We connect a gate to a fence with hinges. We connect doors to walls with hinges. The first century church was the hinge generation; connecting two covenants of God. Dramatic events occurred in this generation, they saw the arrival of the Messiah, the coming of the Holy Spirit, the growth of the new covenant church, times of affliction ending with the great tribulation and finally the coming of the Son of Man in his kingdom. When the last stone of the temple crumbled and the dust settled, a new day arrived. The old disappeared forever while the new forever replaces it. The first Christian believers were a new people of God, not exclusively Jews but Gentiles as well. The new body of people, the body of Christ, was now the new temple. Finally, God has the temple of his dreams. The Old Testament types and shadows pointed to this. The door of the old creation closed, while in the same generation, the door to the new creation opened.

What is missing in a lot of modern preaching is absence of teaching about God's judgment that occurred in the first century.

When we think of judgment, most think of a future final judgment. Yet, there was a day of judgment coming for the people of the first century. It was like a giant black cloud hanging in the sky, reminding them year after year that they were living at the end of an age. Ages usually do not go quietly into the night, but violently end. The New Testament was written in such times. Until we see that the writings of the early apostles were penned under this impending "eschatological tribulation," we will continue to misinterpret large sections of the New Testament.

The New Testament was born within this eschatological age of the "last days." A new beginning arrived when John the Baptist announced that God's kingdom is at hand (Matthew 3:2). Jesus also announced God's arriving kingdom (Mark 1:14). Our difficulty is that the epistles were written to the first churches and their focus was more about what was ending rather than what was beginning, like Peter when he says, *"the end of all things are at hand"* (I Peter 4:7).

Study Questions

1. Why do some say that we are living in the "last days?"

2. Explain how the early church is the "hinge" generation.

3. According to the author of Hebrews, Jesus came at the end of the ages; what does that mean?

4. Explain the three options of the "timing issues" of the "last days." Which view has the most biblical support?

5. What was "ending" in the "last days?"

Chapter 14

Matthew 24 - Part One

Matthew 24 and its counterparts in Mark and Luke are key chapters in the Bible as it pertains to eschatology. Exegetical presuppositions regarding Matthew 24 bring unnecessary obstacles to the text. Too many Christians begin their reading assuming Jesus is giving a prophecy about the end of the world. When these presuppositions are in the mind of the reader, the obvious historical and contextual circumstances are lost. Is Matthew 24 a prophecy about our future? Does it describe conditions that will prevail in the final time of the church? I do not think so.

Where should we begin? The obvious place is with the disciple's questions. The prophecy of Jesus is in response to their questions. Having just heard Jesus declare that the Jewish temple would be "left desolate," the disciples wanted clarification. They first attempted a soft approach by reminding Jesus how great and beautiful the temple was. Maybe that would prompt something positive; but it did not.

Matthew 24:1

"Jesus left the temple and was going away, when his disciples came to point out to him the buildings of the temple."

Luke describes this event in more detail. *"And while some were speaking of the temple, how it was adorned with noble stones and offerings* (Luke 21:5). They described the temple in positive tones with hope Jesus would agree and elaborate more on its future. This is exactly what Jesus did. *"As for these things that you see, 'the days will come when there will not be left here one stone upon another that will not be thrown down (Luke 21:6).* The disciples wanted clarification and received; just not what they anticipated. Therefore, they asked the most important question, *"When will these things happen?"*

Before covering Matthew 24 verse by verse, a step back to see the big picture will help. This prophecy by Jesus may be one of the most important biblical passages determining how we understand the central message of the Bible. At stake is the integrity of the Holy Scriptures and the prophetic ministry of Jesus. Jesus can hardly be the Messiah and Savior of the world, if he made false prophecies. William Kimball explains its importance.

> "The Mt. Olivet discourse is the most important prophecy in the Bible... It is the great pivotal prophecy upon which many teachings either stand or fall. An accurate interpretation of this critical prophecy provides us with invaluable, foundational framework for establishing solid prophetic positions. A sound interpretation supplies us with a balanced counterweight to prophetic extremism, and gives us a reliable set of guidelines to counter many of the misleading interpretations, which often accompany other related passages."[50]

Matthew 24 is the gateway into a revelation of the kingdom. Kingdom centered eschatology cannot be scripturally maintained if a dispensational interpretation is held. How we read this chapter determines a great deal about our eschatology. If we hold onto a futurist's understanding of Jesus' prophecy (our future), then the bulk of the other eschatological passages will also be seen as pertaining to the future. Kimball continues on the importance of Matthew 24 (Mark 13 & Luke 21) and comments on where a poor hermeneutic might lead us.

> "A wrong interpretation of this prophecy has often resulted in a multitude of erroneous concepts, foolish theorizing, and fanciful speculations concerning the prophetic forecasts of the future.

---

[50] William R. Kimball, What the Bible says about the Great Tribulation, Presbyterian and Reformed Publishing Company, Phillipsburg, New Jersey, 1983, page 2

Like the "domino principle" when the Olivet discourse is pushed out of balance, all related prophecies down the line are subsequently out of alignment."[51]

Our reading of Matthew 24 must begin in chapter 21. In Matthew 21:23 Jesus enters the temple and is questioned by the "chief priests" and the "elders of the people." This starts a long dialogue that continues through chapter 25. The original audience of leaders of the Jewish people that begins in chapter 21 is limited to the disciples starting in Matthew 24:1, (Jesus came out from the temple). The parable of the landowner starts in verse thirty-three and it runs to the end of the chapter.

Parable of the Landowner

Matthew 21:33-46

Hear another parable. There was a master of a house who planted a vineyard and put a fence around it and dug a winepress in it and built a tower and leased it to tenants, and went into another country. [34]When the season for fruit drew near, he sent his servants to the tenants to get his fruit. [35] And the tenants took his servants and beat one, killed another, and stoned another. [36] Again he sent other servants, more than the first. And they did the same to them. [37]Finally he sent his son to them, saying, 'They will respect my son.' [38]But when the tenants saw the son, they said to themselves, 'This is the heir. Come, let us kill him and have his inheritance.' [39]And they took him and threw him out of the vineyard and killed him. [40] When therefore the owner of the vineyard comes, what will he do to those tenants?" [41]They said to him, "He will put those wretches to a miserable death and let out the vineyard to other tenants who will give him the fruits in their seasons. [42]Jesus said to them, "Have you never read in the Scriptures: "'The stone that the builders rejected has become the cornerstone; this was the Lord's doing, and it is marvelous in our eyes'? [43]Therefore I tell you, the kingdom of God will be taken away from you and given to

---

[51] Ibid

a people producing its fruits. ⁴⁴And the one who falls on this stone will be broken to pieces; and when it falls on anyone, it will crush him." ⁴⁵When the chief priests and the Pharisees heard his parables, they perceived that he was speaking about them. ⁴⁶And although they were seeking to arrest him, they feared the crowds, because they held him to be a prophet.

Jesus tells a story about a landowner. God is the landowner and the vine-growers are Israel. The landowner invested in land, he built a wall, a winepress, and a tower. When time for the harvest came, he sent servants and finally his own son, and each time the vine-growers killed them. Jesus wants his audience to answer a simple question. *"When the landowner comes what will he do with the tenants?"* Jesus then quotes Psalms 118:22-23 and proclaims the kingdom of God will be *"taken away"* and given to another people, and that this new people will possess the kingdom and will produce the fruits of the kingdom. Israel as a nation was fruitless. Israel as a nation failed to bring forth any spiritual fruit, and in their rebellion seized the Son (Jesus) and killed Him. God is now ready to give the kingdom to another people. Apostle Peter spoke of this nation or people.

I Peter 2:9

"But you are a chosen race, a royal priesthood, a holy nation, a people for his own possession, that you may proclaim the excellencies of him who called you out of darkness into his marvelous light."

The church of Jesus Christ and the nation Jesus spoke of are the same. Paul refers to the church as the *"one new man"* (Ephesians 2:15) and the *"one body"* (Ephesians 2:16) comprising of both Jews and Gentiles. Even though as a nation Israel was fruitless and rejected the Son, God always brings to faith a remnant, and the first members of the Christian church were Jewish. Believing Gentiles once grafted into this remnant (Rom. 11:17) join them as the *"chosen race"* and the *"royal priesthood."*

Matthew 23

In Matthew 23, we see a continuation of the exposure and judgment of the Pharisees. Jesus accuses them of teaching the Law of Moses, but not keeping the law themselves. *"Fill up, then, the measure of the guilt of your fathers. You serpents, you brood of vipers, how will you escape the sentence of hell"* (Matthew 23:32-33). Then Jesus pronounces a final and devastating prophecy on unbelieving Israel, *"so that upon you may fall the guilt of all the righteous blood shed on earth"* (Matthew 23:35). It is at this occasion that He states, *"Behold, your house (temple) is being left to you desolate"* (Matthew 23:38).

Bible Scholar John Bray comments on the temple being "left to you desolate."

> "His statement that their house would be left desolate was His prophecy of the coming destruction of Jerusalem, God's wrath and judgment that would be poured out upon them in A.D. 70, and utter desolation of both the city and the Temple. These tragic and prophetic words of Jesus were uttered at the end of His ministry, just several days before He was crucified. This was the last time He ever went into the Temple."[52]

Jesus gives a timetable for these prophetic judgments. *"Truly I say to you, all these things will come upon this generation"* (Matthew 23:36). About which generation was Jesus talking? What people was judgment about to fall on? The wording here is the same as in Matthew 24:34, so if the people then living were the "this generation" in chapter 23 then it is the same in following chapter. Jesus was speaking to the people in "this generation," the contemporary people that are still living. Attempts to force "this generation" hundreds or thousands years into the future violates

---

[52] John L. Bray, Matthew 24 Fulfilled, John L. Bray Ministries, Lakeland, Florida, 1996, p. 12

sound exegetical principles and distorts the context of what Jesus taught.

Jesus concludes with Israel's leaders and starts towards the Mount of Olives. It is within this background that His disciples began questioning Him about the prophecy just given. There is no doubt that they were stunned to hear about the fate of the temple. They were most likely thinking, "How can the temple become desolate?"

Now we get back to these questions by the disciples. Mark's account says, *"As He was going out of the temple, one of His disciples said to Him, 'Teacher, behold what wonderful stones and what wonderful buildings" (Mark 13:1).*

The temple was one of the greatest buildings of the world. Bray provides some history, "The stones themselves at these buildings were fabulous in size. Those in the foundations were as much as 60 feet long, and others above as much as 67 feet or more long, 7 and a half feet high, and 9 feet wide. To the Jewish people, there was nothing like this building in the whole world."[53] More than architecture, the temple represented the entire Jewish culture and faith. Old Covenant worship with sacrificed animals took place in the temple. The temple was the place of connection, reading of the Law, and exchanging the news of the day. It was central to first century Jewish culture. How could Jesus say that this whole system would become desolate?

A spiritual application is appropriate. When God brings changes either by the moving of the Spirit, or by fresh understanding of the word, we have a difficult time with the changes it brings. We (like the disciples) try to convince God that the old ways (our temple is beautiful) is working just fine. That is what happened to the disciples when they reminded Jesus of how great the temple was. His answer is a prophecy that changed the whole world.

---

[53] John Bray, Matthew 24 Fulfilled, John L. Bray Ministries, Lakeland, Florida, 1996, p. 10

Matthew 24:2

"And He said to them, 'Do you not see all these things? Truly I say to you, not one stone here will be left upon another, which will not be torn down."

Jesus' response to the disciple's comment shocked them even more. How could it be that all this grandeur would soon be gone? Surely, this would mean the end of an age, a change so large that it was beyond their ability to understand. Not only was their house (temple) prophesized to be left "desolate" (empty, without meaning or purpose) but it would also be totally destroyed. Maybe this would happen in connection to the previous words of Jesus about "coming in his kingdom" (Matthew 10:23 & 16:27-28).

Matthew 24:3

As he sat on the Mount of Olives, the disciples came to him privately, saying, "Tell us, when will these things be, and what will be the sign of your coming and of the end of the age?"

The disciple's three questions are imperative to interpreting Jesus' prophecy. What was their primary concern? I do not believe they wanted answers to God's program for the ages. They were not worried about events and circumstances in the distant future. Their basic question was, "when will the temple be destroyed?" Will we be alive? The three separate questions reveal different sides of one basic concern; when will this happen? Because when this does occur, the disciples were convinced it would be the end of the age and linked to his promised "coming on the clouds."For first century followers of Jesus these events belonged together.

Those holding to a futurist interpretation of Matthew 24 believe that Jesus ignored the disciples' first question and jumped 2,000 years in history and told them about the end of the world and his Second Coming. Is this what the disciples had in mind? Our modern attempt to force into this text a particular understanding of the rapture and end of the world does not fit.Why did the disciples ask about his "coming?" I see several factors that lead to this question. First, Jesus prophesied earlier to them that his coming would be within one generation (Matt. 10:23, 16:27-28, 24:30-34,

Mk. 8:38-9:1). The Scriptures provides no evidence that these followers of Jesus would have any notion of yet another coming, far into their future. These questions are really one question. Forcing some future agenda into the text goes far beyond the disciple's comprehension.

The disciples may have thought back to several sayings of Jesus. *"And you will be hated by all for my name's sake. But the one who endures to the end will be saved* (Matt.10:22). Jesus repeats the warning in the Olivet prophecy. *"Then they will deliver you up to tribulation and put you to death, and you will be hated by all nations for my name's sake* (Matt. 24:9). To what end is Jesus referring? *"When they persecute you in one town, flee to the next, for truly, I say to you, you will not have gone through all the towns of Israel before the Son of Man comes* (Matt. 10:23). The "coming" of the Son of Man was to take place within the lifetime of some in the first century. They were to endure until the end. Not the end of the world in the distant future, but to the end of the present age (the disciples were still living in the age of the old covenant), and some experienced the "coming "of the Son 40 years later. *"For the Son of Man is going to come with his angels in the glory of his Father, and then he will repay each person according to what he has done. ^{28} Truly, I say to you, there are some standing here who will not taste death until they see the Son of Man coming in his kingdom* (Matthew 16:27-28)."

Jesus taught His disciples that His coming in His kingdom would take place before some of them died. This is why the disciples connected the questions in Matthew 24. When will these things take place? When will be your coming? (I believe they were thinking about the "coming" Jesus said would happen before some of them died). This 'coming' marks the end of the age. These three questions all ask the same thing.They were anticipating one event, the destruction of the temple.

When dispensationalists place the "great tribulation" into our future, they also place the *"coming of the Son of Man"* right before the start of the tribulation. For them this "coming" is the "rapture." R.C. Sproul states his understanding of the rapture theory. "In my years of study and ministry I have yet to discover a single text of sacred Scripture that teaches a pre-tribulation Rapture. In my opinion the notion, which is quite recent in church history, is pure fiction."[54]

Why ask about the end of the age? If the temple is destroyed, then the end of all things is certainly at hand. The removal of the temple and its ancient worship would be the sign that God is moving on to something new, a new covenant, and a new creation.

Birth Pangs

Matthew 24:4

And Jesus answered them, "See that no one leads you astray."

The first sets of signs given by Jesus are "misleading signs." These signs are general in nature and point to the beginning of the "last days." Followers of Jesus were not to respond to these signs because they would mislead the people. Jesus closes this section in verse eight calling everything "birth pangs." The delivery of the new covenant is at its first stages. These signs occurred many years before the real sign, when all Christians in Jerusalem must flee.

Matthew 24:5

For many will come in my name, saying, 'I am the Christ,' and they will lead many astray.

Of all the different ages and times throughout history, the first generation saw more false Messiahs than probably any other. Jesus' prophetic word came true, as over the next 40 years, many came and proclaimed to be the Messiah. These false Christ's were a sign that everything Jesus prophesied would come true.

Matthew 24:6

And you will hear of wars and rumors of wars. See that you are not alarmed, for this must take place, but the end is not yet.

Dispensational churches use every war, outbreak of violence, earthquakes and famines (etc.) to prove to their people that the "last days," have arrived and Jesus will return soon, maybe before the sun comes up. Yet Jesus said these wars and rumors of wars

---

[54] R.C. Sproul, The Last Days According to Jesus, Baker Books, Grand Rapids, Michigan, 1998, p. 46

were a misleading sign not the real sign to look for. It was a sign to let the followers of Jesus know that His prophecy is coming true, one-step at a time.

Matthew 24:7

For nation will rise against nation, and kingdom against kingdom, and there will be famines and earthquakes in various places.

Every generation experiences wars, famines and earthquakes. The first century had their share. Different from all the following generations, these events in the first century were "signs" the early Christians were to watch for. Bray provides excellent historical insight on these verses.

> "There were wars in the tributaries of Rome and all over Palestine, Galilee, and Samaria in AD 66, preceding the destruction of Jerusalem. They heard of Wars! In AD 40, there was a disturbance at Mesopotamia, which Josephus says caused the death of more than 50,000 people. In AD 49, a tumult at Jerusalem at the time of the Passover resulted in 10,000 to 20,000 deaths. At Caesarea, contentions between Jewish people and other inhabitants resulted in over 20,000 Jews being killed. As Jews moved elsewhere, over 20,000 were destroyed by Syrians. At Scythopolis, over 13,000 Jews were killed. Thousands were killed in other places, and at Alexandria 50,000 were killed. At Damascus 10,000 were killed in an hour's time."[55]

If Jesus had not warned His disciples about these various wars that would take place all around them, they might have mistaken them as the "end" of what Jesus was prophesying. Now they knew to stay put, keep preaching the message of Christ, and continue watching for the final signs. Those living in Jerusalem need not to

---

[55] John L. Bray, Matthew 24 Fulfilled, John L. Bray Ministries, Lakeland, Florida, 1996, p. 28

flee in reaction to any of these wars, and even rumors of impending wars. Jesus predicted that famine would be a sign of His coming in judgment. History records the horrors that came to those in Jerusalem, fulfilling accurately the prophecy of Jesus. The primary historian of these first century events is Flavius Josephus. He was the son of a Jewish priest and eventually traveled with the Roman army. He wrote a complete history of the Jews and gives on-site reporting of the destruction of Jerusalem and its temple. Josephus provides details of the Roman wars against the Jews that would have been lost without his presence. The knowledge he adds to these perilous times is extremely helpful in understanding many passages of our New Testament texts. Josephus provides us the details of this time.

> "It was now a miserable case and a sight that would justly bring tears into our eyes, how men stood as to their food, while the more powerful had more than enough, and the weaker were lamenting (for the want of it). But the famine was too hard...insomuch that children pulled the very morsels that their fathers were eating out of their very mouths, and, what was still more to be pitted, so did the mothers do as to their infants; and when those that were most dear were perishing under their hands, they were not ashamed to take from them the very last drops that might preserve their lives...So all hope of escaping was now cut off from the Jews, together with their liberty of going out of the city. Then did the famine widen its progress, and devoured the people by whole houses and families; the upper rooms were full of women and children that were dying by famine; and the lanes of the city were full of the dead bodies of the aged...Nor was there any place in the city that had no dead bodies

in it, but what was entirely covered with those that were killed either by the famine or the rebellion."[56]

Judgment follows the breaking of covenant. The words of Stephen are appropriate, "*You men who are stiff-necked and uncircumcised in heart and ears are always resisting the Holy Spirit; you are doing just as your fathers did. Which one of the prophets did your fathers not persecute? And they killed those who had previously announced the coming of the Righteous One, whose betrayers and murders you have now become.*" (Acts 7:51-52)

Matthew 24:8
All these are but the beginning of the birth pains.

Birth pangs are what proceeds new life, not the end of life. The misleading signs are just the beginning of what is to come. The event that Jesus wanted them to be watchful of was the "*days of vengeance*" (Luke 21:22) or Matthews term of a coming "*great tribulation.*"

By using the term, "birth pangs" Jesus connects with Jewish eschatological language. There are Old Testament passages that link "birth pangs" with the judgment on a city or nation. Biblical scholar Brant Pitre reviews these passages.

> "As for the ties between 'birth pangs' and the destruction of a city, Old Testament examples abound. Hosea speaks of the "pangs of childbirth" coming upon the northern kingdom of Israel (Ephraim) when the city of Samaria is destroyed and the people taken into exile (Hos. 13:12-16). In Isaiah, a wave 'anguish like a women in travail' – accompanied by earthquakes and the darkening of sun, moon, and stars- comes upon the city of Babylon before it is overthrown and Israel returns from exile Isa 13:6-14:2…Jeremiah repeatedly uses the image of birth pangs to describe the destruction

---

[56] Flavius Josephus, Wars of The Jews, p. 229

of enemy cities, such as Moab (Jer. 48:41) or Babylon (Jer. 50:43)...finally, the book of Micah describes the 'pangs...like a women on travail' that comes upon Zion (Jerusalem) at her destruction by Babylon (Micah 4:10-14)." [57]

Pitre takes us back to Old Testament language and shows that when Jesus uses this term, *"birth pangs,"* first century Jews would hear and associate these words with impending judgment upon a city or nation. What city or nation was Jesus alluding to with such language? It is no doubt that the city is Jerusalem and the nation is Israel. Eschatological judgment is coming and the *"birth pangs"* begins the events that progressively happen over the next forty years.

Difficult Times

Matthew 24:9

Then they will deliver you up to tribulation and put you to death, and you will be hated by all nations for my name's sake.

I cannot imagine how the disciples felt when Jesus prophesied they "will kill you." I have received many wonderful and accurate prophecies during my lifetime, but none spoke about being a martyr. It must have been unsettling to say the least. History shows that many gave their lives for the gospel. The New Testament records the death of James around the year 44 AD at the hands of Herod. According to the Smith Bible Dictionary, Peter and Paul were martyred in Rome. "The time and manner of the apostle's martyrdom are less certain. According to the early writers, he died at or about the same time with Paul, and in the Neronian persecution, A.D. 67, 68."[58]

In Mark 13:9, we find additional information that coincides with verse 9 of Matthew 24. *"But be on your guard; for they will*

---

[57] Brant Pitre, Jesus, The Tribulation, and the End of the Exile, Baker Academic, Grand Rapids, Michigan, 2005

[58] William Smith, Smith Bible Dictionary, Thomas Nelson Publishers, Nashville, Tennessee, 1988 (original 1863), p. 356

deliver you to the courts, and you will be flogged in the synagogues, and you will stand before governors and kings for My sake, as a testimony to them." Kimball comments on this verse.

> "The reference to synagogues and councils limits the timing of this warning to the period prior to 70 A.D. The word councils is translated from the Greek word sunedria and is the same word used for the "Sanhedrin" in Jerusalem... It must be pointed out that with the destruction of Jerusalem in 70 A.D., the entire Jewish polity collapsed. What powers the Jewish rulers were able to wield against the Christians prior to 70 A.D. was effectively terminated after that date. With this fact in mind, we see that the primary thrust of these statements was specifically directed towards the early Christians prior to Jerusalem's destruction. Christ was bracing the disciples of that generation for the opposition they would face before the destruction of Jerusalem. The book of Acts records a variety of persecutions inflicted upon the early believers during the historical period prior to 70 A.D. (Acts 4, 5,68,13,14,18,21,22,24,25)...Looking beyond the historical chronicle of Acts, we discover that Christ's predictions of persecutions were even more aptly fulfilled during the Neronian persecution (64-68 A.D.). Thousands of Christians were butchered in the most fiendish and diabolical manner."[59]

When I hear preachers saying how wonderful it is to be living in the "last days," I wonder if they have read the Bible lately. The Bible paints a clear picture of the period called the "last days." They are not exciting and wonderful days; they were times of great difficulty (II Timothy 3:1). Death, wars, and famines filled the

---

[59] William R. Kimball, What the Bible says about the Great Tribulation, Presbyterian and Reformed Publishing Company, Phillipsburg, New Jersey, 1983, page 43

land. The church faced severe problems with false prophets, unsound doctrine and a two-pronged persecution, from the Jews and from Rome. Christians today should be thankful they are not living in the "last days." Certainly, they were exciting times, the early growth of the church, the miracles, yet as the years past Pentecost progressed, conditions became exceedingly difficult.

Matthew 24:10

And then many will fall away and betray one another and hate one another.

The falling away from the faith is apostasy. One of the signs of the *"last days"* is apostasy. *"But the Spirit explicitly says that in later times some will fall (literally apostatize) away from the faith"* (I Timothy 4:1). When Christians are told to "hang on to the end," it is based upon the assumption that this apostasy occurs at the end of the church age. This takes a jump in logic and exegesis that goes beyond the clear sayings of the New Testament.

Matthew 24:11

And many false prophets will arise and lead many astray.

False prophets will be in abundance during the final days of the old covenant. Jesus warns of their ability to deceive. Warnings concerning false prophets are a common theme through the Olivet discourse and throughout the New Testament. *"Let no one deceive you with empty words, for because of these things the wrath of God comes upon the sons of disobedience"* (Eph.5:6).

Colossians 2:8

See to it that no one takes you captive by philosophy and empty deceit, according to human tradition, according to the elemental spirits of the world, and not according to Christ.

Philippians 3:2

Look out for the dogs, look out for the evildoers, look out for those who mutilate the flesh.

I Thessalonians 2:14-16

For you, brothers, became imitators of the churches of God in Christ Jesus that are in Judea. For you suffered the same things from your own countrymen as they did from the Jews, [15] who killed both the Lord Jesus and the prophets, and drove us out, and displease God and oppose all mankind [16] by hindering us from speaking to the Gentiles that they might be saved—so as always to fill up the measure of their sins. But wrath has come upon them at last!

I Thessalonians 5:9

For God has not destined us for wrath, but to obtain salvation through our Lord Jesus Christ,

The wrath was the coming tribulation prophesied by Jesus in Matthew 24.

II Thessalonians 2:2-3

Not to be quickly shaken in mind or alarmed, either by a spirit or a spoken word, or a letter seeming to be from us, to the effect that the day of the Lord has come. [3] Let no one deceive you in any way. For that day will not come, unless the rebellion comes first, and the man of lawlessness is revealed, the son of destruction.

Reading Matthew 24 as prophecy pertaining to events occurring within the contemporary generation of the disciples brings unity and increased understanding the whole of the New Testament. Instead of tearing much of the New Testament out of its prophetic and historic sitting and skipping 2,000 years for the fulfillment; applying the time frame of Jesus is the best hermeneutic. *"Truly I say to you, this generation will not pass away until all these things take place* (Matt. 24:34).*"*

Study Questions

1. Is there evidence of apostasy in the early church? Give at least five Scriptures.

2. Explain the biblical usage of "birth pains."

3. Why is Matthew 24 key in understanding eschatology?

4. Give first century events that may have fulfilled Jesus prophecy of coming earthquakes, famines and wars and rumors of wars.

5. Why is the historian Josephus helpful in understanding the prophecy of Jesus in Matthew 24?

Chapter 15

Matthew 24 - Part Two

Matthew 24:12
And because lawlessness will be increased, the love of many will grow cold.

The breakdown of law leads to famine and other calamities during the days preceding the fall of Jerusalem. There was such an overthrow of laws that hording and theft became common. The famine became so severe, that a prophecy from the Old Testament about eating their children became a reality during the siege of Jerusalem. When respect for law breaks down, our love for one another fades quickly. Remember, this is not a prophecy for the end of the church age, there is no such age spoken of in the Scriptures. These prophecies were to a specific generation, the first, not ours. Lawlessness became a major theme throughout the first century. Years after the cross Apostle Paul named an individual as the *"man of lawlessness."* (II Thessalonians 2:3).

Matthew 24:13
But the one who endures to the end will be saved.

What end is Jesus speaking of? The clear implication of the context along with the strong historical evidence is that He spoke about the "end" of the city and temple. Jesus promised salvation, physical survival for those who "endured." When the Roman armies invaded the city bringing death and destruction, the Christians were gone. They were "saved" because they knew the "signs" and followed them carefully.

Chilton writes about the church during this time.

> "The early Church looked forward to the coming of the new age. They knew that, with the visible end of the Old Covenant system, the Church would be revealed as the new, true Temple; and the work of Christ came to perform would be

accomplished. This was an important aspect of redemption, and the first generation Christians looked forward to this event in their own lifetime. During this period of waiting and severe trial, the Apostle Peter assured them that they were, 'protected by the power of God through faith for a salvation ready to be revealed in the last time' (I Peter 1:5). They were on the very threshold of the new world. The Apostles and first generation Christians knew they were living in the last days of the Old Covenant age. They looked forward anxiously to its consummation and the full ushering in of the new era. As the age progressed and the 'signs of the times' increased and intensified, the Church could see that the Day of Judgment was fast approaching; a crisis was looming in the near future, when Christ would deliver them 'from this present evil age.'"[60]

Matthew 24:14

And this gospel of the kingdom will be proclaimed throughout the whole world as a testimony to all nations, and then the end will come.

Jesus gives a positive sign to watch for. As news of the spreading message of Jesus returned to Jerusalem believers checked off one more sign of the coming end. Again, we must ask, "Is this the end of the physical world?" In context, the "end" in verse 14 is the same as in verse 3. The end is not the end of the world but the end of the events leading to the destruction of the temple and city. It is the end of temple worship, the end of the old priesthood, and the end of the old covenant. Grady Brown gives his view on which end was in mind. "What "end" was he talking about? Not the "end of the world" as we know it, not the "end of time," but the end of that "present age," the age of the Old

---

[60] David Chilton, Paradise Restored, Reconstruction Press, Tyler, Texas, 1985, page 119

Judaistic economy that must come to a close before the fullness of the Messianic Age could be ushered in."[61]

There are Bible teachers who link verse 14 with Matthew 28:18-20 (great commission). Although the language seems similar at first glance, there is a difference between "witness" and "making disciples." In Matthew 24, the gospel of the kingdom is proclaimed as a "witness" to the known world before the end of the old age. Yet, the task for us is more than just preaching the gospel; we are to *"make disciples of all nations."* Is it possible that the word of the kingdom spread that far in the first century? Paul writing several years before the end of the temple and Jerusalem (which ended the age of the old covenant) said, *"the hope of the gospel that you heard, which has been proclaimed in all creation under heaven, and of which I, Paul, became a minister* (Colossians 1:23)." The witness about God's kingdom coming to earth was indeed fulfilled. Paul says to the Romans, *"But I ask, have they not heard? Indeed they have, for "Their voice has gone out to all the earth, and their words to the ends of the world* (Romans 10:18)."

We should note here that the term "world" in Romans 10 as well as in Matthew means the same as in Luke 2:1, *"In those days a decree went out from Caesar Augustus that all the world should be registered.* This 'world' is the known world of the Roman Empire. We should not attempt to force this to mean the ancient civilizations of China or South American. For the first century Jew, their world was the Roman Empire.

The Final Sign

Matthew 24:15

So when you see the abomination of desolation spoken of by the prophet Daniel, standing in the holy place (let the reader understand).

The end is near. When this final sign is evident then an escape must be immediate. The *"abomination of desolation"* is the final

---

[61] Grady Brown, That All May be fulfilled, Daysprings Publishing, Bryan, Texas, 2006, p. 171

sign before the city and the temple come under its final assault. Anyone missing this final sign would likely be among those killed during the siege of Jerusalem.

Speculation of what or who is "*abomination of desolation*" has seen an abundance of possibilities. Both Mark and Luke repeat the Olivet discourse and include this portion of Jesus' prophecy. Matthew is writing to a Jewish audience and therefore expects them to be familiar with Old Testament prophecy, especially Daniel. Luke makes no such assumptions, as his audience is gentile. They are not educated in the Hebrew Scriptures and would have difficulty understanding the phrase, "*abomination of desolation*" which has its origins in the Old Testament. Therefore, Luke changes the wording and in so doing answers the mystery of this "*abomination of desolation*."

Luke 21:21-22

"But when you see Jerusalem surrounded by armies, then know that its desolation has come near. ²¹ Then let those who are in Judea flee to the mountains, and let those who are inside the city depart, and let not those who are out in the country enter it, ²² for these are days of vengeance, to fulfill all that is written."

Kimball explains the need for a sign that believers would clearly recognize.

> "Even a casual examination shows that in order for something to effectively serve as an early warning for the disciples to escape, it would have to be a clear sign which would appear before a forceful penetration of the city even commenced. The sign could not possibly appear after the city had been forcefully seized, for at this point, it would be too late for the Christian community; however, the presence of heathen troops gradually approaching the city of Jerusalem would be an unmistakable sign for the disciples to flee, as was the historical case. Therefore, it is clear that the placing of an idolatrous image in the temple could not logically be the abomination of desolation. Matthew and

Mark's accounts instruct the disciples to flee to the mountains at the first appearance of the abomination of desolation standing in the holy place. The abomination was to be clearly visible to the disciples both in Jerusalem and the surrounding Judean countryside."[62]

Chilton indentifies these heathen armies as the Edomites. He describes the events when this heathen army invaded Jerusalem.

"This was the last opportunity to escape the doomed city of Jerusalem. Anyone who wished to flee had do so immediately, without delay. The Edomites broke into the city and went directly to the Temple, where they slaughtered 8,500 people by slitting their throats. As the Temple overflowed with blood, the Edomites rushed madly through the city streets, plundering houses and murdering everyone they met, including the high priest. According to the historian Josephus, this event marked "the beginning of the destruction of the city...from this very day may be dated the overthrow of her wall, and the ruin of her affairs."[63]

Chilton links the final sign of "*armies surrounding Jerusalem*" to the Edomites; yet Jesus may have been referring to another circumstance. Josephus tells us about a Roman Army commander named Cestius who had the opportunity to take the city, but for an unknown reason he withdrawals the troops. He "took his whole army along with him, and put the Jews to flight, and pursued them to Jerusalem."[64] The Jews were greatly afraid and "retreated into

---

[62] William R. Kimball, What the Bible says about the Great Tribulation, Presbyterian and Reformed Publishing Company, Phillipsburg, New Jersey, 1983, page

[63] Ibid. (page 92-93)

[64] Flavius Josephus, Translated by William Whiston, Hendrickson Publishers, Peabody, MA., 2001, p. 631

the inner part of the city and into the temple."[65] The next few days the Romans and the Jews engaged in fierce battle. A few officers under the command of Cestius persuaded him not to launch a final and devastating attack on the city but to retreat. William Whiston (translator of The Works of Josephus) comments on this sudden and unexpected withdrawal.

> "There may be another very important and very providential reason here assigned for this strange and foolish retreat of Cestius; which Josephus had been now a Christian, he might probably have taken notice of also; and that is, the affording of the Jewish Christians in the city an opportunity of calling to mind the prediction about thirty-three years and a half before, that "when they should see the "abomination of desolation" (the idolatrous Roman armies, with the images of their idols in their ensigns, ready to lay Jerusalem desolate,) "stand where it ought not:" or "in the holy place"..."they should flee to the mountains." By complying with which those Jewish Christians fled to the mountains of Perea, and escaped this destruction."[66]

When Nero heard his army had retreated, a "concealed consternation and terror fell upon him...and he was very angry."[67] Nero replace Cestius with a commander with experience and skill who will "best able to punish the Jews for their rebellion, and might prevent the same distemper from seizing upon neighboring nations also."[68] Whom did Nero choose? He picked Vespasian, who was experienced and had the loyalty of his sons. He would oversee the East for Nero. Vespasian's son Titus had command of the armies that eventually destroyed Jerusalem and burned the

---

[65] Ibid.

[66] Ibid.(p. 631-632)

[67] Ibid. (p.639)

[68] Ibid.

temple. This seems like a great fit; except for the timing; Nero died in June of 68 AD and that leaves, maybe, too much time between the withdrawing of Cestius and the actual destruction of the city. Yet, we must take into account that the Roman wars against the Jews continued for several years before the destruction of the city and temple. We do not know the exact date the Christians safely fled out of the city, so the Cestius withdrawal just might be the sign prophesied by Jesus. This is one case where it would help if the book of Revelation were actually written in 95AD instead of much earlier. If John wrote after the destruction of Jerusalem, he surely would have given us some of the miraculous details of the Christians escape.

Was it the event of the Edomites or the withdrawal of Cestius that fulfills the prophecy of Jesus? We cannot be certain and therefore historical studies must continue. Maybe some future Christian archeologists will dig up an old parchment of a firsthand account of these events. As contemporary studies of the preterists interpretation of Matthew 24 continues, we will understand much more than we do today. Whatever the exact event that triggered the Christians to flee, the important thing is we know they did, and every believer escaped almost certain death.

Pitre comments on this.

> "Jesus is not only alluding to Daniel's use of the abomination of desolation image, he is also alluding to the angel's declaration that at "the time of the end," there would be those who had "understanding" and as such would be able to interpret the book of Daniel. And this precisely what Jesus is enjoining his disciples to do, by saying, in effect: "When you see the abomination of desolation, let he who reads (Daniel) understand that the time of the end, the time of 'unsealing' of

the words of Daniel's prophecy-the time of the Great Tribulation-is at last at hand."[69]

These events were not the "great tribulation" that Jesus had talked about, but they were the signs leading up to it. The worst for those remaining in Jerusalem was still ahead.

Matthew 24:16-17

Then let those who are in Judea flee to the mountains. Let the one who is on the housetop not go down to take what is in his house.

The local geography is important. If this were a message to believers in our day, what would Christians do that live in areas without mountains? We must not overlook the obvious. This "great tribulation" was a local event dealing with Jerusalem and Judea. We know from history that local believers remembered the words of Jesus and fled just at the right time. The mountains gave them protection during the terrible siege where over one million people perished. Kimball comments on the miracle of the Christians escape. "Miraculously, not a single believer perished in the holocaust which engulfed Jerusalem in 70 A.D. under the leadership of Symeon, a cousin of the Lord, withdrew (the entire Christian community) to the village of Pella in Perea which lay in the mountainous regions east of the Sea of Galilee.[70] The Christians in Jerusalem must heed these prophetic warnings of Jesus. Even though the final events were almost 40 years in the future, the church must keep the fervency of the prophecy alive.

Most people in the western world do not spend a lot of time on their housetops, but for those living in Jerusalem during the first century it was common to spend time on their housetops. The warning is so explicit that when the final sign appears and the news spread, people were to flee immediately, do not even pack.

[69] Brant Pitre, Jesus, The Tribulation, And the End of the Exile, Baker Academic, Grand Rapids, Michigan, 2005 p. 313

[70] William R. Kimball, What the Bible Says About The Great Tribulation, Presbyterian & Reformed Publishing Co., Phillipsburg, New Jersey, 1983, page 78

Matthew 24:18-19

And let the one who is in the field not turn back to take his cloak. ¹⁹ And alas for women who are pregnant and for those who are nursing infants in those days!

The statement concerning the coat is all about the urgency of the moment. This is not a warning for us today, in our modern world, but a clear message to those first century Christians living in Jerusalem. The comment concerning women who may be pregnant or nursing at the time of escape was Jesus expressing compassion. During my lifetime, there have been a few occasions where misinformed preachers gave warnings to married couples not to have children based upon this verse. It is a sad commentary on Christian leadership when occurrences like this happen. When I hear, "eschatology does not matter" these kinds of events scream the opposite. Eschatology is one of the most practical doctrines we have. What we believe about the future is the foundation on how we live our lives in the present.

The mention of women who are pregnant or have small babies is because travel will be more difficult for them. God does not always remove times of difficultly; yet we are to pray for the best possible outcome.

Matthew 24:20

Pray that your flight may not be in winter or on a Sabbath.

Why is he warning about the time of year? Travel in winter may cause delay and slow their escape from the quick invading forces. Christians must have prayed, because we know that their flight was not during the winter months but came towards the end of summer. God's grace prevailed again. The comment about the Sabbath is necessary because under Jewish law travel was limited on this day. If Christians would begin their escape from the city on the Sabbath, others would notice. We are not sure of the exact day of the week they began to flee, but it was likely a day other than the Sabbath because they left Jerusalem without being stopped.

Matthew 24:21

For then there will be great tribulation, such as has not been from the beginning of the world until now, no, and never will be.

The great tribulation is not in our future, Jesus said before the current generation would pass *"all these things"* would take place. One of the central themes of Matthew 24 is the "Great Tribulation." Christian teachers over the last few generations have spread fear to millions concerning the coming "tribulation." In seminars on the kingdom, I have seen believers so gripped of fear that when the truth that the "Great Tribulation" is over, they began to cry. Teaching a victorious future is the best way to free people and give them a biblical reason to hope again.

Dispensational authors argue that Jesus said the tribulation would be the worst of all history. Does the destruction of Jerusalem reach that level? First, if we evaluate it only in building destroyed and lives taken, it is bad, but others surpass it. It would be very difficult to match what happens in Noah's day. The circumstances occurring during the three and one half years of tribulation in Jerusalem and surrounding Judea were horrific, possible surpassing suffering from any previous war or disaster, yet we cannot calculate in this manner. The destruction of Jerusalem with its temple was covenantal judgment. This will never occur again. The new covenant is for all eternity. No other generation will pay for the sins of all previous ones. Jesus makes this abundantly clear in Matthew 23.

Thus you witness against yourselves that you are sons of those who murdered the prophets. [32] Fill up, then, the measure of your fathers. [33] You serpents, you brood of vipers, how are you to escape being sentenced to hell? [34] Therefore I send you prophets and wise men and scribes, some of whom you will kill and crucify, and some you will flog in your synagogues and persecute from town to town, [35] so that on you may come all the righteous blood shed on earth, from the blood of righteous Abel to the blood of Zechariah the son of Barachiah, whom you murdered between the sanctuary and the altar. [36] Truly, I say to you, all these things will come upon this generation (Matthew 23:31-36).

Placing the 'great tribulation' in the first century opens the door to pursue cultural advancement. If everything is to be lost, then why bother creating ministries to transform culture? Those advocating both cultural transformation and a future worldwide tribulation (destroying culture) are revealing their theological Schizophrenia. Pastors teaching the seven mountains of cultural transformation on Wednesday and preaching a future great tribulation on Sunday may need to enroll in addition theological studies, or see a Christian psychiatrist. The church needs a clear message. The great tribulation Jesus predicts occurred exactly when he said it would, within one generation. It is time to invest in ministries building the kingdom of God.

Some Bible teachers equate the tribulation of Matthew 24 with the tribulation mentioned in the book of Revelation. Bray makes a distinction between the two.

> "When Jesus spoke of "great tribulation" in Matthew 24:21, He was referring to the awful horrors and tragic events of those days on the Jewish people back in AD 67-70, in Jerusalem and Judaea. When John the Revelator spoke of the "great tribulation" in Revelation 7:14 he was referring primarily to the awful persecutions being brought upon the Christian people of his day, mainly at the instigation of the roman Emperor Nero but including the tribulation and persecutions they were having under the Jewish leaders. The tribulation under Nero lasted approximately three and one half years, from AD 64 until AD 68 when Nero committed suicide. This period of time is mentioned several times in the book of Revelation. John called himself their *'brother and companion in tribulation'* (Revelation 1:9), for it was during those approximate days which we have been discussing that those early Christians themselves had been undergoing tremendous tribulations and persecutions by Nero the Emperor of Rome."[71]

---

[71] John L. Bray, Matthew 24 Fulfilled, John L. Bray Ministries, Lakeland, Florida, 1996, p.94

Matthew 24:22

"And if those days had not been cut short, no human being would be saved. But for the sake of the elect those days will be cut short."

To whom is Jesus speaking? Who are the "elect?" Does the word "elect" refer to Israel since they are the covenant people of God at this time (this is before the cross)? On the other hand, is Jesus speaking of Christians? First, we must realize the accuracy of Jesus prophecy. The siege of Jerusalem almost annihilated the entire Jewish population. Around 90% were killed and most that remained were taken as slaves. God cut short the tribulation in order to save a few. I think it is safe to say that the days being cut short is addressed to the Jews. The second part deals with the "elect." The "elect" are clearly those people Jesus is giving the signs to; those who follow him, and who become (after the cross) the new people of God; the church. The church is now the elect of God. They are the ones saved by departing Jerusalem at the right moment.

Matthew 24:23-25

Then if anyone says to you, 'Look, here is the Christ!' or 'There he is!' do not believe it. [24]For false Christ's and false prophets will arise and perform great signs and wonders, so as to lead astray, if possible, even the elect. [25]See, I have told you beforehand.

During the time of the early church (30-70 AD), false prophets were plentiful. Reading through the New Testament one can see how important this warning was. Repeatedly Paul, Peter, and other inspired authors brought this subject up making sure the church did not forget the words of Jesus. The term "elect" applies to the same people of verse 22; believers in Christ.

Matthew 24:26

"So, if they say to you, 'Look, he is in the wilderness,' do not go out. If they say, 'Look, he is in the inner rooms,' do not believe it."

Jesus was warning his followers that after he is gone false prophets and false Messiahs would come and deceive people into searching for him in the wilderness or in the temple. Jesus tells them plainly, "*do not believe them.*" "During the siege of Jerusalem, a common belief among the Jews was that God would intervene and save them. God would deliver Israel from certain destruction from Rome. In these words of Jesus, he is making it clear that they were not to expect any deliverance.[72]

Matthew 24:27-28

"*For as the lightning comes from the east and shines as far as the west, so will be the coming of the Son of Man. ²⁸ Wherever the corpse is, there the vultures will gather.*"

What does this mean? It may at first glance seem a little out of place. Verse 27 states the coming of the Son of Man can be compared to lighting. Then, vultures are to gather around a corpse. *"Immediately after the tribulation of those days the sun will be darkened, and the moon will not give its light, and the stars will fall from heaven, and the powers of the heavens will be shaken* (Matthew 24:29.)"

The language he used was familiar; it was the words of the Old Testament prophets. In the Hebrew tradition when God declared judgment upon a nation, be it Israel or surrounding people's, "apocalyptic" language was used. A common theme was a "collapsing universe." When people heard the prophets speak about the sun and moon losing their lights and about stars falling from heaven, everyone knew judgment was coming. No one stared at the sky for falling stars; they knew it was not literal. The lights represent authorities, and these powers were about to fall; literally, their lights of influence were being shut off.

There are several of these judgment passages in the Old Testament; three is sufficient to show how they worked.

Judgment on Babylon

Isaiah 13:9-10

Behold, the day of the LORD comes, cruel, with wrath and fierce anger, to make the land a desolation and to destroy its

---

[72] William R. Kimball, The Great Tribulation, Presbyterian and Reformed Publishing, Phillipsburg, New Jersey, 1983, p. 142

sinners from it. [10] For the stars of the heavens and their constellations will not give their light; the sun will be dark at its rising, and the moon will not shed its light.

Judgment on Egypt

Ez.32:7-8

When I blot you out, I will cover the heavens and make their stars dark; I will cover the sun with a cloud, and the moon shall not give its light. [8]All the bright lights of heaven will I make dark over you, and put darkness on your land, declares the Lord GOD.

Judgment on Edom

Isa.34:4

All the host of heaven shall rot away, and the skies roll up like a scroll. All their host shall fall, as leaves fall from the vine, like leaves falling from the fig tree.

Matthew 24:29 is viewed by dispensationalists as events in the future because the stars still shine. Yet, if taken literally, it causes exegetical problems, because in the book of Revelation, it also talks of stars falling, and yet, later, the earth continues. If a third of the stars (which most are many times larger than the earth) would literally fall from the sky, the earth would be in serious trouble. The best approach is not to force our doctrines into the Scripture, but to see how the Bible itself uses such language. Exegesis rule number one is to allow the Bible to interpret itself. Our first task is to ask, "Are there other passages in the Bible that speaks of the sun and moon losing their light and stars falling from the sky?" The answer is of course, yes. We have seen how the Old Testament prophets used similar language to pronounce judgment on a nation. The stars represent the light of these authorities. By proclaiming the sun, moon and stars will fall means one thing; the light of the nation will go out. DeMar explains;

> "The Old Testament is filled with solar, lunar, and stellar language depicting great political and social upheaval. The rise of kingdoms is compared to the brightness of the sun, moon, and stars. The

brightness of these heavenly bodies means a nation is in ascendancy. When a nation is described as falling-coming under the judgment of God-it is compared to the sun and moon going dark and stars falling from the sky."[73]

Although the best method is not forcing a wooden literal interpretation on the "collapsing universe" language, Pitre sees a balance between symbolic and literal, and that we should not be too quick to dismiss any literal reading.

"The imagery of the "abomination of desolation" strongly suggest that the darkening of the heavenly lights and the shaking of the celestial powers should be interpreted as cosmic signs of the destruction of Jerusalem...however...I see no absolutely reason to suggest that the cosmic imagery being employed in this instance is any less "literal" because it is meant to signify the destruction of Jerusalem. Such imagery is much more than "metaphorical language" meant to invest a "historical" event with "theological" significance. Rather, I would suggest that it is in fact literal language meant to describe the cosmic effects of an event that is both historical and eschatological: the destruction of Jerusalem."[74]

Pitre brings up a valid point because according to first century historian Josephus there were indeed unusual signs in the sky around the time of the destruction of Jerusalem and the temple.

Josephus records strange events that occurred the days of and preceding Jerusalem's destruction. "star resembling a sword, which stood over the city, and a comet, that continued a whole

[73] Gary DeMar, Last Day Madness, American Vision, Atlanta, Georgia, 1997, p. 139

[74] Brant Pitre, Jesus, The Tribulation, And The End Of The Exile, Baker Academic, Grand Rapids, Michigan, 2005, page 336

year…on the eight day of the month Nisan, and at the ninth hour of the night, so great a light shone around the altar and the holy house, that it appeared to be bright day time, which lasted for half an hour."[75] Even with these physical occurrences in the sky, we must be careful about applying a literal interpretation of these "end of the universe" passages. Even if we have some physical manifestations surrounding the destruction of Jerusalem, we would be hard pressed to show the same in cases where similar language is used (Ez.32:7-8, Isa.34:4). It is best to conclude that because of the theological importance of the destruction of Jerusalem and the temple, we have the normal "apocalyptic" (symbolic) language in describing the falling starts, etc., but it also backed up with real and literal signs in the heavens.

One of the first things done by the Romans as the army readied to approach Jerusalem was to cut down all the trees that circled the city. Josephus said that if any foreigner seeing the city beforehand would lament and mourn and its present state. Now the landscape was like a desert with its tress and pleasant gardens demolished.[76] The time of war had come.

Titus was leading the armies and he used Josephus to speak with the Jews. He wanted them to stop fighting and therefore, save their beautiful temple. Titus desired to leave the temple untouched. Yet he was pressured the actions by the Jews. Here is part of the conversation Josephus had with the Jews in Jerusalem. "And are not both the city and the entire temple now full of the dead bodies of your countrymen? It is God therefore, it is God himself who is bringing on this fire, to purge that city and temple by the means of the Romans, and is going to pluck up this city, which is full of your pollutions (Josephus notes he spoke these words with tears in his eyes)."[77]

With Josephus failing to persuade the Jews, Titus comes and engages them.

---

[75] Josephus, The Works of Josephus, Edited by William Whiston, Hendrickson Publishers, Peabody, MA., 1987

[76] Ibid.

[77] Ibid

"Now Titus was deeply affected with this state of things, and reproached John and his party…I appeal to the gods of my own country…I also appeal to my own army, and to those Jews that are now with me, and even to you yourselves, that I do not force you to defile this your sanctuary; and if you will but change the place where on you will fight, no Roman shall either come near the sanctuary, or offer any affront to it; nay, I will endeavor to preserve you and your holy house, whether you will or not."[78]

Our understanding of Roman power is that they crushed peoples with little concern for life, custom or buildings. This is true in many cases, but here in Jerusalem, they were very deliberate, even careful, before completely demolishing the city. Finally, Titus gives up in any negotiating with the Jews. "When Titus saw that these men were neither to be moved by commiseration towards themselves nor had any concern upon them to the holy house spared, he proceeded, unwillingly, to go on again with the war against them."[79] There was no turning back. Titus knew what must be done and proceeded to do so.

Conditions got worse. As food became scarce, famine set in. Hunger and misery was the people's portion. Josephus; "Thus did the miseries of Jerusalem grow worse and worse every day, and the seditious were, still more irritated by the calamities they were under, even while famine preyed upon themselves, after it had preyed upon the people. And indeed the multitude of carcasses that lay in heaps one upon another, was a horrible sight."[80]

Matthew 24:30

Then will appear in heaven the sign of the Son of Man, and then all the tribes of the earth will mourn, and they will see the Son

---

[78] Ibid

[79] Ibid

[80] Ibid

of Man coming on the clouds of heaven with power and great glory.

The first thing to notice is the "sign" appears in heaven. Which heaven is Jesus referring to? Is it the heaven of God or the heavens that we see (the sky and clouds)? The context fits best the heavens that we see, because this sign is what sparks the response of mourning. Jesus is saying to his disciples that there will be a sign in the heavens, which gives witness that he is coming on the clouds in power and great glory. It does not say that the Son of Man appears in the sky, but the sign of him appears. Then it goes to say that they will see the *"Son of Man coming on the clouds of heaven with power and great glory."* The second phrase is the common way of expressing God coming in judgment. Jesus spoke these exact words regarding his coming in Matthew.

Matthew 16:27-28

For the Son of Man is going to come with his angels in the glory of his Father, and then he will repay each person according to what he has done. Truly, I say to you, there are some standing here who will not taste death until they see the Son of Man coming in his kingdom.

Jesus states of a judgment coming to *"repay each person."* Since the "coming" is clearly an event within the apostolic era, so must the judgment.

Matthew 24:31

And he will send out his angels with a loud trumpet call, and they will gather his elect from the four winds, from one end of heaven to the other.

Is this the final harvest? Is this what is happening today? No, it is not. Over the years, preachers have told their congregations, "This is the final harvest." How do they know it is God's final harvest of souls? They do not know, and over time, this reasoning has proven false. Since this verse falls within the *"all these things"* of verse 34, we must look for answers within the time limits Jesus provides.

The Bible uses the word "angels" many times in referring to his "ministers." When the church began, the gospel went to the

Jew first. Until the temple came down there was common confusion between Christians and Jews. Once the old covenant practices stopped, a new day opened up for the gentile nations. A harvest now begins for the gospel to spread to all nations.

What about the trumpet call? If angels are his ministers in this case, should we take trumpet lessons? The Scriptures speak of trumpets on numerous occasions. DeMar writes...

> "The 'great trumpet' of verse thirty-one is the call of the gospel. It refers to Numbers 10:1-10, where silver trumpets were made to call the people together for worship and set them on their march. It also alludes to the year of Jubilee, the year when the world reverts to its original owners, the year when Satan is dispossessed and Christ reclaims the world (Acts 3:19-21)...The Jubilee year was announced by trumpets and signified the coming of Christ kingdom...With the destruction of Jerusalem the gospel went out to the gentiles in new fullness and with the expectation that the nations (Gentiles) would be discipled...the trumpet is symbolic of a great work about to commence, the great gathering of God's people into a new spiritual nation."[81]

We often think this *"coming of the son of man"* in the first century is only about judgment; yet, it also brought many positive blessings. With the ending of the old covenant, a new day has come.

Matthew 24:32-33

From the fig tree learn its lesson: as soon as its branch becomes tender and puts out its leaves, you know that summer is near. [33]So also, when you see all these things, you know that he is near, at the very gates.

Jesus now turns to the *"fig tree"* to bring home his point. The Bible makes numerous uses of the fig tree imagery. Starting with

---

[81] Gary DeMar, Last Day Madness, American Vision, Atlanta, Georgia, 1997, p.172

the Garden of Eden, when after the fall, Adam and Eve made clothing out of fig leaves. In Old Testament language, *"sitting under a fig tree"* (I Kings 4:25) was symbolic of peace and experiencing God's blessing. Jesus curses the fig tree and makes a case against fruitless Israel (Matt. 21:19).

In the context of Matthew 24, how does Jesus use the image of the fig tree? Does this fig tree image represent the nation of Israel? It appears that Israel is not in view in this text. By reading Luke's version, we see what the image stands for. He said the when the fig tree-and all trees-burst forth with leaves, then summer is near. The fig tree is the example but all trees are included. Likewise, when the signs Jesus gave happens in progressive manner, then we know for sure, *"the kingdom of God is near"* (Luke 21:29-32). The coming of the *"son of man"* is for judgment of the covenant breaking Israel and for the arrival of the kingdom of God in its fullness. The kingdom came in progressive steps (see Appendix 2) and his spiritual coming in 70 AD is the final step.

Matthew 24:34

Truly, I say to you, this generation will not pass away until all these things take place. [35] *Heaven and earth will pass away, but my words will not pass away.*

How we interpret a vast amount of eschatological passages depends on how Matthew 24:34 is interpreted. If a futurist view is adopted (dispensationalism), then that becomes the standard on interpretation for the rest of the Bible. If a preterist position is adopted (victorious eschatology), then it follows that other passages are seen in the same light. If Matthew 24 is the Bible's most important chapter concerning eschatology, then, verse 34 is the most important verse in the Bible, at least concerning eschatology. We can even take another step if verse 34 is the most important verse about eschatology, then, the word "generation" becomes the most important single word in the Bible. It comes down to one question. What did Jesus mean by saying that *"all these things"* would take place within a *"generation?"*

Matthew 24:34 is interpreted primarily in three ways.

1. Generation means race (the Jewish race continues until all is fulfilled).

2. Generation means the people living at the time when the signs are seen in the earth.

3. Generation means the generation of contemporary people to which Jesus spoke.

The first interpretation removes the prophetic element. To give a prophecy centered in "signs" to watch for and then lengthen the period to centuries, defeats the entire point. If Jesus were speaking as an "eschatological prophet" then where is the vindication?

The second attempt to interpret "generation" is that Jesus was speaking to a future generation, a generation that will actually see the signs. Many modern dispensationalists take this view and conclude that we are now the generation seeing the signs; therefore, we are living in the last days.

What did Jesus mean by '*this generation*?' First, we must consider a few basic questions. Who is the "you" in the verse? Jesus says, "I say to you." Was he talking to the generation of the protestant reformation in the 16th century? Was he speaking about the people in the 10th century? Was Jesus speaking to the people living in the 21st century? Can we honestly put "us" as the people to whom Jesus speaks? The correct answer to all three questions is no. Jesus was speaking to his disciples. The disciples of the first century were the "you" to whom he spoke.

Second, we must ask, to what does "*all these things*" refer? Going back to verse four, we find that Jesus begins to speak about the things that will happen before the destruction of the temple. That is the primary concern of the disciples. They were not asking questions about the far future, they were very concerned about their own. The last question leads back to the word "*generation*." If Jesus was speaking to his followers about the "things" he spoke of, to be consistent, the generation he speaks of must be the contemporary people then living.

The words *"this generation"* gives a timetable for all these events. The same Greek words are used in Matthew 23:36 *"Truly I say to you, all these things will come upon this generation."* Chilton provides a good review on how other passages use the term, 'this generation."

"Some have sought to get around the force of this text by saying that the word generation here really means race, and that Jesus was simply saying that the Jewish race would not die out until all these things took place. Is that true? I challenge you: Get out your concordance and look up every New Testament occurrence of the word generation (in Greek *genea*) and see if it ever means "race" in any other context. Here are the references for the Gospels: Matthew 1:17; 11:16; 12:39,41,42,45; 16:14; 17:17; 23:36; 24:34; Mark 8:12,38; 9:19; 13:30; Luke 1:48,50; 7:31; 9:41; 11:29, 30,31,32,50,51; 16:8; 17:25; 21:32. Not one of these references is speaking of the entire Jewish race over thousands of years; all use the word in its normal sense of the sum total of those living at the same time. It always refers to contemporaries...The conclusion, therefore...is that the events prophesied in Matthew 24 took place within the lifetime of the generation which was then living. It was this generation which Jesus called *"wicked and perverse"* (Matthew 12:39, 45; 16:4; 17:17); it was this "terminal generation" which crucified the Lord; and it was this generation, Jesus said, upon which would come the punishment for "all the righteous bloodshed on the earth" (Matthew 23:35)."[82]

A biblical interpretation that settles on the literal meaning of generation has devastating implications for dispensational

[82] David Chilton, Paradise Restored, Reconstruction Press, Tyler, Texas, 1985, page 86-87

eschatology. Even though their system insists upon a "literal interpretation" of Scripture, at this very critical verse, the 'literal' is abandoned. J. Stuart Russell in The Parousia (1887) gives a good commentary on verse 34. "Surely there can be no pretence of a primary and a secondary reference here. No expositor will deny that these words have a sole and exclusive application to the generation of the Jewish people then living upon the earth."[83] The words of Jesus are clear; everything prophesied will happen and all within the present generation.

Study Questions

1. Explain the "abomination of desolations?"

2. Explain the warning about fleeing on the Sabbath or in winter.

3. Explain the key verse and key word in Matthew 24.

4. In verse 30, is Jesus appearing in the sky or is it a sign that appears? Why is this important?

5. Is the nation of Israel in view in verse 32? What is the meaning here of the "fig tree?"

---

[83] J. Stuart Russell, The Parousia, Baker Books, Grand Rapids, Michigan, 1999 (originally published in 1887),p. 50

Chapter 16

The Destruction of Jerusalem

If we want to grasp New Testament theology, we must not overlook the importance of the Jewish temple. As long as the temple stood, animals sacrificed and the old priesthood remained in power; the glory of the "new creation" remained obscure. Kimball explains,

> "Had the Jewish nation not been destroyed, the spiritual concepts of the kingdom of God taught by Christ and the apostles would have been more difficult to enforce. As long as the old city and temple remained, the true spiritual nature of the kingdom of God would have been clouded by the Jewish concept of a natural and temporal kingdom of God. The destruction of Jerusalem, the center of Judaism, meant that the break with the old dispensation was final and complete. It resulted in great blessing to the entire world, for with the demise of Judaism, the true nature of the kingdom was no longer obscured, and the gospel of grace could be presented to the world in all its intended purity and simplicity."[84]

Jesus came as a first century Jew to his people. As a prophet, Jesus denounces the temple. Here is this unknown man from Galilee, wanting the temple replaced. The temple is the center of Judaism; and Jesus declared its value gone and within a generation, it will be left desolate (Matt. 24:2, 23:38). Did Jesus imagine Yahweh would rebuild a new temple, or did Jesus see himself as the new temple?

---

[84] William R. Kimball, What the Bible says about the Great Tribulation, Presbyterian and Reformed Publishing Company, Phillipsburg, New Jersey, 1983, page 203

The temple had become not a house of prayer but a den of robbers (Matt. 21:13). Jesus declared that something better than the temple was here (Matt. 12:6). Like most religions, Judaism found tradition difficult to break with. The events during the crucifixion did not change many hearts. After the temple's curtain was torn, Jews sewed it back and everything went back to normal. Something must jolt the Jews into recognition that Jesus is their Messiah. Something must dramatically declare the coming of a new covenant. What action could accomplish this? The destruction of the temple was the only event that would end the old worship patterns and officially set Christians apart as the new people of God.

Wright addresses Jesus warnings about the temple's destruction;

> "In language drawn not least from Jeremiah and Daniel, that the Temple would be destroyed by foreign armies, and that this event should be seen as the outpouring of YHWH's wrath upon his recalcitrant people. The state of the house would be worse than the first. As the Temple symbolized and drew together the themes of Israel's national life and self-understanding, so Jesus offering as he was (like some other movements of the time) a new and subversive way of being Israel, naturally conceived of this in terms of the Temple. The house built on sand would fall with a great crash. Only that built on the rock of Jesus' kingdom-announcement would stand."[85]

This new way of being Israel is at the heart of the Christian gospel. First century Judaism had extreme difficulty with this concept and today many believers still struggle. The remaking of Israel into the new people of God (Jews and Gentiles together) does not deny God's intentions for Israel but is the true fulfillment

---

[85] N.T. Wright, Jesus and the Victory of God, Fortress Press, Minneapolis, Minnesota, 1996, p. 416

of these intentions. God, in my way of thinking, has little interest in someday re-creating old Israel with a new temple of stone; God has a people already; and it is the people of his dreams, it is the church.

Why is the destruction of Jerusalem and its temple rarely included in much of our modern exegesis? Why do sermons seldom mentioned it? Why is it that many Christians have little knowledge about this history? The answer is that until recently the destruction of Jerusalem and its temple had no theological significance; therefore, it received little attention. The eschatology of dispensational-premillennialism is committed to a futurist interpretation; therefore the events of the Roman war against the Jews garnered scant interest; again no theological significance.

The last few decades we have seen a resurgence of New Testament studies that include these events. Scholars such as N.T. Wright have helped with his work in the New Testament and early Christian origins. Many others are now writing about the importance of 70 A.D. and the events leading up to the temples destruction. Fresh approaches to New Testament theology are coming on the scene.

What happened in Jerusalem during the years of 66-70 A.D.? Was there a divine purpose behind the destruction of the second temple? The writings of Josephus help immensely, without this history (or better, ignoring the history) many have forced a futuristic reading where it is not warranted. His writings are translated into numerous languages and invaluable for understanding the conditions of Jerusalem in the first century.

Serious students of the New Testament must make themselves acquainted with the works of Josephus. He paints a vivid picture of the events surrounding the invasion and conquest of Jerusalem by the Romans. We can gain amazing insight by reading his writings side by side with the New Testament.

James 5:1-6 (NKJV)
"Come now, you rich, weep and howl for your miseries that are coming upon you! ² Your riches are corrupted, and your garments are moth-eaten. ³ Your gold and silver are corroded, and

*their corrosion will be a witness against you and will eat your flesh like fire. You **have heaped up treasure** in the last days. ⁴ Indeed the wages of the laborers who mowed your fields, which you kept back by fraud, cry out; and the cries of the reapers have reached the ears of the Lord of Sabbath. ⁵ You have lived on the earth in pleasure and luxury; you have fattened your hearts as in a day of slaughter. ⁶ You have condemned, you have murdered the just; he does not resist you."*

James is the half-brother of Jesus and one of the early apostles. He is the leading elder in Jerusalem and was the moderator at the Jerusalem council. Most scholars date James around 49-50 A.D., before the council meet in Jerusalem and certainly before Jerusalem is destroyed. James describes a time that is coming; it is a pronouncement of judgment against the wicked.

The rich living in Jerusalem should have read James. His prophetic insight about coming events may have saved them their money, and their lives. Josephus writes about the destruction of the temple. He uses language very similar to James. "They also burnt down the treasury chambers, in which was an immense quantity of money, and an immense number of garments, and other precious goods, there it was that the entire riches of the Jews were heaped up together."[86]

These wealthy Jews *"laid up treasure in the last days."* Just as James prophesied, their riches were literally *"heaped up."* Now it was aflame with fire. The apostle warned them. The day of slaughter arrived; and their riches and garments were ashes. Christians knowing the prophecy of Jesus and James refrained from putting their treasure in the temple area, and they escaped before the horrible day.

Josephus was a God fearing Jew, yet to his fellow Jews he offered little support. His conclusion was simple; the hand of God was at work. "So Titus retired into the tower of Antonia, and

---

[86] The Works of Josephus Translated by William Whiston, Hendrickson Publishers, Peabody, MA. 1987,page 741

resolved to storm the temple the next day, early in the morning, with his whole army, and to encamp round about the holy house; but, as for that house, God had for certain long ago doomed it to the fire; and now that fatal day was come."[87]

The destruction of Jerusalem and its temple is a fact of history. Yet overwhelming numbers of evangelical Christians have vaguely heard of it, and those who do, seldom make any connection to biblical interpretation. We previously said that it was because it had no theological significance for many Evangelicals. With that being true, there is another reason for its lack of attention. When believers read their New Testament, its pages are silent about this historical event. The reason is simple; the Temples destruction came after the completion of the New Testament. Therefore, we hear warning about coming judgments and difficult days but never get to the actual event. The majority of apostles were dead by the time Rome finally burned the Temple.

How does this unfold throughout the New Testament? Starting with the gospels, we will proceed onward looking for those passages where the importance of the coming destruction of Jerusalem and the temple are highlighted. Once this theme is apparent, many parts of the eschatological puzzle begin to fit.

The Gospels

John the Baptist paints a picture for those refusing to repent and enter the kingdom. He says, "*even now the axe is laid to the root of the tree.*" The coming judgment is put in graphic language of cutting down a tree at its roots (Matt. 3:10). Even though rebellious Israel looks alive, its religious systems appear strong and secure; yet, the prophetic word is true; it is only a matter of time. It will not be long before "death" appears on the tree.

Large portions of Matthew's gospel show Jesus exposing the "death" within rebellious Israel.Jesus continuously shows Israel her hypocrisy. He teaches that Yahweh is doing something new, something superior to the old ways. There is a sense of urgency in

---

[87] Ibid, page 739

Matthew's gospel; it is time to repent. Judgment is coming, not in some distance generation but *this generation* (Matt. 23:32-36).John the Baptist was correct. The axe of God was striking at the root of Israel's hypocrisy and unbelief. The 40-year gap between John's words and the final judgment shows not slowness on God's part, but the vital time for strengthening the church in the midst of fierce opposition. The axe has already been applied to the tree; now the important thing is, who is sitting in the tree when it falls (I find it amusing that Zacchaeus came out of the tree)?

Jesus uses the image of a tree in Matthew chapter seven.

Matthew 7:17-20

So, every healthy tree bears good fruit, but the diseased tree bears bad fruit. A healthy tree cannot bear bad fruit, nor can a diseased tree bear good fruit. Every tree that does not bear good fruit is cut down and thrown into the fire. Thus you will recognize them by their fruits.

If our lives are bearing bad fruit, we should focus not on the fruit but on the tree, that produces the fruit. The church should stop railing against people's bad fruit and begin to heal the disease causing it. As a nation, Israel was a diseased tree and was about to be cut down.

Matthew 10:16-23

Behold, I am sending you out as sheep in the midst of wolves, so be wise as serpents and innocent as doves. [17]Beware of men, for they will deliver you over to courts and flog you in their synagogues, and you will be dragged before governors and kings for my sake, to bear witness before them and the Gentiles. When they deliver you over, do not be anxious how you are to speak or what you are to say, for what you are to say will be given to you in that hour. For it is not you who speak, but the Spirit of your Father speaking through you. Brother will deliver brother over to death, and the father his child, and children will rise against parents and have them put to death, and you will be hated by all for my name's sake. But the one who endures to the end will be saved. [23]When they persecute you in one town flee to the next, for truly, I say to you, you will not have gone through all the towns of Israel before the Son of Man comes.

Jesus explains the coming persecution. He refers to those bearing his name and message as *"sheep in the midst of wolves."* He is preparing them for future problems with governmental officials. He encourages them that they are not alone. They will have a helper, the Holy Spirit. When the need arises, the Spirit will be there. He tells them to endure to the end. Repeatedly we must realize that Jesus is not speaking about the end of the physical universe. Nor, is the end of the church age in view. No, none of these would have make sense. The Jewish age is rapidly ending and before it does, there will be difficult days.

Jesus gave them a promise; he would return. When is he coming? It will be before the disciples finish going *"through the towns of Israel."* He uses the term *"Son of Man"* which is based upon the language of Daniel. He encourages them to be faithful despite the increased persecution. Something big is on the horizon. At this point, the disciples knew two certainties; difficult days were ahead and Jesus would return. This language of return must have puzzled the disciples. Where is he going that he must return?

Matthew 12:41

"The men of Nineveh will rise up at the judgment with this generation and condemn it, for they repented at the preaching of Jonah, and behold, something greater than Jonah is here."

Jesus is pronouncing judgment to the religious leaders. He tells them *"the men of Nineveh will rise up at the judgment with this generation and condemn it."* What is striking is that the judgment is upon a *"generation."* It does not seem to be a universal threat, but very narrow indeed to those of Israel who refuse to repent and enter the kingdom.

Matthew 12:43-45

When the unclean spirit has gone out of a person, it passes through waterless places seeking rest, but finds none. Then it says, 'I will return to my house from which I came.' And when it comes, it finds the house empty, swept, and put in order. Then it goes and brings with it seven other spirits more evil than itself, and they

enter and dwell there, and the last state of that person is worse
than the first. So also will it be with this evil generation.

In Matthew's account, Jesus follows the *"sign of Jonah"*
pronouncement with an example of demons returning in greater
number to a person. Jesus says that this will be like *"this*
generation." Some have tried hermeneutical tricks to avoid a
literal interpretation of this verse, and I would say, proceed at great
caution. The point of Jesus is not teaching about demon
possession (but he does anyway), but in the awful condition of first
century Israel. It would be far greater to live in another generation,
even a wicked one, than to live in this one and reject Yahweh's
Messiah.

I & II Peter

The writings of Peter present a challenge, even the most
skillful exegetes approach with caution. His second epistle is
disputed as to its authenticity. A number of scholars have
attempted to prove it was written by someone other than Peter, and
in the second century, this being a case of pseudepigrapha writing.
The evidence affirming Peter authorship by evangelical scholars is
fine with me. For those wanting to read the various arguments
(pro and con) there are many resources available.[88] When the
evidence is in, I strongly support two conclusions; I and II Peter
were written by Peter, and written before 70 A.D. A likely date
for First and Second Peter is from 60 A.D. to 64 A.D. The
parameters for setting these dates are narrow since we know that
Peter died at the hand of Nero around 65 A.D.

Acceptance of authorship and its approximate date is only the
start. Now, we come to the difficult process of understanding what
Peter writes. He writes two letters, both dealing with the same
subject, the coming of Jesus. A preterist reading of Peter is the
best approach to understand his writings. The letters deal with a
coming of Jesus but a coming, which was promised to happen in
the lifetime of Peter's readers. This is a spiritual coming in glory

---

[88] "The Promise of His Appearing" a book on II Peter by Peter J. Leithart.
Cannon Press, Moscow, Idaho

and judgment, not a physical coming. Times are getting tough, persecutions are increasing, some believers are forsaking the faith; and Jesus has not come. Why is there a delay? Will it really happen? When will our enemies be judged? This is the contour of Peter's epistles.

Peter was there when Jesus foretold the temple's destruction. Early Christians reading Peter's letter were aware of this prophecy. For over 30 years, the stories and prophecies of Jesus reminded early church members about coming events. Also, since the gift of the Spirit now operates in the church, it can be surmised that prophesies and words of knowledge are regular occurrences. The Holy Spirit was at work, admonishing the church that Jesus was a true prophet and the events he spoke about would soon arrive. What seems like a delay is only man's reasoning, God is right on schedule.

Peter writes about mockers who are questioning if Jesus is coming. These mockers point out that the "fathers" are dying and still nothing is happening. These "fathers" are not Old Testament saints but refer to the Apostles who by now have begun to die off. These mockers were talking about the delay of the "coming" Jesus prophesied, the coming that would occur within their generation. This is brought out by Peter J. Leithart's book The Promise of His Appearing. Leithart makes a convincing case that these "fathers" were New Testament Apostles and the mockers are not attacking the delay of the first coming (which makes little sense), but directing their doubts on the promise that Jesus would return in his kingdom, before the end of the present generation.

Leithart explains...

> "There are indications within chapter 3 that Peter is talking about a "day of judgment" that would occur within the first century. Peter is concerned with mockers who arise in the church in the "last days," and this and similar phrases refer throughout the New Testament to the apostolic era, not some future period of history...Peter warns that mockers will come in the first century (II Peter 3:3),

and this implies that their "destruction" must also take place within that period. As noted above in chapter 2, the mockers are the same as the false teachers of 2 Peter 2; the false teachers are the "ungodly men" of 3:7 and the "unprincipled men" of 3:17. Thus the "day of God" (3:12) is the "day" for the destruction of false teachers (3:7). If the mockers have already appeared in the first century, and their destruction is predicted, that destruction must also take place in the first century. It would hardly be worthwhile for God to destroy the false teachers long after they have died."[89]

Throughout the Apostle Peter's two books, there is clear evidence of eschatological expectations. These expectations were now turning into reality as false prophets reveal themselves. The time of the end must be soon; according to Peter. The "*coming*" of the "*son of man*" is approaching and the signs of his coming are increasing in intensity as the day draws closer. Surely, Peter and his readers are living in this hinge generation. The old was about to disappear with the appearing of the son of man in judgment.

John

John wrote his gospel, the book of Revelation and three epistles. With the exception of Paul, we have more material from John than from any other New Testament author. As we saw earlier, his gospel is different from the synoptic gospels. He is less concerned about telling the story of Jesus as a man and more concerned we see the Christ, God's son. His letters take a different tone.

In his epistles, John writes as a father ministry to those whom he loves and cares about deeply. Time is getting short on the eschatological chart. John knows it, and he is determined that his

---

[89] Peter J. Leithart, The Promise of His Appearing, Cannon Press, Moscow, ID, 2004, p.80-81

readers know it. His three letters are short, but very enlightening to the times that they live in.

John in his three epistles has the end of the old covenant in view. Leithart explains, "John's letters are part of the New Testament's final response to Judaism. They are part of the last-ditch New Testament address to Israel and the problems surrounding Israel's unbelief...John's epistles are part of a climactic confrontation with Judaism."[90] The mood of the letters conveys a sense of urgency. The believers receiving these letters must know what God has in store for their times. John reveals that the antichrists have arrived. This fact among others confirms that the time of the end is near; that is the Jewish days, and as for the Christians, they will see the kingdom of God.

Hebrews

The book of Hebrews is a case where the preterists view simply makes sense. Even though authorship is unknown, it makes little difference in how it prepares Christians for the end of one age and the beginning of a new. Hebrew believers living in Jerusalem were in crisis. Falling away is very real and some have already gone back to Judaism. Hebrews reveals Christ as superior to the old sacrifices and priesthood.

The Mosaic age is ending and the Messianic age is near. Should we follow Jesus or Moses? Is the keeping of the ancient traditions the best way to follow Jesus? Many were confused and some were backsliding into Judaism. The author reveals Christ as superior in every aspect. A new age of Yahweh's Messiah is here.

As we read New Testament literature, the occasion for the letter is vital for its interpretation. Why was the letter written? Who are the people needing this letter? The position that Hebrews is written to Jewish Christians in Jerusalem only a few years before its destruction is the proper place to begin. This is clear in a number of texts. One passage often misunderstood is, *"not to fail at gathering together, as they see the day appearing."* To what

---

[90] Peter J. Leithart, From Behind the Veil, Athanasius Press, Monroe, Louisiana, p. 8

day is he referring? Some place "the day" far off in the distance future. No, the "*day*" that was approaching was the day of the "son of man" coming in judgment. Jerusalem and the temple fall to the Romans. This is the "*day*" where over a million Jews would lose their lives, and the remainder would be taken as slaves. Meeting regularly for worship means they would hear the Spirit speak to them; they would be prepared. As they gathered prophets would speak, others moved by the Spirit would offer encouragement and comfort. Missing church during these final days may lead to a failure in discerning the times resulting in the loss of their very lives.

With these things in mind, the writer of Hebrews gives us a timetable for certain events. The "*last days*" are not the final generation before the second coming of Christ; rather it was the beginning point for the Christian Church. For the nation Israel with its old covenant laws and practice of worship, the end had come. With the death of Christ upon the cross, the old covenant regulation of worship now was without merit or value. With the coming of the Messiah, there was the introduction of a new age, the age of the Kingdom.

The Apocalypse of John

John's apocalypse is fiercely debated. What should we make of these images, these symbols and his out of this world visions. Is this a literal picture of our future? Will two-thirds of the population soon face annihilation? Will beasts and dragons soon be after us? Will the next sly politician institute tattoos for our foreheads? With speculations abounding and books enough to fill the ocean, it is time for some biblical sanity. The journey to common sense is not easy. Many evangelicals believe John's prophecy is about our generation. We are the generation specifically portrayed in Revelation. It seems quite exciting-at least for some. Yet, Revelation may have a different story. It may, and I believe it does, complete our view of how the rest of the New Testament books reveal, one age is dying and another age is coming to birth. The writing style of John in his use of "apocalyptic literature" is not easy to interpret, yet, he conveys the same message; Jesus is coming soon-once the old is judged.

The difference between prophecy and apocalyptic writing needs clarification. Our knowledge of apocalyptic literature is limited because it is no longer in use. Like a lost language, its meaning has passed away through time. We assume we understand far more than we do. Two basic rules will help immensely with understanding the book of Revelation.

1. Understand the Old Testament Background

2. Understand Apocalyptic Literature

How did the people receiving John's letter understand the strange images and visions? Were they better prepared to interpret John's images than we are? First, they were acquainted with Old Testament imagery. There are over 500 images and allusions in the book of Revelation taken from the Old Testament. When Jewish Christians fled Jerusalem after the stoning of Stephen, many settled in Asia Minor; the churches John writes to. Therefore, the Jews in the church helped the gentiles with the Old Testament background.

Secondly, the people of the first century understood apocalyptic literature. Apocalyptic literature was common in the first century. Our difficulties are not theirs. John was not masking his message in strange codes; he used a familiar form, one that they understood.

What is apocalyptic literature and how does it differ from prophetic literature? First, prophecy is a spoken word that later was copied on scrolls by scribes. In the Old Testament, Prophets spoke for God (they did not write for God). That is why many Jewish scribes did not group Daniel among the Prophets, since Daniel wrote his message. Apocalyptic literature is different as it is always in written form. Secondly, in Biblical writings the source is important. Who is responsible for this word? Authorship was vital in determining canonicity. The book of Revelation is apocalyptic literature; yet it was the opposite of other similar writings, John ascribes himself as the author. Apocalyptic writings of the time were usually anonymous. Thirdly, there is a difference in the type of the images used. Prophecy primarily uses dreams, statutes, common animals (like bears, goats, lions, etc.), trees or plants, things that are known and understood. Apocalyptic literature used images that were unfamiliar, almost alien to our thinking, like animals with men's faces, bugs wearing crowns of gold, and numerous images that only a writer of fiction would imagine. It has an otherworld feeling to it. Fourthly, apocalyptic literatures express some approaching catastrophic event. It brings to light conflicts that are about to implode. This explains that when prophecy is used to pronounce judgment, it includes elements of the apocalyptic (the collapsing earth images are common). Prophecy also includes predictions of future events, which is not the norm in apocalyptic writings.[91] With these basic differences in mind, the overall message of Revelation becomes a little easier to grasp.

A complete book (a large one) is necessary for a comprehensive study of Revelation. No matter what underlining theology one has, interpretation of John's book is difficult. Futurists have problems with certain passages and likewise preterists may find particular passages unyielding to standard hermeneutics. Our goal here is to lay out a basic guide to help keep the overall perspective.

John is telling his readers that Jesus is coming soon. Remember, the New Testament uses the "coming" of the Lord in various ways. More often than not, it refers to a coming in the first century that results in the coming of the kingdom. Why is Jesus coming? Because the kingdom is near. The bulk of Revelation's visions of judgment describe the destruction of Jerusalem using apocalyptic language. It is over the top, almost like viewing a violent cartoon; and that is exactly how this type of ancient literature reads. Modern attempts to understand the small details will lead to frustration or to faulty conclusions. Read for the big

---

[91] Gordon D. Fee, Douglas Stuart, How to Read the Bible for All Its Worth, Zondervan, Grand Rapids, Michigan, 2003, page 187

picture, and then study some trusted commentaries for the minor points of interest.[92]

Now that we have reviewed some New Testament passages dealing with the coming disaster, we move to some actual events of the destruction of Jerusalem and its temple. Josephus is again our guide back into history.

One interesting note is that when the Romans propelled large white stones into the temple area, the watchmen on the walls would shout, "The Son Cometh."[93] Is this a simple mistake in translation? In Hebrew, the word for Son is "ben" and stone is "eben." If only available in Hebrew, it seems logical to conclude that a mistake was made and the watchmen were simply warning the people that a "stone" was coming in. Since we have Josephus in other languages[94], where he clearly wrote "The Son Cometh" this argument is weakened. We can never be sure of the reasoning behind this odd way of warning. It may be that the many dire predictions of Jesus remained in the conscience of the Jewish nation. In addition, the concept of the "coming of the son of man" in the clouds had clear overtones of pending judgment. Did the Jews think this was their God flying through the sky coming to judge Israel? Did these Jews remember the words of Jesus, God's eschatological prophet? We are not sure of their thinking. What we do know is that it was God moving in covenantal judgment against a rebellious and unbelieving people.

Consistence Hermeneutic

The destruction of Jerusalem is the primary consideration of the Olivet discourse. This is the partial preterists position. Even theologians not adopting the preterists hermeneutic see Matthew 24 as partially fulfilled in the destruction of the city and the temple

---

[92] David Chilton, The Days of Vengeance, Dominion Press, Fort Worth, Texas, 1987, page 236

[93] Josephus, The Works of Josephus, William Whiston, Editor, Hendrickson Publishers, Peabody, MA, page 710

[94] William Whiston, Editor, The Works of Josephus, Hendrickson Publishers, Peabody, MA, 1987, page 710

in 70 A.D. J. Rodman Williams wrote a complete Systematic Theology from a charismatic perspective. His Renewal Theology established that charismatics do take the biblical text serious (at least they should). He argues that Matthew 24 has a two-fold fulfillment, one in the destruction of Jerusalem and the other at the end of the current age (Second Coming). Williams reviews the variety of ways Jesus talked about his "coming." He mentions the transfiguration, his resurrection, Pentecost, his incarnation, his coming to the people of Israel, his triumphal entry, and the destruction of Jerusalem.[95] It is imperative that we understand how Jesus and the apostles use the language of "coming." The mistake we make is that whenever the text has the word "coming" used in reference to Jesus, we automatic think Second Coming and interpret the passage on that assumption. For the majority of New Testament passages this "rush to judgment" will result in faulty exegesis and wrong doctrines. Williams gives Matthew 10:23 as an example on a first century coming of Jesus.

Matthew 10:23

When they persecute you in one town, flee to the next, for truly, I say to you, you will not have gone through all the towns of Israel before the Son of Man comes.

Williams writes, "The charge, which begins in 10:1, is related to much more than a brief journey. There is no doubt that a fairly long period is envisaged in such words as *"you will be dragged before governors and kings for my sake, to bear testimony before them and the Gentiles.* (vs. 18)" This coming seems to represent God's visitation upon the Jews by the Romans in A.D. 70...Thus, the coming referred to in Matthew 10:23 was likely fulfilled in the desolation and destruction of Jerusalem."[96] The next passage Williams brings up in his discussion about the 'coming of Jesus' is Matthew 26:63.

---

[95] J. Rodman Williams, Renewal Theology, Zondervan Publishing House, Grand Rapids, Michigan, 1997,page 309 Vol. 3

[96] Ibid.

Matthew 26:63-64

But Jesus remained silent. And the high priest said to him, "I adjure you by the living God, tell us if you are the Christ, the Son of God." Jesus said to him, "You have said so. But I tell you, from now on you will see the Son of Man seated at the right hand of Power and coming on the clouds of heaven.

The Sanhedrin questions Jesus. The high priest demands that Jesus answer him. Jesus responds but he does not say, "I am the Christ, the Son of God" directly, but answers the question in the affirmative. He tells the Jewish leaders (the *you* is plural) that they *"will see the son of Man seated at the right hand of Power and coming on the clouds of heaven."* William's comments, "Jesus words apparently refer to an occurrence within the lifetime of the members of the Jewish high council. The fulfillment, at least in the primary instance, would occur in the coming judgment and destruction of Jerusalem in A.D. 70. For this happened within forty years of the time Jesus spoke the words."[97] From this background of how Jesus uses words of his "coming" Williams addresses Matthew 24:30.

Then will appear in heaven the sign of the Son of Man, and then all the tribes of the earth will mourn, and they will see the Son of Man coming on the clouds of heaven with power and great glory.

"Let us now reconsider Jesus' words in Matthew 24:30 about his coming...It is noteworthy that the language is almost identical with that of Matthew 26:64...this suggests that Jesus is referring basically to the same event. If Matthew 26:64 refers primarily to the event within the lifetime of the Sanhedrin members (as seems likely), then Matthew 24:30 could do so as well. This seems to be confirmed by the later words of Jesus in Matthew 24:32..."*Truly, I say to you, this generation will not pass away till all these things take place.*" A review of Jesus' earlier words in Matthew 24 reveals that "all these things" finds its primary focus in the

---

[97] Ibid.

destruction of the temple"[98]. Even though the overall eschatology of Williams may have directed him towards an inclusive futurist's interpretation, he allows the text to direct the outcome. He brings our attention to the events surrounding the destruction of Jerusalem as the primary meaning of these texts. He does add a secondary meaning of another judgment at the end of the current age. I believe Williams is consistent in interpreting the primary meaning of Matthew 24. I am disappointed to find in another section that he reverts to the "secondary meaning" of Matthew 24 in discussing circumstances of the *last days.*"

Matthew 24:12-13

"And because lawlessness will be increased, the love of many will grow cold. But the one who endures to the end will be saved."

Williams, "This suggests that the decline of Christian love-the love of God and all people that Christ makes possible-will be prevalent toward the end. This points to a falling away, or apostasy...This departure from love is the core of apostasy, for when love is gone, there is little left. Toward the end of the age, such tragic lovelessness will be the true of most men."[99] I see an inconsistency here. Williams admits earlier that the primary meaning of Matthew 24 is found in the destruction of Jerusalem, and then when addressing another subject he uses Matthew 24 as Scriptural proof for circumstances surrounding the Second Coming. Why should the secondary meaning take precedent? Why should the apostasy be understood for the end of the church age when Matthew 24 is primarily about the end of the Jewish age? The New Testament has many warnings about apostasy.When the contexts of these texts are considered carefully, it is an apostasy of the first century, not some "falling away" of generations in the future.

Did Jesus refer both to the destruction of Jerusalem and the events of his future Second Coming in the Olivet discourse? I see

---

[98] Ibid.

[99] J. Rodman Williams, Renewal theology, Zondervan Publishing House, Grand Rapids, Michigan, 1997, page 327 Vol. 3

no biblical evidence that points to a double fulfillment. Scripture and history can explain everything Jesus spoke about, and it points to a complete fulfillment in the coming horrific events of Jerusalem. We must be consistent when we interpret the Scripture. This is not easy; it takes time and work, but is always worth it.

The old covenant with its temple worship was ending. Before its complete collapse, many events will take place. There will be false Messiahs and prophets, wars and rumors of wars, earthquakes and famines, and a time of apostasy. All of this happened during the first century. The destruction of Jerusalem and the temple is one of the most theologically significant events in the New Testament. We need our New Testament back; and understanding of how the destruction of Jerusalem lies beneath many of the passages is a good start. Wright states it well; "When Jerusalem is destroyed, and Jesus' people escape from the ruin just in time, that will be YHWH becoming king, bringing about the liberation of his true covenant people, the true return from exile, the beginning of the new world order."[100]

Study Questions

1. Explain the theological importance of the destruction of Jerusalem.

2. Why do we not have a description of Jerusalem's destruction in the New Testament?

3. Give Scriptures where language of Jesus' coming is not the future Second Coming.

4. Explain the key elements of Apocalyptic Literature.

5. Discuss "Peter's eschatological expectations?"

---

[100] Gary DeMar, Francis X. Gumerlock, The Early Church And the end of the World, American Vision, Powder Springs, Georgia, 2006, P. 8 (introduction)

Chapter 17

The Antichrist

This will be the shortest chapter. There are two reasons for this. First, the amount of Scriptures mentioning the antichrist is amazingly few. Secondly, the shortness of the chapter is symbolic of the attention the Bible gives the subject. Indentifying the antichrist is very helpful in getting shelf space in Christian bookstores. Countless individuals are tagged with the term, "antichrist" and then in time they are replaced by someone else. What is true about these many predictions is that no one writes a book apologizing for being mistaken; they just pick another candidate and begin driving the eschatological bus off another cliff.

Advocates of the kingdom-centered eschatology are committed to progressive victory. We are not looking for the world to get worse, but actually better. Where do we begin to unravel the confusion? Since the Apostle John is the first to use the term "antichrist" this is the best place to start.

I John 2:18-19

Children, it is the last hour, and as you have heard that antichrist is coming, so now many antichrists have come. Therefore we know that it is the last hour. [19] They went out from us, but they were not of us; for if they had been of us, they would have continued with us. But they went out, that it might become plain that they all are not of us.

I John 2:22

Who is the liar but he who denies that Jesus is the Christ? This is the antichrist, he who denies the Father and the Son.

I John 4:1-3

Beloved, do not believe every spirit, but test the spirits to see whether they are from God, for many false prophets have gone out into the world. [2] By this you know the Spirit of God: every spirit that confesses that Jesus Christ has come in the flesh is from God,

³and every spirit that does not confess Jesus is not from God. This is the spirit of the antichrist, which you heard was coming and now is in the world already.

II John 7

For many deceivers have gone out into the world, those who do not confess the coming of Jesus Christ in the flesh. Such a one is the deceiver and the antichrist.

The Apostle John is not only the first to use the term "antichrist;" he is the only biblical writer to do so. These four passages are the entire basis of biblical knowledge that we have on the antichrist. It fits into the overall apostasy that Jesus prophesied in Matthew 24. John writing only a few years before the destruction of Jerusalem warns the believers to test the spirits and remain faithful to the truth about Jesus.

Chilton summaries the New Testament's meaning for antichrist.

> "First, the Christians had already been warned about the coming of antichrist. Second, there was not just one, but "many antichrists." The term antichrist, therefore, cannot be simply a designation of one individual. Third, antichrist was already working as John wrote…Obviously, if the antichrist was already present in the first century, he was not some figure who would arise at the end of the world. Fourth, antichrist was a system of unbelief, particularly the heresy of denying the person and work of Jesus Christ. Fifth, the antichrists had been members of the Christian Church, but had apostatized. Now these apostates were attempting to deceive other Christians, in order to sway the Church as a whole away from the Jesus Christ."[101]

Since the Bible refers so little to "antichrist," where do popular books find their material? Most dispensational authors

---

[101] David Chilton, Paradise Restored, Reconstruction Press, Tyler, Texas, 1985, page 110-111

combine a number of terms and figures of speech and call it "antichrist." They take the man of lawlessness (II Thess. 2), the beast of Revelation (Rev. 13), the abomination of desolation (Matt. 24), and the prince (Daniel 9) and create an evil superhuman called antichrist. This is not only bad exegesis but also just plain wrong. It leads people astray and tends toward wild speculation. It causes harm to individuals who really believe these predictions and makes a mockery of Christians in general. The Bible uses the term "antichrist" in a unique way and connects these false teachings and the people to the first century-not the 21st century.

Study Questions

1. Why is the chapter on "antichrist" so short?

2. How do dispensationalists find enough information about "antichrist" to fill entire books?

3. Explain what the Apostle John taught about "antichrist."

4. Paul uses the terms, "last days" and "last times" whereas John uses the term, "last hour;" explain the possible significance.

Chapter 18

The Man of Lawlessness

The increase in lawlessness and the revealing of what Paul calls a *"man of lawlessness"* are features of the last days. Paul's *"man of lawlessness"* is a mystery that many have found difficult to solve; even biblical scholars and theologians disagree on almost every point.[102] Additionally this *"man of lawlessness"* fuels wild speculations when connected to Apostle John's *"antichrist."*

II Thessalonians 2:1-12

"Now concerning the coming of our Lord Jesus Christ and our being gathered together to him, we ask you, brothers, ²not to be quickly shaken in mind or alarmed, either by a spirit or a spoken word, or a letter seeming to be from us, to the effect that the day of the Lord has come. ³ Let no one deceive you in any way. For that day will not come unless the rebellion comes first, and the man of lawlessness is revealed, the son of destruction, ⁴who opposes and exalts himself against every so-called god or object of worship, so that he takes his seat in the temple of God, proclaiming himself to be God. ⁵Do you not remember that when I was still with you I told you these things? ⁶And you know what is restraining him now so that he may be revealed in his time. ⁷For the mystery of lawlessness is already at work. Only he who now restrains it will do so until he is out of the way. ⁸And then the lawless one will be revealed, whom the Lord Jesus will kill with the breath of his mouth and bring to nothing by the appearance of his coming. ⁹The coming of the lawless one is by the activity of Satan with all power and false signs and wonders, ¹⁰and with all wicked deception for those who are perishing, because they refused to love the truth and so be saved. ¹¹Therefore God sends them a strong delusion, so that they may believe what is false, ¹²in order that all may be

---

[102] Keith A. Mathison, Postmillennialism An Eschatology of Hope, P&R Publishing, Phillipsburg, New Jersey, 1999, p. 228

condemned who did not believe the truth but had pleasure in unrighteousness."

The first thing to be aware of is that we are missing key facts in the passage. Paul reminds these believers in Thessalonica *"⁵Do you not remember that when I was still with you I told you these things?"* It is precisely *"these things"* that we are not privileged to know. Therefore, we pick up Paul's letter, written to people living about 2,000 years ago, and we attempt to piece the puzzle together. We must be careful here or we will lapse into futuristic speculations like many holding dispensational views. How did the readers in the first century understand this passage? Without all the information, it can be difficult to know, but it is not impossible.

What is the context? Why did Paul bring up this *"man of lawlessness"* in the first place? The context is the *"coming of the Lord."* A false teaching was circulating throughout the church that the *"day of the Lord"* had already come. An interesting note here is that they seem to not be concerned about themselves (why they were left behind) but had questions about those who had died. What was their status? Paul hears about this and writes to correct their misunderstanding.

This *"coming of the Lord"* is not the Second Coming. This is the first mistake we must avoid. Since the New Testament uses this type of language for different "comings" of Jesus, we must stop, and allow the context to lead us and not our presuppositions. It is always necessary to ask, which coming of Jesus is this passage referring to? As the passage develops, Paul refers to events in his day, not ours. We will also see that the "coming" is in connection with the *day of the Lord*, which speaks of the judgment of Israel.

Do we know why Paul wrote in such cryptic language? Was he intentionally hiding something in his public letter? His prior private teaching must have revealed more facts than we have in his letter. It is possible that Paul did not want the name of the *"man of lawlessness"* revealed in public at this time. It could be used against him or bring additional persecution to the churches.

Andrew Perriman, author of <u>The Coming of the Son of Man</u> argues Paul's language comes from the Old Testament, especially Daniel.

> "Allusions to Old Testament texts have commonly been noted, but not in any very coherent way: we tend to suppose merely that Paul has constructed his narrative in a magpie fashion out of phrases and images pilfered from various Old Testament texts. This is where interpretation has consistently missed the point of Paul's account-by not taking seriously enough the intertextual indicators that are found in it. The argument that we will put forward here is that Daniel's multilayered story of the crisis provoked by Antiochus Epiphanes, mediated in all likelihood by a tradition of interpretation that is largely invisible to us, provides the narrative background needed to make sense of the disjointed synopsis of 2 Thessalonians 2:3-7."[103]

The argument of Perriman is not that this *"man of lawlessness"* means Antiochus Epiphanes, but a person like him. This leads to the conclusion that the "man" Paul addresses is pagan. The pagans are Roman, probably Titus, and at the time of the temples destruction. There are historical accounts where the Romans placed their ensigns in the temple area and offered sacrifices.[104]

J. Stuart Russell also thinks Paul's "man" is pagan. Paul assures his readers that the "dead" are not forgotten; and that the "Day of the Lord" has not come yet. Paul knows this because two events that must precede the "Day" have not happened. First, the apostasy must occur. This is a general overall falling away that

---

[103] Andrew Perriman, The Coming of the Son of Man, Paternoster, London, 2005, page 132

[104] Josephus, The Works of Josephus, Translated by William Whiston, Hendrickson Publishers, Peabody, MA.,1987, page 743

Jesus warned of in his Olivet Discourse. Second, the *"man of lawlessness"* must be revealed. Russell, "the apostasy is a system, the man of sin an individual." [105] Russell provides a list of characteristics to begin our search.

1. 1. It is not a system but a man, an individual.

2. 2. It is not private, but a public person.

3. 3. It is a person holding the highest rank and authority in the State.

4. 4. The person is heathen and not Jewish.

5. 5. He claims divine names, prerogatives and worship.

6. 6. He pretends to exercise miraculous powers.

7. 7. He is characterized by enormous wickedness, the incarnation and embodiment of evil.

8. 8. He is distinguished by lawlessness as a ruler.

9. 9. He had not arrived at the fullness of his power when the apostle wrote; there existed some hindrance or check to the full development of his influence.

10. 10. This hindrance was a person, who was known by the Thessalonians; and soon would be taken out of the way.

11. 11. The "man" was doomed for destruction.

12. 12. His full development or "manifestation" and his destruction are immediately to precede the Parousia. "The Lord will destroy him with the brightness of his coming." [106]

Who does Russell think this man is? "When the apostle wrote he was on the steps of the Imperial throne-a little longer and he sat on the throne of the world. It is NERO, the first of the persecuting

---

[105] J. Stuart Russell, The Parousia, Baker Books, Grand Rapids, Michigan, reprinted in 1999 from the 1887 original, p. 178

[106] Ibid.

emperors; the violator of all laws, human and divine; the monster whose cruelty and crimes entitle him to the name, 'man of sin."[107]

Russell makes a compelling case for Nero. Yet, there are some unanswered questions about how Nero fits the text. First, we have no record that Nero sat in the temple and proclaimed himself God. Knowing the perverse personhood of Nero, he would have no fear of doing so, if he was in Jerusalem. The other objection I would have of Nero is Paul says this "man" will be destroyed by the "appearance of his coming (Jesus)." Nero died in June of 68 A.D.[108] the coming of the "son of man" took place in 70 A.D. Russell does answer this objection. "It is the coming of the Lord, the Parousia, which is to be the signal of his destruction...the man of sin was destined to perish, not in the full blaze of the Parousia, but at its first dawn or beginning."[109] Russell thinks the word *"appearance of his coming"* may be that "brightness" which precedes the actual event. Russell makes some good points. He has done his research, which is superior to many today. Most people today pick people out of thin air, with little exegesis of Paul's words.

This may be what Paul had in mind, but there are other views. Gary DeMar in his book, Last Day Madness, states the possibility that the *"man of lawlessness"* is Jewish. He takes a strong first century interpretation of the timing issues and then proceeds in indentifying this man of mystery.

> "The man of lawlessness was the principal religious leader of Israel-the high priest who officiated over Jewish law and did not concern himself with using the law in a God-honoring way (Matthew 26:32-36). In addition, the defilement of the temple was the result of their lawless acts. Josephus describes how the Zealots dismantled the

---

[107] Ibid.

[108] Herbert W. Benario, Emory University, De Imperatoribus Romanis, http//www.roman-emperors.org

[109] Ibid.

biblically prescribed method of choosing priests and "ordained certain unknown and ignoble persons for that office." Their choice for high priest was Phannias."[110]

Author John Bray has another first-century man in mind; John Levi of Gischala. He quotes Josephus who provides a character description of John Levi of Gischala. He was a "treacherous person...his character was that of a very cunning and very knavish person...he was a ready liar...and thought it a point of virtue to delude people...he was a hypocritical pretender of humanity...he had a peculiar knack of thieving."[111] Certainly, the Christian community knew his lawless behavior. Points in favor of John Levi are several. First, he had access to the temple. Second, being in Jerusalem, he was likely killed in the destruction of the city.

There are items that we can be certain. First, this *"man of lawlessness"* is not a person in our future. He has been dead for generations.The important factor about the *"man of lawlessness"* is his appearance in the 'last days.' He was a man of the first-century. Second, we must connect Paul's *"man of lawlessness"* to events occurring in the "last days" of the old covenant. These simple, but textual honest conclusions, strikes a blow to the dispensational scheme of building a case for a future antichrist. Take away the leg of *"antichrist"* and now remove another leg of the *"man of lawlessness"* and the stool of dispensationalism falls.

Who was the real "man of lawlessness"? We can never know for sure; yet, we can be sure he lived during the days of Paul and the early apostles. Even though Russell makes a good case for Nero, John Levi of Gischala seems a better fit; he is my "Man of lawlessness."

---

[110] Gary DeMar, Last Day Madness, American Vision, Inc., Atlanta, Georgia, 1997, pages 284-285

[111] Ibid. p. 635

Study Questions

1. Why does Paul connect the "man of lawlessness" with his overall theme of the "coming" of the Lord?

2. Why is this passage difficult for modern readers?

3. According to Paul should the church today be active in watching for this "man of lawlessness?"

Chapter 19

Satan and the Kingdom

Since Adam ate the forbidden fruit, God's people have been at war with Satan. He is the great deceiver and the enemy of our souls. For two-thousand years, Christians developed strategies to defeat this devil, yet the battle continues. 21st century Christianity, especially those in charismatic churches have led the way in this epic battle. Books are written, seminars conducted, and new prayer formulas are created; all wanting control over the "roaring lion." Spiritual warfare is big business. Lots of money is spent, a lot of time invested, and now time for serious evaluation is here. Is the church stronger? Have we grown spiritually? Is Satan finally defeated? Should the battle with Satan continue? What have we learned from all this battle strategy? One thing is clear; all the intercession and preaching, all the binding and casting out, has produced at least one thing; a worn out church. The sad element is that people with problems for the most part, still have problems. Government still has problems. Churches have problems. Can we point to one positive cultural change resulting from our attempts to "bind the devil?" As is in every spiritual enterprise, there are victories; nevertheless, in comparison to the commitment made, the positive results are few. Time has come for a new theological model for spiritual warfare.

The new model needed is the partial-preterist hermeneutic and an eschatology embracing victory. Once we rethink eschatology, the role of Satan can be seen with a fresh perspective.This has immense practical applications, and it will free the church to pursue her true mission of preaching Jesus and his kingdom.

A Bound but partially free Satan

Those favoring the partial-preterist view of eschatology believe that Satan is defeated but differ in the scope of his defeat. A number of partial preterists see Satan as hindered in his work, defeated at the cross, yet still possessing significant influence. Christians are "mopping up" the forces of evil in light of his defeat. Revelation 20 has Satan chained, thrown in a pit and then the pit sealed over. The reason for this binding is to prevent him from deceiving the nations. Yet Satan roams freely even if he drags his chains. The clause about not deceiving the nations takes precedence over the binding symbolism. He cannot prevent the spread of the gospel in the nations, but continues his work of warring against individuals.

There is an even a stronger view that also fits within a partial-preterist understanding of eschatology. Here, the scene in Revelation 20 is the next step in restricting Satan from any present involvement. The language of binding has theological consequences. The time has come for a more restricted view of Satan.

A Bound and Restricted Satan

Jesus battled Satan during his earthly ministry. He cast out demons and confronted Satan in person. Reading the gospels, we see demons everywhere. It was likely that they were making one last stand, one great battle to stop Jesus from accomplishing his mission. As the ministry of Jesus unfolds, there is a progression of restriction.

If Jesus defeated Satan on the cross, why then, was the early church warned about his evil intentions (I Peter 5:8-9)? Could it be that the final sentence on Satan is not complete?Through the cross, Satan is defeated. Yet he continues harassing God's people. The reason for this is that he is given a few years before being bound in a pit of God's choosing. His doom is waiting; his imprisonment is near. Within one generation, he is restrained to a pit. Twenty-eight years after the cross [112] Paul encouraged Christians in Rome that Satan's time is about up, *"The God of peace will soon crush Satan under your feet"* (Rom.16:20).

---

[112] Dating for the cross is disputed as well as dating the book of Romans. Assuming the crucifixion was in 30 A.D. and Paul wrote the book of Romans in 58 A. D., then a twenty-eight year difference is created.

"*Soon,*" does not mean hundreds or thousands of years, but it can mean twelve years. In twelve years, Roman armies will destroy Jerusalem and its temple. The early church experienced a Satan that was free to roam looking for "*someone to devour*" (I Peter 5:8). Yet, this freedom does not last long.

Witness of the Early Church

Compared to the number of references in the gospels, the rest of the New Testament has amazingly few references to Satan. He is still an evil power but the emphasis has moved away from his influence. As an example, the book of Romans is cited as the greatest doctrinal statement of the Christian faith. Paul lays out the great truth of the gospel. Where is Satan in the book of Romans? He has only one reference in the final chapter.

The God of peace will soon crush Satan under your feet. The grace of our Lord Jesus Christ be with you (Rom. 16:20).

The book of Galatians is called the "Magna Carta" of Christian liberty. How much space does Paul give Satan? There is not a single reference. Now in fairness, Paul does mention Satan (devil) in several occasions in other letters, yet the amount of focus on Satan and his activity compared with the gospels is quite small.

"Therefore, rejoice O heavens and you who dwell in them! But woe to you, O earth and sea, for the devil has come down to you in great wrath, because he knows that his time is short (Rev.12:12)." Partial-preterists normally align with an early date for dating the book of Revelation, most likely close towards the end of Nero's reign in 66-68 (Nero died June 68A.D.). John says the devil has only a short time and with his binding occurring in the "coming of the son of man" in 70 A.D., he is chained, thrown in the pit sealed (to prevent any escape). We now need further exegesis on the binding of Satan in Revelation 20.

Revelation 20

Theologian J. Rodman Williams correctly addresses the time period of the reign of Christ (which is the same time period of the binding of Satan).

"The reign of the saints with Christ is said to be for a thousand. How are we to understand the figure of a thousand? Does this refer to a literal calendar period? In light of the symbolic use of figures in the Book of Revelation, it is more likely to express a complete but indeterminate period of time. Indeed, the reference to a thousand years in regard to the reign of the saints sets it apart from the age to come when, *"they shall reign forever and ever"* (Rev. 22:5), and places it within the limits of the present age. Hence, the thousand years specifies the period between His first coming and His final advent-that is, the gospel age. Upon Christ's return the thousand years will be complete, and the eternal reign begin."[113]

Partial preterists agree, the age of the Messianic kingdom (God's general rule is eternal) is between the first and final comings of Jesus. It is the present kingdom where Jesus rules over his people and leads them into victory. The thousand years have already gone over two-thousand and no one knows how long it will continue. During these symbolic thousand years, Satan is bound. How restricted is he? We are not sure and there are different interpretations of this passage.

A Theological Model

Adopting models that advocate a "progression of truth" is critical at this junction. Does theological truth advance over time? Does the revelation from God progress in chronological time? Theology teacher C. Michael Patton writes, "there would certainly be little quibble from someone who suggested that doctrine develops. There would also be no problems when someone suggests that earlier writers of the Old Testament knew less than the later writers. The idea here is doctrinal development within the

---

[113] J. Rodman Williams, Renewal Theology, Zondervan Publishing house, Grand Rapids, Michigan, 1996, page 429

canon, often referred to as the doctrine of progressive revelation."[114]

Patton offers up a term, "progressive revelation." I like the term. That means that at certain times the church possesses truth that is present for them, their present truth. It also means we must avoid the denominational trap of creating inflexible doctrinal statements that cannot adapt to ongoing revelation. On the other side, it does not mean we someday will deny the physical resurrection or devalue the cross; only that our understanding of these events will grow.

Are there examples where a truth or principle in Scripture undergoes change by later passage? A chronological approach is easy to spot when viewing the massive change from the Old Testament to the New. Christians no longer worship on Saturday. Christians eat pork. Most importantly, Christians no longer sacrifice animals for forgiveness of sins. In the New Testament, things are more subtle. Is there evidence of any such change? If the binding of Satan occurred in the first century, then, it is in direct contradiction to other New Testament passages, which speak of him as roaming free. How can Satan be bound in a pit and be roaming free, seeking Christians to devour?

Do New Testament authors express everything there is to know about any particular doctrine? No, we build our doctrines by pulling all the Scriptures on a specific area together. No single author is writing a complete set of doctrines. This being true, all New Testament doctrine is based upon the totality of the New Testament cannon. When applying the "doctrine of progressive revelation" to the defeat of Satan, then all of the New Testament comes into play, not just a few isolated passages.

Most people modify the binding in Revelation to match other passages in the New Testament. When reading that Satan is bound, most preachers retreat and warn the people about the dangers of the devil. Yes, he is bound, but he is still free. Our illogical

---

[114] C. Michael Patton, Case Studies In Inerrancy: Can Doctrine Develop within the Cannon, 2010, http://www.reclaimingthemind.org/blog/

thinking casts doubt on a reasonable approach to Scripture. Yet, because we are so positive that Satan is a constant threat, we become blind to our faulty exegesis. Preachers prefer to read Peter's warning, *"your adversary the devil prowls around like a roaring lion, seeking someone to devour"* (I Peter 5:8). Yet, upon a closer exanimation, a case can be made for synthesis of the two concepts. We need a reasonable synthesis of Scripture is seeing Satan bound by successive acts of the Christ event[115] and his coming in AD 70 as the final act in destroying the works of Satan.

If progressive development of doctrine is part of the New Testament, it opens the door then for a genuinely bound Satan. It is now possible that the teaching of Revelation 20 (Satan bound) takes precedent over the teaching of I Peter (free to roam). Are there any examples of instructions given in the New Testament that undergo alteration? An example comes from comparing a passage in Matthew to one in Acts.

Matthew 10:5

"These twelve Jesus sent out with the following instructions: "Do not go among the Gentiles or enter any town of the Samaritans."

Acts 1:8

But you will receive power when the Holy Spirit has come upon you, and you will be my witnesses in Jerusalem and in all Judea and Samaria, and to the end of the earth."

The first text says, do not go to any town of the Samaritans and the second text says, *"Be my witnesses in Samaria."* Which one do we follow? We have little difficultly following the instructions in Acts. We believe that the fuller understanding of Jesus' work is now in view, and the previous instructions were only for a short period.

---

[115] The Christ Event is used to describe the major events in the life of Jesus in relation to his salvation acts. These events are his birth, life, death, resurrection, his coming in the Spirit at Pentecost, ascension and last, his coming in judgment in AD 70. See Appendix 2

Taking into consideration the eschatological implications of the New Testament era, a final and complete binding of Satan seems a better fit than to project this binding far out into some unknown future date. Premillennial theologian Wayne Grudem views the language in Revelation about Satan as too strong to avoid a total restriction in his activities.

> "Although Matthew 12:28-29 and Luke 10:18 do speak of a "binding" of Satan during Jesus' earthly ministry, the binding of Satan described in Revelation 20 seems to be much more extensive than that. The passage does not simply say that Satan is bound at this time, but speaks of "the bottomless pit" and says that the angel that came down from heaven *"threw him into the pit, and shut it and sealed it over him, that he should deceive the nations no more, till the thousand years were ended"* (Revelation 20:2-3). More than a mere binding or restriction of activity is in view here. The imagery of throwing Satan into a pit and shutting it and sealing it over him gives a picture of total removal from influence on the earth."[116]

Grudem states it well; the language of Revelation, metaphoric as it is, has meaning. John paints a picture of Satan's influence, not just reduced, but taken away.

Who is the Angel?

First, who is the angel of Revelation 20:1? Is it Jesus, or another angel? By examining John's use of 'angel' in other passages, a case for the angel being Jesus is reasonable. The movement of the angel descending from heaven is important. He is coming from God's place, the highest court of the universe. He brings symbols of authority with him, keys and a chain.

---

[116] Wayne Grudem, Systematic Theology, Inter-Varsity Press, Leicester, England, 1994, page 1117

Revelation 1:18

I died, and behold I am alive forevermore, and I have the keys of Death and Hades.

Revelation 9:1

And the fifth angel blew his trumpet, and I saw a star fallen from heaven to earth, and he was given the key to the shaft of the bottomless pit.

Jesus saw Satan fall to earth. Then Satan, for a short time holds the key. He opens the abyss and releases "all hell" upon the land. When we get to Revelation 20, something has changed, it is not Satan who possesses the keys; it is the resurrected Christ. Satan is about to be cast into the abyss.

Revelation 10:1

Then I saw another mighty angel coming down from heaven, wrapped in a cloud, with a rainbow over his head, and his face was like the sun, and his legs like pillars of fire.

Revelation 18:1

After this I saw another angel coming down from heaven, having great authority, and the earth was made bright with his glory.

These passages make the case for Jesus being the angel in chapter twenty much easier. David Chilton identifies the angel in Revelation 20, he says, "Again as in 10:1 and 18:1, this is the Lord Jesus Christ."[117] Chilton is right; all three angels refer to Christ.

When is Satan Bound?

Our second question is, "When did Jesus bind Satan?" The view taken here is Jesus returned in spiritual power during the destruction of Jerusalem in AD 70, and at this time Satan is bound. Wayne Grudem defines the Amillennial view. "According to the Amillennial interpretation the binding of Satan in verses 1-2 is the binding that occurred during Jesus' earthly ministry. He spoke of binding the strong man in order that he may plunder his house

---

[117] David Chilton, The Days of Vengeance, Dominion Press, Fort Worth, Texas, 1987, page 499

(Matt.12:29)." [118]   Author of <u>Renewal Theology</u> J. Rodman Williams says, "The statement that Satan was 'cast' into the pit (or abyss) likewise is to be understood as happening through the work of Christ in His first coming."[119] Through Jesus' life, death and resurrection Satan progressively was bound. Even after the resurrection, Peter declared he was free to harm believers. Therefore, even though a partial binding took place, a final binding lays shortly in the future. When Christ returns in spiritual power in 70 A.D., Satan is bound, the pit sealed, and his personal activity is halted (the Scripture does not mention demons in this binding).

What scriptural evidence shows the return of Jesus (not the Second Coming) in 70 A.D. is the correct timing of Revelation 20? Waiting until chapter 20 to sort out timing issues will take us straight into an exegetical fog, with the danger of falling into some doctrinal bottomless pit.The first chapter of Revelation is the best place to start.   Revelation is foremost a letter to first century Christians. They were facing difficult times and impending tribulations. The events disclosed by John, although in apocalyptic language of metaphor and symbol, are speaking about circumstances and events soon to take place. John begins his book by giving us key time references.

Revelation 1:1-3

The revelation of Jesus Christ, which God gave him to show to his servants the things that must soon take place. He made it known by sending his angel to his servant John, who bore witness to the word of God and to the testimony of Jesus Christ, even to all that he saw. Blessed is the one who reads aloud the words of this prophecy, and blessed are those who hear, and who keep what is written in it, for the time is near.

John does not want his readers to be confused about when these events will take place. Twice in his first three verses he tells us plainly, *"the things that soon must take place,"* and *"the time is*

---

[118] Wayne Grudem, Systematic Theology, InterVarsity Press, Leicester, England, 1994, pages 1114-1115

[119] J. Rodman Williams, Renewal Theology, Zondervan Publishing House, Grand Rapids, Michigan, 1996, page 423

near." Reading chapter twenty in this light, then, the binding of Satan is very much at hand. Taking an early date for Revelation of 67-68 A.D., then it was only a matter of months before Satan is bound. What significant event after the resurrection could represent this binding? Jesus foretold his coming in Matthew 10:22-23. *"And you will be hated by all for my name's sake. But the one who endures to the end will be saved. When they persecute you in one town, flee to the next, for truly, I say to you, you will not have gone through all the towns of Israel before the Son of Man comes."* His return at the end of the world is not in view. This event occurs within one generation. Again, Jesus states, *"For the Son of Man is going to come with his angels in the glory of his Father, and then he will repay each person according to what he has done. [28]Truly, I say to you, there are some standing here who will not taste death until they see the Son of Man coming in his kingdom" (Matt. 16:27-28).* Jesus tells the crowd around him that some will live to see his return. Even though 70 A.D. was about 40 years in the future, some of the younger ones were alive to see the prophecy fulfilled. In the Olivet discourse, Jesus gives details of what will take place before he returns. He equates the destruction of the temple with the great tribulation and then in the same context, he speaks of his return. Then in verse 34, he says all this will take place within one generation (Matt. 24).

John sees the "angel" coming down from heaven. At the ascension, Jesus ascended to heaven. Then, Jesus returns from heaven and finishes the binding of Satan. The binding of Satan at this time, is part of Jesus coming in power. There is no other event spoken of in Scripture that can fit this event. The timing of the angel equates with Jesus coming from heaven at the time of the temple's destruction. This was to be the sign that Satan was bound, the Old Testament system of worship and practice was formally over.

Revelation is like a verbal motion picture to first century believers. It describes the events that many will experience. The language is apocalyptic, it is symbolic, yet it was to be understood by its readers. Revelation is not about the end of the physical world in our future. It is about the coming of Christ and His victory over evil. It is about how worship prevails and how the saints of God overcome. Revelation is a book of victory.

How long is Satan Bound?

The third question is easier than the first two. The Bible states that Satan is bound *"until the thousand years are completed"* (Rev. 20:3). The thousand years are not literal years as the theology of premillennialism teaches.[120] The thousand years are symbolic. It represents a large quantity of time. Williams correctly addresses the time of the reign of Christ (which is the same period of the binding of Satan).

"The reign of the saints with Christ is said to be for a thousand. How are we to understand the figure of a thousand? Does this refer to a literal calendar period? In light of the symbolic use of figures in the Book of Revelation, it is more likely to express a complete but indeterminate period of time. Indeed, the reference to a thousand years in regard to the reign of the saints sets it apart from the age to come when, "they shall reign forever and ever" (Rev. 22:5), and places it within the limits of the present age. Hence, the thousand years specifies the period between His first coming and His final advent-that is, the gospel age. Upon Christ's return the thousand years will be complete, and the eternal reign begin."[121]

When the term "one thousand" is interpreted consistently throughout the Bible, it becomes clear that a symbolic interpretation is the best understanding of the authors' intent. "Satan is to remain bound, St. John tells us, for a thousand years-a

---

[120] Millard J. Erickson, Christian Theology, Baker Books, Grand Rapids, Michigan, 1983, pages 1216-1217

[121] J. Rodman Williams, Renewal Theology, Zondervan Publishing house, Grand Rapids, Michigan, 1996, page 429

large, rounded-off number. We have seen that as the number seven means a fullness of quality (in Biblical imagery), the number ten contains the idea of a fullness of quantity; in other words, it stands for manyness. A thousand multiplies and intensifies this (10x10x10), in order to express great vastness." [122] Two Old Testament verses show how this is the case.

Psalms 50:10

For every beast of the forest is mine, the cattle on a thousand hills.

I Chronicles 16:15

Remember his covenant forever, the word that he commanded, for a thousand generations.

Does God own cattle beyond a literal thousand hills? Will God's covenant continue past one-thousand generations? No serious Bible student limits the term of a thousand to a literal number in these passages. Likewise, the thousand years of Revelation 20 is also a symbolic number. It is a large round number representing more than a thousand years, many more. The time period for the reign of the saints and the binding of Satan runs from the first coming of Christ in the first century to his Second Coming.

We have provided possible answers to our three questions concerning Revelation 20. Who is the angel? When did the binding take place? Finally, what is the length of the binding? Arguments have shown that Jesus is the angel, the binding takes place in 70 A.D., and the length of binding of is the same as the millennial reign of Christ, which is unknown, but much longer than a literal one-thousand years.

Because many Evangelicals come from dispensational churches, the eschatological age of the New Testament is foreign to them. Prophecies of tribulation, antichrist, and the coming of Jesus are placed far out into the future. This approach overlooks many passages where the issues of timing are clear (Matthew

---

[122] David Chilton, The Days of Vengeance, Dominion Press, Ft. Worth, Texas, 1987, page 506

10:23, Matthew 16:28, Matthew 24:34, I Peter 1:20, I Peter 4:7, I John 1:18, Revelation 1:1-3).   Taking into consideration the eschatological implications of the New Testament era, a final and complete binding of Satan seems a better fit rather than to project this binding far out into some unknown future date.

As partial preterism is new to many, the acceptance that Satan is bound is difficult to grasp. Studies will continue to see how the New Testament deals with Satan. This view is a starting point for further investigation. In time, it will need adjusting, but I am firmly convinced that Satan, antichrist, demons, and the forces of wickedness receive far too much attention and needs to replaced by a greater understanding of Jesus as the Lord of Lords and the King of Kings.

Study Questions

1. Why is interpreting the book of Revelation difficult?

2. Discuss the timing of Revelation 20. Is this the first century or our current century John has in mind?

3. Explain how the Bible uses the number 1,000?

4. If Satan were presently bound, how would that affect current "spiritual warfare?"

5. Give examples of progressive doctrine.

Chapter 20

The 1,000-Year Millennium

The belief that Jesus returns and sets up a kingdom for 1,000 years is popular among current evangelicals. Nevertheless, throughout history it has been a minority view. Today the 1,000-year millennium finds itself on the shelf of left behind doctrines. Renewed eschatological studies are finding little support for the once popular teaching. The millennium of premillennialism is a literal interpretation of Revelation 20:1-5. Dispensationalists and Premillennialists adhere to a literal 1,000-year reign of Christ. Amillennial, Postmillennial, and those advocating a kingdom centered victorious view do not. How then, should we interpret the thousand years found in Revelation chapter 20?

An optimistic view of God's kingdom and premillennialism does not fit. The only system of theology that accepts a literal 1,000-year kingdom is premillennialism/dispensationalism. According to dispensationalism, every age ends in failure and therefore God judges it and begins anew with a different age. If we endorse that God needs another kingdom, another age beyond that of the present one, then we must also see the present age ending in failure. Too many moving from dispensationalism to a kingdom view still build their overall theology from dispensational doctrine. On the practical level, attempting to squeeze a premillennial kingdom into any victorious eschatology will lead to the weakening of optimistic thinking about our future.

Revelation 20:1-5

Then I saw an angel coming down from heaven, holding in his hand the key to the bottomless pit and a great chain. And he seized the dragon, that ancient serpent, who is the devil and Satan, and bound him for a thousand years, and threw him into the pit, and shut it and sealed it over him, so that he might not deceive the nations any longer, until the thousand years were ended. After that he must be released for a little while. Then I saw thrones, and seated on them were those to whom the authority to judge was committed. Also I saw the souls of those who had been beheaded for the testimony of Jesus and for the word of God, and those who had not worshiped the beast or its image and had not received its mark on their foreheads or their hands. They came to life and reigned with Christ for a thousand years.

How long is a Thousand Years?

Although the issues in Revelation 20 are many and interpretation difficult, the mention of Christ reigning for a thousand years is not difficult. First, Revelation is not a letter, not even a prophecy in the strictest sense; it is apocalyptic literature (chapter 4). The use of symbolic numbers is prominent in apocalyptic writing. Therefore the numbers used in the book of Revelation are likely symbolic. We previously saw two verses where 1,000 are used as more than the literal number. In addition, there other passages in the Bible use the number "thousand" in a symbolic fashion.

Psalms 84:10

For a day in your courts is better than a thousand elsewhere.

Deuteronomy 1:11

May the LORD, the God of your fathers, make you a thousand times as many as you are and bless you, as he has promised you!

Deuteronomy 7:9

Know therefore that the LORD your God is God, the faithful God who keeps covenant and steadfast love with those who love him and keep his commandments, to a thousand generations.

Every one of these Scriptures uses "a thousand" as symbolic. The thousand is more than a literal thousand. It connotes fullness, a vast quantity and the sense of largeness, which if taken "literally" loses it meaning. Likewise, the thousand years of Revelation 20 is a vast amount of time. It began with the advent of Jesus in the first century and continues today. Charismatic theologian Williams in his summary of the millennial debate states it simply. "The

Millennium is now. Christ is presently reigning, and his people reign with him."[123]

Where does the term "millennial" come from? It is a theological concept based from two Latin words *mille*, meaning "thousand," and *annus*, meaning "year." The Greek word for a thousand is *"chilia ete"* and means a "thousand years." The early church referred to this view as "chiliasm" and its use was normally pejorative.

Concerning the actual length of the millennium, no one knows. We are now two-thousand years past its beginning. Some think we are close to the end, while others sense we are only getting a good start. In the Anglican Book of Common Prayer, they provided a method to calculate the feasts until the year 6000 AD.[124] They were no dispensationalists on that committee. I would side with Leithart in his view.

> "Finally, and drawing not from specific texts but rather from the penumbra of Scripture, it would seem odd if the Lord gave Adam a commission to rule and subdue the earth, sent his Son to die and rise again as the Last Adam to restore humanity to that task, and then ended the whole process after a couple thousand years, just when we were beginning to make a few meager advances in our dominion over creation."[125]

The day must end where churches live by a five-year plan because the return of Jesus is expected. The church must tear up their short term strategies and prepare (with help from the Holy Spirit) a 100-year plan for growing the church and kingdom. What decisions would you make if you believed your great-great grand

[123] J. Rodman Williams, Renewal Theology-Systematic Theology from a Charismatic Perspective, Zondervan Publishing House, Grand Rapids, Michigan, 1996, Vol. 3, page 443

[124] Peter J. Leithart, From Behind the Veil, Athanasius Press, Monroe, Louisiana, 2009, page 95

[125] Ibid

children would continue walking in the kingdom? What advice would you give your children? What advice would you give your local church? Eschatology makes a difference!

The doctrine of the millennial kingdom is as much about the nature of the kingdom as its duration. Noticed in the text (Rev. 20) John never tells us where Christ is located. We assume he is on earth, but the text never says that. The better understanding would be that Christ is ruling from his throne in the heaven over a kingdom on the earth.

The premillennial millennium is vastly different from the kingdom advocated by those of a victorious view. Premillennialists have Jesus returning to a rebuilt temple in Jerusalem where Jesus sits on a throne made by man. The worship in this newly built temple includes "animal sacrifices." Although premillennialists deny these "sacrifices" are for the remission of sin (memorial purposes only) the very thought of returning to the Old Testament priesthood would be unthinkable to Christians of the first century. During this 1,000-year millennium, Israel is restored to its former glory. This concept of returning to the old covenant finds absolutely no support from the New Testament. In fact, the opposite is true. There is not a single passage in the New Testament that Israel is to return to the land and the old priesthood restored.

Without Revelation and its symbolic construction, where would we go to support our 1,000-year kingdom? If this is an important doctrine, why is the New Testament quiet about it? Jesus never taught it; neither did Paul, Peter, James, or any other Apostle.

The difference between millennial views goes much deeper than whether the 1,000 years is taken literally or symbolically. The doctrine strikes at the core of Christian living. For the premillennialists, the millennium is where God fulfills all the promises to Israel. Dispensationalists teach the church has no part in any prophecy found in the Old Testament; therefore, a different age must be constructed.

Dispensational author Charles C. Ryrie makes this clear. "The doctrine of the millennial kingdom is for the dispensationalist an integral part of his entire scheme and interpretation of many biblical passages."[126] This means, Christians have no part of Abraham, no part of David, no part of any promise made by the ancient prophets; the church is left out. The New Testament teaching is clear; gentiles are now in Christ and made one with believing Israel and heirs of the promises of God. There is no need for a separate age to fulfill these promises; all of God's promises are fulfilled in the church.

Ephesians 2:11-13

"Therefore remember that at one time you Gentiles in the flesh, called "the uncircumcision" by what is called the circumcision, which is made in the flesh by hands— remember that you were at that time separated from Christ, alienated from the commonwealth of Israel and strangers to the covenants of promise, having no hope and without God in the world. But now in Christ Jesus you who once were far off have been brought near by the blood of Christ."

Paul argues for the inclusion of gentiles into the *"commonwealth"* of Israel. He reminds the Ephesians that at *"one time"* they were not included but *"separated"* and *"strangers to the covenants of promise."* This separation left Gentiles with *"no hope"* and *"without God."* What happened to these people? They came to Christ and everything changed! They now possess everything promised to Israel. In Christ, they are transformed and are now heirs of the promises.

Paul goes further in his letter to the Ephesians. He goes beyond saying they are *"brought near."* He perhaps was concerned that his words would be misinterpreted. Maybe Paul was concerned about a possible teacher in the future trying to prove that 'near' does not mean "included" (dispensationalism attempts this). The stronger words are *"one new man in place of*

---

[126] Charles C. Ryrie, Dispensationalism, Moody Press, Chicago, Illinois, 1966, page 148

the two.'' Since God took two men (Jews and Gentiles) and made them one in Christ, we must be very careful not to divide them again. These once separate peoples (believing Jews and believing gentiles) now have access to the Father by the Spirit, and become the new temple of God.

Ephesians 2:14-22

"For he himself is our peace, who has made us both one and has broken down in his flesh the dividing wall of hostility by abolishing the law of commandments expressed in ordinances, that he might create in himself one new man in place of the two, so making peace, and might reconcile us both to God in one body through the cross, thereby killing the hostility. And he came and preached peace to you who were far off and peace to those who were near. For through him we both have access in one Spirit to the Father. So then you are no longer strangers and aliens, but you are fellow citizens with the saints and members of the household of God, built on the foundation of the apostles and prophets, Christ Jesus himself being the cornerstone in whom the whole structure, being joined together, grows into a holy temple in the Lord. In him you also are being built together into a dwelling place for God by the Spirit".

Chilton comments on Paul's words to the Ephesians.

> "There is, properly, no such thing as a 'Hebrew Christian,' any more than there are separate biblical categories of 'Indian Christian,' 'Irish Christians,' 'Chinese Christians,' or "American Christians." The only way for gentiles to be saved is by becoming grafted into the one 'olive tree,' the faithful covenant people. And the only way for a Jew to be saved is by becoming a member of God's people. There is no difference. By his finished work Christ 'made both groups into one.' Believing Jews and gentiles have been united 'in one body,' the church. There is one salvation and one church, in which all believers, regardless of ethnic heritage, become children of God and heirs of the promises

to Abraham. The creation of a special Jew-gentile distinction within the body of Christ is ultimately a denial of the gospel."[127]

The premillennialists set Revelation 20 in the future. When Jesus returns to earth, then the 1,000- years begin. By their own system, they create a new problem that is much bigger than misunderstanding the Bible's use of 1,000. They create two separate periods for the resurrection of the dead. The dispensational scheme of multiple resurrections is necessary to fit their eschatological system. First, Christians are raptured and enter into resurrection. Then seven years later, when the Second Coming occurs, there is possibly another resurrection for those "saved" during the tribulation. Then one thousand years later, another resurrection occurs. There is no other passage in the Bible that hints at various stages of resurrection. Premillennialism takes a very difficult section of Scripture (Rev. 20) and creates a complete doctrine that runs contrary to the rest of the Bible. Jesus made it clear about the timing of the resurrection.

John 5:28-29

Do not marvel at this, for an hour is coming when all who are in the tombs will hear his voice [29]and come out, those who have done good to the resurrection of life, and those who have done evil to the resurrection of judgment.

Jesus gives no hint of any separation of the resurrection of life from the resurrection of judgment. Both take place at the same time, at the last day.

"If this is the millennium then I am very disappointed" When Christians hear about the present kingdom, they often experience a letdown. First, many learned a fairy tale version of the kingdom. Our image from premillennial eschatology is Jesus ruling the world from Jerusalem and everything being perfect. We do not live in a perfect world, so how can this be the great millennial kingdom? Is this all we get? We accept an 'other world' view of

---

[127] David Chilton, Paradise Restored, Reconstruction Press, Tyler, Texas, 1985. Page 130

the kingdom. The truth is simple; the kingdom is the life you have, the family you are in and the work you do. If Jesus was ruling his kingdom living in Jerusalem, how could he keep the peace in Africa, Asia or in your neighborhood? Will Jesus need an army? Will he hire the United Nations peacekeepers? NO! Jesus reigns over people through spiritual transformation; a changed heart. This is the core of present kingdom realities and reveals a substantial flaw in the premillennial scheme.

Second, God is not finished. The best is yet to come. The biblical concept of the kingdom is its continual growth. Isaiah said it best. If you are not satisfied with the state of things, get to work.

Isaiah 9:7

Of the increase of his government and of peace there will be no end, on the throne of David and over his kingdom, to establish it and to uphold it with justice and with righteousness from this time forth and forevermore. The zeal of the LORD of hosts will do this.

The question of the millennium is of great importance. If we are not living in the millennium (age of the kingdom) then we have no right to the prophecies and promises that flow from the prophets of old. If Jesus must return so that we can walk in the fullness of God's purposes, then we restrict Christianity to a very narrow set of biblical truths. Yet, the glorious fact is that we are already in the kingdom. Jesus is crowned king. We reign with him. The kingdom is growing! The millennial kingdom is here, it is the kingdom of God Jesus preached, Paul preached and what we proclaim and teach to the nations.

Study Questions

1. According to dispensational eschatology what is the primary purpose of the 1,000-year millennial kingdom?

2. Discuss how the passage in Ephesians 2:11-22 is important in the debate over the millennium kingdom.

3. According to John, is there a large time gap between the resurrection of the righteous and the unrighteous?

4. Why would a church create a prayer book with a calendar continuing to the year 6,000?

5. If the church is now living in the Messianic kingdom, why is there still evil and corruption in the world?

Chapter 21

The Rapture

When are we raptured? If you mean, when does Jesus fly down from heaven to meet Christians in the clouds and everyone returns to heaven for a large banquet, if that is the question, then, the New Testament teaches nothing of the sort. Some explanation and a little history are in order. What is commonly known as the "rapture doctrine" is new in the Christian church (compared with 2,000 years of history). It began in the 1830's and became mainstream doctrine in the early 20th century. The difference in Darby's dispensational scheme from the historical teaching of the church is the creation of two "second comings" of Christ. Darby insisted that natural Israel and the church are separate peoples. Israel is God's earthly people whereas the church is God's heavenly people. Each has a separate covenant and future. Since the "great tribulation" is a judgment upon Israel, Darby needed a method to remove Christians from the earth; hence the rapture of the saints. Darby goes to I Thess. 4:17 and declared the events described are not the second coming of Christ but a separate coming, and called it the "rapture." The Second Coming takes place seven years later, following the great tribulation.

Is there evidence for "two" second comings as dispensational eschatology demands? Williams is correct when he states; "there is utterly no biblical justification for a twofold future coming."[128] The creation of a "secret rapture" found its way into mainstream Evangelical churches and our challenge today is its removal before the church incurs additional damage.

The doctrine of the rapture as taught by Darby and later C.I. Scofield and Charles C. Ryrie of America became a popular teaching, especially after World War I. Dispensational eschatology

---

[128] J. Rodman Williams, Renewal Theology, Zondervan Publishing House, Grand Rapids, Michigan, 1996, page 379, Vol. 3

(the only theology with a secret rapture) made its way into numerous Bible Colleges and publishing houses, spreading its teaching around the world (largely by American missionaries).

We have used the terms premillennial and dispensational as referring to the same eschatological position. The degree that dispensationalists have captured the bulk of the premillennial audience and the majority of modern evangelical Christians is amazing. Stanley J. Grenz comments on this phenomenon.

"By the midpoint of the century (20th) this eschatological orientation (dispensationalism) had become the most widely held viewpoint among fundamentalist and evangelical Christians in America. Not only did it replace what had been the dominant eschatology of the nineteenth century, it also so overwhelmed other varieties of premillennialism that in the minds of many it came to be seen as the only legitimate representative of that viewpoint."[129]

It is true that a resurgence of historic premillennialism is challenging traditional dispensationalism, yet in percentages, it remains small. The primary difference centers on the understanding of the rapture. Dispensational eschatology has two-second comings of Jesus. The first is the rapture, and then seven years later is the Second Coming (where Jesus returns to earth). Historic premillennialism teaches a single coming; therefore no rapture in the modern sense (although some refer to the Second Coming as the rapture).

Those advocating a kingdom centered eschatology and convinced of a victorious outcome within time and history believe in a single day (one event) where at the appearance of Christ the dead are raised and the final judgment occurs. This does not take place until the kingdom of God has filled the earth and every nation is discipled. Some propose this might happen within our

---

[129] Stanley J. Grenz, The Millennial Maze, InterVarsity Press, 1992, page 91

generation, I suspect it will take many generations; which means we have the responsibility and privilege to train up the coming generation with the message of the kingdom. A book by Harold R. Eberle and Martin Trench called <u>Victorious Eschatology</u> explains the rapture.

"Victorious Eschatology depicts the rapture in the following way. Jesus will continue to build his church, and though Christians will face many trials and setbacks, they will experience more successes than failures. This progressive building will continue until the 'Last Day," a day which only God knows. On that day, without any warning signs, Jesus Christ will return in the clouds and every eye will see him. All believers-living and dead-will be caught up to meet him as He returns. As they ascend to Jesus, believers will be transformed, their bodies being changed into glorified bodies."[130]

Partial preterists view the return of Jesus as connected to the resurrection of the dead and the final judgment. Jesus does not physically return in the *"last days"* (that was his spiritual return in the first century) but comes on the *"last day."* At the death of Lazarus, Martha understood that he will *"rise again in the resurrection on the last day* (John 11:24). Jesus teaches a two-step process of resurrection, first the spiritual resurrection and then a physical one.

John 5:25-29

"Truly, truly, I say to you, an hour is coming, and is now here, when the dead will hear the voice of the Son of God, and those who hear will live. For as the Father has life in himself, so he has granted the Son also to have life in himself. And he has given him authority to execute judgment, because he is the Son of Man. Do not marvel at this, for an hour is coming when all who are in the tombs will hear his voice and come out, those who have done good

---

[130] Harold R. Eberle, Martin Trench, Victorious Eschatology, Worldcast Publishing, Yakima, WA., 2006, page 135

to the resurrection of life, and those who have done evil to the resurrection of judgment"

Jesus said that even in his time, the dead are hearing his voice and receiving life (born again). Yet, that is not the end of the story, for *"an hour is coming"* that even those in the grave will hear and be resurrected, some to life and others to judgment.

The Challenge of Thessalonians

Paul's two letters to believers in Thessalonica contain a large amount of eschatological material. That is the good news; but the bad news is, they are difficult to interpret. We can like many today, claim Paul exclusively talks about events surrounding the future Second Coming. Yet in so doing, we must close our eyes to exegetical problems this creates. In I Thessalonians 4, we have the passage concerning the "coming of the Lord." These early Christians had a question for Paul. "Have we missed the 'coming of the Lord?" We must not smile at their question. They had good reason to believe that Jesus would come in their lifetime (as we have already covered).

Paul writes to assure them that no one missed the day of resurrection. In chapter five, he changes the term from "coming of the Lord" to the "Day of the Lord," and this is where a simple interpretation (making all passages refer to the same coming) breaks down because the events of this "Day" are connected with first century circumstances. Reading I Thessalonians, we must take notice that at the close of every chapter Paul brings up the subject of the "coming of the Lord."

I Thessalonians 1:10

And to wait for his Son from heaven, whom he raised from the dead, Jesus who delivers us from the wrath to come.

Paul tells them to wait for the Son (who comes from heaven). If this refers to the future Second Coming, then Paul provided false and rather cruel information (how can first century Christians wait several thousand years). This clearly fits into the passages dealing with the "coming of the Son of man" that is associated with the coming judgment on apostate Israel. The words echo that of John the Baptist, *"But when he saw many of the Pharisees and Sadducees coming to his baptism, he said to them, "You brood of vipers! Who warned you to flee from the wrath to come* (Matt. 3:7)?" This "wrath" comes upon the generation Jesus spoke of in Matthew twenty-three.

Woe to you, scribes and Pharisees, hypocrites! For you build the tombs of the prophets and decorate the monuments of the righteous saying, 'If we had lived in the days of our fathers, we would not have taken part with them in shedding the blood of the prophets.' [31]Thus you witness against yourselves that you are sons of those who murdered the prophets. Fill up, then, the measure of your fathers. You serpents, you brood of vipers, how are you to escape being sentenced to hell (Matt. 23:29-33)?

Paul's first mention of the "coming" (in my view) best fits within a first century event.

I Thessalonians 2:14-16 & 19-20

For you, brothers, became imitators of the churches of God in Christ Jesus that are in Judea. For you suffered the same things from your own countrymen as they did from the Jews, who killed both the Lord Jesus and the prophets, and drove us out, and displease God and oppose all mankind by hindering us from speaking to the Gentiles that they might be saved—so as always to fill up the measure of their sins. But God's wrath has come upon them at last! [19] For what is our hope or joy or crown of boasting before our Lord Jesus at his coming? Is it not you? [20]For you are our glory and joy.

Paul closes chapter two by returning to the theme of judgment upon the Jews (who oppose all mankind) in connection with a "coming of Jesus." We cannot claim to take the biblical text seriously if these timing issues are ignored. Whatever the exact nature of this coming, it must not be divided from the judgment prophesied to occur in less than twenty years from this letter. Once again Paul reminds his readers of the words used by Jesus, *"Fill up, then, the measure of your fathers (Matthew 23:32)."*

I Thessalonians 3:11-13

"Now may our God and Father himself, and our Lord Jesus, direct our way to you, and may the Lord make you increase and abound in love for one another and for all, as we do for you, so that he may establish your hearts blameless in holiness before our God and Father, at the coming of our Lord Jesus with all his saints."

Paul was a spiritual father and an Apostle to those believers living in Thessalonica. He had great concern and love for them. He wants them "established" in their faith, so they will not fall away in the coming years. This established in the faith is connected with the *"coming of our Lord Jesus."* If this "coming" was a trip to heaven then Paul's concern for them is not necessary. Paul adds new information here, that this "coming" is *"with all his saints."* This must be the future Second Coming because it says the saints are coming back with him, right. I am not so sure. When Scripture speaks of God's "coming" it often includes others, mainly clouds of angels. Are these "saints" angels? Jude uses similar wording and by examining the context of his "coming" passage, it sheds light on the present verses in Thessalonians.

Jude 14-19

It was also about these that Enoch, the seventh from Adam, prophesied, saying, "Behold, the Lord comes with ten thousands of his holy ones, to execute judgment on all and to convict all the ungodly of all their deeds of ungodliness that they have committed in such an ungodly way, and of all the harsh things that ungodly sinners have spoken against him." These are grumblers, malcontents, following their own sinful desires; they are loud-mouthed boasters, showing favoritism to gain advantage. But you must remember, beloved, the predictions of the apostles of our Lord Jesus Christ. They said to you, "In the last time there will be scoffers, following their own ungodly passions." It is these who cause divisions, worldly people, devoid of the Spirit.

Jude refers to those coming with the Lord as "holy ones." He also links the "last days" with the judgment upon the boasters, scoffers (etc). If the judgment is in the "last days" then also the coming with his "holy ones" must also be in the "last days" (remember, the last days is biblical language for the first century ending of the Mosaic covenant). This helps to place the words of Paul about the coming with the saints in the same period.

Now, the question remains, who are these "saints" mentioned by Paul? It may be that both Jude and Paul are referring to angels; but interpreting "saints" and "holy ones" as those believers in heaven at the time of Christ's return in judgment in 70 A.D. must be considered. In the book of Revelation, John writes about the destruction of the great city Babylon.

Revelation 18:19-20
"And they threw dust on their heads as they wept and mourned, crying out, "Alas, alas, for the great city where all who had ships at sea grew rich by her wealth! For in a single hour she has been laid waste. Rejoice over her, O heaven, and you saints and apostles and prophets, for God has given judgment for you against her!"

John calls the "great city" Babylon (vs. 21). John wrote previously in chapter 11 about a city symbolically called "Sodom and Egypt" that is the "great city." He then removes any speculation of this city by saying it is where the Lord was crucified (Rev. 11:8). The "great city" Babylon is Jerusalem, the city filled with the blood of the prophets and saints (vs. 24). The point made is when Jerusalem faces judgment, it is in part for the blood of those dying in the great tribulation. They are not left in heaven, but ride with Jesus when he comes in the clouds in judgment on unbelieving Israel. John writes, *"for God has given judgment for you against her!"*

When Scripture is compared with Scripture, we see that the conditions of the "last days" are in view here. Therefore, it is likely that Paul's *"coming of the Lord"* with his saints in 3:13 is the same coming spoken of in his two previous references.

I Thessalonians 4

Most agree that I Thessalonians 4 is about the Second Coming and not the coming in 70 AD.[131] Most partial preterists would also agree. However, why should we now change our interpretation from the previous three uses? There must be a reason (if our exegesis is correct) that Paul now speaks of a coming far in the future and not the "coming" in the first century. Why did Paul change how he uses the term? First, the text and then a simple explanation of what Paul possibly may have meant.

I Thessalonians 4:13-18

But we do not want you to be uninformed, brothers, about those who are asleep, that you may not grieve as others do who have no hope. For since we believe that Jesus died and rose again, even so, through Jesus, God will bring with him those who have fallen asleep. For this we declare to you by a word from the Lord, that we who are alive, who are left until the coming of the Lord, will not precede those who have fallen asleep. For the Lord himself will descend from heaven with a cry of command, with the voice of an archangel, and with the sound of the trumpet of God. And the dead in Christ will rise first. Then we who are alive, who are left, will be caught up together with them in the clouds to meet the Lord in the air, and so we will always be with the Lord. Therefore encourage one another with these words.

Many Bible teachers use these few sentences from the hand of Paul to promote a multitude of sensational occurrences. From books, films, charts and graphs, to Sunday morning sermons, the rapture has captivated the minds and souls of the evangelical church. False prophecies of the rapture have caused enormous damage to the reputation of the church. It has created a subculture where Christians retreat from the world waiting for their trip to heaven. Instead of engaging the world with the kingdom, too many believers have shed their responsibly towards the earth.

---

[131] Those who advocate a Full Preterist view would not agree. They see all New Testament citations of a "coming of the Lord" as the coming in Judgment in 70AD.

Why carry any responsibility when the world is scheduled for destruction. It is pure and simple dualism. It is a false understanding of Paul and of the very nature of the gospel. Rebuilding the mentality of the church as to God's purpose for his people and the earth must be a priority in our generation. This includes taking on the modern "rapture" theory. Normal biblical principles of interpretation are in need here.

We know from Paul's second letter that confusion was wide spread in the church. They were concerned about those dear believers who had died; would they miss the Lord's coming? I find it interesting that they were not concerned about themselves, but only those who have died. Why were the living believers not concerned about being "left behind?" This is the key to understanding why Paul goes from an arrival of the Lord in a soon coming judgment to a coming many generations in the future. Since Jesus ascended into heaven, the prophecy concerning the circumstances of the "last days" (Matt. 24) was circulated by word of mouth, apostolic teaching, and by prophetic ministry to the churches. They understood the soon coming of the Lord; that it was the final event ending the old Jewish system. And with this coming, they will be set free and fully engage with the kingdom of God. They were not expecting to fly off into space, they were not expecting to leave earth for heaven; there is no other Scripture that points us in that direction. Therefore, in their minds, the thinking may have been that the Lord did come, as they were not expecting any physical or bodily changes for themselves. Yet, the question remains, what about the dead? This was their concern. Therefore, Paul, now turns to the "coming" that deals with the "resurrection of the dead" in order to give them comfort and so they will not grieve over those who have died.

When Paul writes we will "meet" the Lord, he is not meaning what modern rapture teachers say. The text says nothing about Jesus taking Christians to heaven. The opposite is true. The word "meet" is used to go out and greet someone (like outside the city walls) and then joyfully return. Jesus uses this word in the parable of bridegroom (Matt. 25:1-13). When the bridegroom arrives, those waiting go out to "meet" him, and then return to the feast. This is the meaning in Paul's description to meet the Lord. When the day of resurrection arrives, believers will "meet" the Lord and usher him back to earth, to continue the great work of God's kingdom. Of course, heaven is not part of the physical universe-so we must be careful on how we describe this meeting the Lord. The Lord is already in the air we breathe, he is already reigning in his corporate body, the church.

What about us, do we fly up into the air to meet the Lord? In studying this passage, I read many books by preterists (full and partial) on how they interpret this text. For the most part, I admit being disappointed by many authors; they hover over the text like a helicopter but never land. One author brave enough to land on Paul's rapture text is N.T. Wright.

Wright begins with background information.

> "The word 'parousia' occurs in two key passages in Paul (I Thessalonians 4:15 and I Corinthians 15:23), and is found frequently elsewhere in Paul and the New Testament. It seems clear that the early Christians knew the word well, and knew what was meant by it. People often assume that the early church used *parousia* simply to mean 'the second coming of Jesus' and that by this event they all envisaged, in quite literal fashion, the scenario of I Thessalonians 4:16-17 (Jesus coming down on a cloud and people flying upward to meet him). Neither of these assumptions is in fact correct. "[132]

On the use of "parousia" in the first century, he writes, "When a person of high rank or emperor visits a colony or province" then this coming is called the "parousia." Wright continues; "The word for such a visit is royal presence: in Greek, *parousia*. In neither setting, we note, obviously but importantly, is

---

[132] N.T. Wright, Surprised By Hope, Harper One, New York, New York, 2008, p. 128

there the slightest suggestion of anybody flying around on a cloud. Nor is there any hint of the imminent collapse or destruction of the space-time universe."[133]

I have long suspected that Christians will never fly off in mass to meet the Lord in the physical air; yet, that is what Paul says, or at least what we think he says. The popular scenario of planes crashing, school buses left without drivers and a host of other "rapture" speculations, does not to fit the overall biblical message. It just seemed odd, that, God will bring about a glorious change in his reign on earth amidst such massive confusion. What then, can we make of Paul's statement?

Write quotes I Thessalonians 4:16-17 and then gives his commentary.

> "The point to notice above all about these tricky verses is that they are not to be taken as a literal description of what Paul thinks will happen. They are simply a different way of saying what he is saying in I Corinthians 15:23-27 and 51-54, and in Philippians 3:20-21. We had better get those other passages straight in our minds to start with. In I Corinthians 15:23-27 Paul speaks of the *parousia* of the Messiah as the time of the resurrection of the dead, the time when his secret rule will become manifest in the conquest of the last enemies, especially death. Then in verses 51-54, he speaks of what will happen to those who, at Jesus coming, are not yet dead. They will be changed, transformed. This is the same event as he is speaking of in I Thessalonians 4; we have the trumpet in both, and the resurrection of the dead in both; but whereas in I Thessalonians he speaks of those presently alive being "snatched up in the air," in I Corinthians he speaks of them being "transformed." So too in Philippians 3:21, where

---

[133] Ibid.

the context is quite explicitly ranging Jesus over Caesar, Paul speaks of the transformation of the present lowly body to be like Jesus' glorious body, as a result of his all-conquering power."[134]

If I understand Wright, he is saying Paul is talking about being "transformed" on the day of resurrection. Paul's highly charged metaphors in Thessalonians is just another way of saying we will be changed. I would suggest as I did earlier, that the reason for such language rests in the confusion of his readers. He wanted them to understand, "Do not worry or be confused, you will know when the day of resurrection happens." It seems Paul builds his vocabulary from the Old Testament, building upon at least three stories. The first is Moses coming down the mountain with sounds of a trumpet, and then appears after being absent. The second story comes from Daniel 7 where the "son of man" comes in the clouds. Now, in Paul's understanding at the day of resurrection it is believers who also "come on the clouds." Third, Paul uses the Greek word "parousia" as a way to describe how citizens would greet an emperor or high-ranking authority. [135] With Paul's understanding of the Old Testament, the fog begins to thin as he uses language to explain the transformation occurring in the day of resurrection.

It may be that in coming years, better exegesis will unlock unseen truth about what it means to be "caught up in the air" to meet the Lord. For the present, it is commonly accepted as occurring at the "Last Day," the day of the resurrection of the dead, which is future, and is unlikely a literal event; just another way of describing the Lord's presence and our transformation.

I Thessalonians 5:1-5

As we move into chapter five, we must follow Paul's line of thought and not blindly force our doctrines into the text. Is Paul continuing the same subject (the future resurrection of the dead), or

---

[134] Ibid.
[135] Ibid.

does he use similar language in addressing a different subject; that is the "coming of the son of man" that takes place in the first century. Dispensationalism claims Paul keeps on message (second coming) throughout his two letters. I do not. After changing directions in chapter four to clarify their confusion about when the dead are raised, he now goes back to his previous teaching about the "coming" that they must be ready for; because it will happen in their life time.

Teaching concerning the far distance day of resurrection was less understood (because it was taught less) than the soon arriving "Day of the Lord." Paul begins this next section by reminding them, that what he is about to teach, is common teaching, and they are *"fully aware"* of these events. His introduction of *"concerning the times and seasons"* sounds familiar. Verses throughout the New Testament mention the soon approaching *"last days."* It was a common theme, because the day was fast approaching. The comparison to Matthew 24 is striking. Jesus said the first wave of signs (false Christ's, wars and rumors of war, nation against nation, famines and earthquakes) are but the *"beginning of the birth pains* (Matt. 24:8)." Paul uses the same words in describing the "times" they are entering. He says when people are talking peace then, *"sudden destruction will come upon them as labor pains come upon a pregnant women* (Ch. 5:3)." Yet, believers in Jesus are not in the dark because they are children of the light. I agree with the comments of Mathison. "If Paul taught in I Thessalonians 5 that the day of the Lord would occur at the same time as the bodily resurrection and the "catching up" into the air of all believers (Chapter4), then why would anybody have believed that the day had already come (2Thess. 2:2)?"[136]

Paul finishes his letter with one last exhortation concerning the coming of the Lord. He frames his words in a form of a blessing, where he asks God to keep the saints blameless in spirit, soul and body at the coming of our Lord Jesus Christ (vs. 23).

---

[136] Keith A. Mathison, Postmillennialism an Eschatology of Hope, P&R Publishing, Phillipsburg, New Jersey, 1999, p. 226

From Paul's first letter, we now briefly look at his second.

II Thessalonians

Paul is not finished teaching about the soon coming "Day of the Lord." Persecution of believers is intensifying; the churches need understanding concerning the times. Enemies of God are bringing *"affliction"* upon them. Paul reminds the believers they are suffering for the kingdom, and God is just. He will repay these with *"affliction"* when Jesus comes *"in flaming fire inflecting vengeance on those who do not know God and those who do not obey the gospel of our Lord Jesus Christ* (Ch.1:8).*"*

The question must be answered that if believers in the first century were to receive relief from these who *"afflict"* them, how would a *"coming"* long after they are dead bring any relief? Paul was reminding them; once again, of events surrounding the coming Day of Judgment that Jesus prophesied would come.Paul writes about a *"man of lawlessness"* and the subject of apostasy in general. Since the *"man of lawlessness"* is covered in another chapter, we will not repeat it here. Yet, notice how all of this fits with a "coming" and the "Day of the Lord" that Paul (from the teaching of Jesus) believed would happen within a few years. In addition, the wicked are judged at the appearance of the Lord. This judgment is not thousands of years in the future, but within the lifetime of those living.

How should the student of the Bible understand Paul's message about the "coming" of the Lord in I and II Thessalonians?" Does Paul speak only about a "coming" in the first century or only events of our future? Mathison provides us with the only reasonable conclusions.

1. All the chapters refer to the second coming of Christ (dispensationalism).

2. All the chapters refer to the coming of Christ in judgment upon Jerusalem (full preterism).

3. All chapters except II Thessalonians 2 refer to the Second Coming.

4. All chapters except I Thessalonians 4 refer to the coming of Christ for judgment in 70 AD [137](partial preterism).

Mathison believes, and I agree, that number four is the best choice taking into consideration how Paul uses these terms here and elsewhere. A close reading of both letters reveal that only in I Thessalonians 4 does Paul teach anything about a "coming" of Jesus that is future for us. All other passages teach a "coming" within their generation. This is the same coming of the "son of man" Jesus spoke about. This is the coming in judgment upon unbelieving Israel and for the Christians it will be the full realization of the new covenant and his kingdom.

Signs of Jesus Return

When will Jesus return? Will it be soon? Dispensationalism teaches a soon coming of Jesus because of the belief that we live in the last days and the prophetic clock is ticking. Partial preterists place the emphasis on the growth of God's kingdom and they see this advancement as the "signs" of the day of resurrection.

1. The Enemies of Christ are Defeated

I Corinthians 15:20-25

But in fact Christ has been raised from the dead, the firstfruits of those who have fallen asleep. For as by a man came death, by a man has come also the resurrection of the dead. For as in Adam all die, so also in Christ shall all be made alive. But each in his own order: Christ the firstfruits, then at his coming those who belong to Christ. Then comes the end, when he delivers the kingdom to God the Father after destroying every rule and every authority and power. [25]For he must reign until he has put all his enemies under his feet.

When will Jesus come? Paul reveals the mystery; the day of resurrection occurs when his enemies are under his feet. We have

---

[137] Keith A. Mathison, Postmillennialism, P&R Publishing, Phillipsburg, New Jersey, 1999, p. 224-225

work to do. No one knows how long it will take. Our role is to engage in advancing the kingdom according to gifts we have received. Every generation has responsibility. The joy of living in the kingdom is that no one knows how far the kingdom can advance within any given generation. Throughout history, we see some generations that made only meager progress, while others made gigantic advancement. I believe we are connecting with a younger generation that will see kingdom growth on many fronts, more than we ever imagined.

2. The Nations are Discipled

Matthew 28:18-20

And Jesus came and said to them, "All authority in heaven and on earth has been given to me. Go therefore and make disciples of all nations, baptizing them in the name of the Father and of the Son and of the Holy Spirit, teaching them to observe all that I have commanded you. And behold, I am with you always, to the end of the age.

Jesus left the church with a job. To preach the gospel, make disciples and advance God's kingdom. This begins with conversion of individuals in each nation, but must not stop there. Evangelism is only the beginning. Even if the whole world converted to Christ today, the work of the church would still be at its beginning. Jesus gives us a commission to "disciple the nations." This means each people group in the world must follow the teachings of Jesus. Each nation will submit to the authority of Christ and walk in his ways. We need people with vision to create biblical strategies to see transformations of entire nations. This is not impossible. This is the purpose of the church. We must start small, build upon our successes and learn from our failures.

3. The Knowledge of God's Glory Covering the earth

Habakkuk 2:14

For the earth will be filled with the knowledge of the glory of the LORD as the waters cover the sea.

The knowledge of God's glory covers all areas. The glory of God is the visible manifestation of everything he is. The earth will see God in thousands of different ways. They will see God in our love, our wisdom, our spiritual power, our gifts, our creativity; the church will manifest God in every aspect of life.

The traditional "signs of the end" of dispensational eschatology are not biblical signs of the future return of Christ; they are signs of the destruction of Jerusalem and the temple. The dispensational doctrine of the "rapture" has confused, manipulated, and been the source of untold harm to the church. It is time to move on. Move on to the biblical signs and work towards the growth of God's kingdom on the earth.

When the day arrives and the Lord appears in the day of resurrection, it will be the conclusion of his increasing presence with his children. The veil between heaven and earth will progressively weaken. We are seeing episodes of heaven "breaking in' more and more. As the earth begins to resemble heaven, the Lord will appear, his 'presence" will be fully known, at that time, our bodies will be transformed and experience the resurrection.

Study Questions

1. Why do you think the doctrine of the rapture is popular in certain churches?

2. Do you think many advocates of the rapture realize it is a modern doctrine?

3. What are the biblical signs pointing towards the day of resurrection and coming of Jesus?

4. Why was the doctrine of the rapture created?

5. Is there any verse in the Bible where it says Jesus will come and take us to heaven?

Chapter 22

The Earth: Will it be destroyed by Fire?

Despite what we have seen in Scripture, despite church history, and despite practical considerations, there are evangelicals that still object to a present and growing kingdom. Most are sincere Christians who are committed to their traditions. They point to particular sections of the New Testament and conclude that the world is heading towards apostasy and judgment. They see the world as getting worse and only the Second Coming brings true hope. They often point to II Peter 3 as a passage that supports their view. Although this passage belongs in an advanced study of the kingdom and not an introductory one, a beginning exegesis will be offered based upon the fact that many Christians point to Peter's words to deny any "Victorious Eschatology."

II Peter 3:10

But the day of the Lord will come as a thief in the night; in which the heavens shall pass away with a great noise, and the elements shall melt with fervent heat, the earth also and the works that are therein shall be burned up (King James Version).

But when the Day of God's Judgment does come, it will be unannounced, like a thief. The sky will collapse with a thunderous bang, everything disintegrating in a huge conflagration, earth and all its works exposed to the scrutiny of Judgment (The Message).

But the day of the Lord will come like a thief, and then the heavens will pass away with a roar, and the heavenly bodies will be burned up and dissolved, and the earth and the works that are done on it will be exposed (English Standard Version).

The King James Version ends the passage by stating the earth and it works shall be *"burned up."* If this is true then any kingdom growth and impact upon culture will be dissolved and have no lasting influence. Then the dispensational attitude would be correct, "we are not here to build a better world (cultural transformation) but to save people for the next world (heaven)."

This is the standard dispensational approach. Other versions have keyed off the King James and have translated the ending with similar words. Yet, versions like The Message and the ESV Bible translate it much differently.

The Message ends verse ten with the *"earth and all its works exposed to the scrutiny of Judgment."* The ESV says *"the earth and the works that are done on it will be exposed."* Being exposed is a lot different from *"burned up."*

Will the works of our hands, our cultural achievements in life, be burned up or are they exposed and then judged by God? Also, when is this "Day of the Lord?" Do these events happen at the Second Coming or does Peter have something else in mind? Wim Rietkerk author of The Future Great Planet Earth writes about how the popular understanding of II Peter 3 is opposite of what the Bible teaches. It teaches not the total destruction of the world but its renewal.

> "For biblical scholars, however, the manuscripts should decide the meaning. The main manuscripts and the most authoritative ones have a reading contrary to the King James translation. They read *"the earth and the works upon it will be found."* Two of the three ancient manuscripts, the Sinaiticus and the Vaticanus (both from the 4th century) and many others of a later date, have this reading of the text. Therefore the most authoritative edition of the Greek New Testament, Nestle, gives the reading (*heureteseti*)...I prefer this literal translation *"will be found"* to the Scofield Bible's *"will be laid bare"*, although here it is at least implied that the earth and its works will come through the fire and not be totally destroyed...further support for the literal translation *"will be found"* is provided by comparison with the other texts in the New Testament where we read the same words, Luke 15:9 and 24: *"My son here was lost but now he is found"*(Luke 15:24). He went

through a deep crisis but he has happily come through. In the same way, the earth and the works upon it will go through the fire of God's judgment, but they will come through. This is good news, and completely in harmony with Revelation 14:13: "*And their works do follow them*,"…When everyone expects Peter to say that the earth and the works upon it-that is nature and culture- are going to be crushed and lost beneath a passing heaven and burning elements, he professes quite the opposite. His argument is as follows: "what all the Stoics believe, namely that in this way nature and culture will disappear, we, as Judeo-Christian believers in the wake of God's covenant with Noah, do not believe. We can rest assured that the earth and all its works *will be found.*"[138]

II Peter as a whole is difficult. Exegesis is not easy, nevertheless, chapter three must fit into the overall message of Peter. As in I Peter, the theme is the coming of Jesus. This coming is not his coming at the end of history, but his promised coming within a generation. Peter is answering critics who ask, "*where is the promise of his coming*" (3:4). Christians and Jews were keenly aware of the prophecies made by Jesus.

Matthew 10:23

When they persecute you in one town, flee to the next, for truly, I say to you, you will not have gone through all the towns of Israel before the Son of Man comes.

Matthew 16:27-28

For the Son of Man is going to come with his angels in the glory of his Father, and then he will repay each person according to what he has done. Truly, I say to you, there are some standing here who will not taste death until they see the Son of Man coming in his kingdom.

---

[138] Wim Rietkerk, The Future Great Planet Earth, Good Books, page 18-19

Jesus said clearly that people then living (not all but some) would live to see the "*Son of Man coming in his kingdom.*" How can this be true? If Jesus returned to earth in the first century, where is he? Our failure at this junction comes from thinking the New Testament uses the word "coming" only to an event in our future and to a physical coming. These predictions must take place within a literal generation or we have a far bigger problem, Jesus giving false prophecies.

We must distinguish between a physical coming and a coming of a spiritual nature. Both are "real" comings. Both bring about the intended purpose. Is there any precedent for a "spiritual coming" of God? Yes, we already provided Old Testament passages where the Prophets use similar language when God visited nations with judgment (Ez. 32:7-8, Is. 34:4, Isaiah 9:9-10).

These events happened, not in the physical creation, but in real terms of judgment and taking away the "light" of the judged nation. God came down and brought judgment to these nations in the Old Testament era; likewise, Peter uses symbolic words to teach a coming judgment. Peter J. Leithart in his commentary on II Peter helps clarify the timing issues.

> "There are indications within chapter 3 that Peter is talking about a "day of judgment" that would occur within the first century. Peter is concerned with mockers who arise in the church in the "last days," and this and similar phases refer throughout the New Testament to the apostolic era, not to some future period of history (I Cor. 10:11, Heb. 1:1-2, I Peter 1:20). Peter warns that mockers will come in the first century (2 Peter 3:3), and this implies that their "destruction" must also take place within that period. As noted above in chapter 2, the mockers are the same as the false teachers of 2 Peter 2; the false teachers are the "ungodly men" of 3:7 and the "unprincipled men" of 3:17. Thus the "day of God" (3:12) is the "day" for the destruction of the false teachers (3:7). If the mockers have already

appeared in the first century, and their destruction is predicted, that destruction must also take place in the first century. It would hardly be worthwhile for God to destroy the false teachers long after they have died."[139]

Apostle Peter announces that mockers and false teachers will soon face their day of judgment. This will happen in conjunction with the *"heavens melting away"* and the *"earth and its works are found (discovered)."* It is illogical that one aspect of creation is destroyed and another part not. Can the created universe (heavens) come under utter destruction and not destroy the earth in the process? [140] The heavens here refer the old covenant and its elements; they are about to end and be replaced with the reality of the new covenant and the coming of the kingdom in power and glory.

If we can get the correct reading about the earth being 'found' and not burned up, then Peter's use of "elements" makes more sense. Peter is not talking about the physical elements here, but about spiritual elements. Paul uses this same word, elements, and he clearly has something different in mind from a physical fire.

Colossians 2:8

See to it that no one takes you captive by philosophy and empty deceit, according to human tradition, and according to the elemental spirits of the world, and not according to Christ.

Colossians 2:20-22

If with Christ you died to the elemental spirits of the world, why as if you were still alive in the world, do you submit to regulations-Do not handle, Do not taste, Do not touch (referring to things that all perish as they are used)-according to human precepts and teaching.

In both verses, the *"elements"* refer to the teaching of man, elementary principles, to which we are not to be enslaved. I

---

[139] Peter J. Leithart, The Promise of His Appearing-An Exposition of Second Peter, Canon Press, Moscow, Idaho, 2004, p. 80-81

[140] ibid

believe Peter has the same meaning in mind about the passing of the old heavens and the destruction of these "elemental" spirits and teaching. The timing of these events are the same as his coming as judge upon the city and temple of Jerusalem.

The author of the book of Hebrews says in chapter 8:13 *"In speaking of a new covenant, he makes the first one obsolete. And what is becoming obsolete and growing old is ready to vanish away."* The best date for Hebrews in the 60's and therefore it was only a few years away from when the temple would vanish from sight. When the author of Hebrews wrote his letter the temple was standing, but within a few years, it was aflame and destroyed forever. The old system (heavens) is gone forever and what remain is the new people of God that become the temple of God in the earth.

The doctrine that God destroys the earth by fire has no basis in Scripture. God is renewing the earth and has no plan of destroying it. Sin and evil are destroyed, Christ's enemies are being destroyed; but the physical earth will last a very long time. How long? The Bible tells us.

Ecclesiastes 1:4

A generation goes, and a generation comes, but the earth remains forever.

Study Questions

1. Discuss the doctrinal implications of a reading of "found" compared to "burned up" in I Peter 3:10.
2. Do you think the temple in Jerusalem was standing when the book of Hebrews was written? How does knowing the date help in interpreting the letter?
3. Discuss the language of the Old Testament when God came in judgment against nations.
4. Explain how translations that rely on earlier copies of the New Testament are better than one translating from much later documents. The Bible that you read, is it translated from early or late copies?
5. Discuss how the mockers Peter talks about will be judged.

6. How would the truth that God is working towards renewing the earth, and not destroying it, affect the work of the church?

Chapter 23

Eternal Life

We now take a little deviation from the central topic of the kingdom; at least from first appearances. Most Christians link eternal life with heaven. Spending eternity in heaven worshipping God is our goal. Being delivered from this evil world fills our minds and provides strength to struggle through another day. If that is our thinking, then, we may be wrong again. This manner of thinking has filled the imaginations of many believers, nevertheless, the Scripture tells us very little about heaven and the afterlife. Why is that? It goes back to the beginning where God created earth and placed mankind there. We are humans and God prepared a special place for us, we call it earth.

Nature of Eternal Life

Christians have competing concepts on where they spend eternity. We know our future is secure in Christ. We know we will spend eternity in God's presence. The question remains, where will this eternity be? The Bible presents a variety of pictures and images that if stood side by side would seem contradictory. We have images of heavenly worship and people setting under a fig tree, all representing God's eternal blessing for us.

The answer is not easy. We do not have a clear passage of Scripture that settles the question. We must integrate Scriptures so that a full picture of eternal life emerges. Our journey through this study will cause some to rethink their traditional understanding. For others it may be confirmation on some matters that you are already considering. I hope this short study will stimulate more conversation about the nature of eternal life. We begin with one firm truth; the Bible promises eternal life to those who believe in God's Son, Jesus Christ.

John 3:16

For God so loved the world, that he gave his only Son, that whoever believes in him should not perish but have eternal life.

John 3:16 may be the best-known verse in the Bible. It is the source of comfort and faith for millions of believers. The offer of eternal life begins with God's love. God loved us so much, that He sent His Son to earth. This is important because God is eternal; therefore, his love has no beginning or end. The eternal life we possess in our salvation is like that of God's, it always exists in the present reality. herefore bringing time into the concept of eternity is bringing it where it does not belong. We have eternal life; now. Yet, we live with the constraints (and blessing) of time.

If then, we as Christians have eternal life through our relationship with Christ, what is our state of being once we die? Is heaven and eternal life the same? If heaven and eternal life are the same in Scripture, we then have a dilemma. Paul sees believers as presently *"raised with Christ"* or seated in heaven at the right hand of God (Col. 3:1). If heaven is eternal life and we are not there yet, how can the Bible speak of believers presently possessing eternal life? Many adopt the view that eternal life is waiting for us in heaven, and heaven is our eternal rest and dwelling place. As we will see, the Bible may support the view that heaven may NOT be our final destination place, and eternal life has more to do with work than rest. Please read on.

In John 17, Jesus prays to his Father concerning his followers. *"And this is eternal life, that they know you the only true God, and Jesus Christ whom you have sent* (John 17:3). Ask any Christian believer, "What is eternal life?" and see how few would respond with the description given by Jesus. The knowledge God is eternal life! Knowing Jesus Christ as Lord and Savior is eternal life! John writes not a word about going to heaven and not a word about living forever. They can be included, but are the by-products of knowing God. Receiving eternal life (born again) begins a relationship with God through Jesus Christ. Eternal life is a present reality. Likewise, this translates into heaven as a present reality. In the final analysis, God is eternal and those united with Him by faith; enter into the world of eternity. The gospel is more than acceptance of Jesus, so we get a ticket to heaven and escape hell; rather, it is entering into an eternal relationship with the one and only true God. Our first step into heaven is the day we embrace Jesus as God's Son, and are born again by the Spirit.

"Whoever believes in the Son has eternal life (John 3:36). Have we believed in the Son? Then we have eternal life. The future is not measured in years. The church throughout history has expressed two primary views on the nature of eternal life. The terms for these different approaches are the "spiritual vision model," and the second is the "new creation model."[141]

Spiritual Vision Model

The "spiritual vision" model emphasizes biblical texts speaking of a future state of blessing within a "heavenly" context. Heaven is the dwelling place of God, and at death, all believers enter eternity in heaven with God. This "spiritual vision" model creates in Christians a sense that earth is a temporary dwelling and our true home is in heaven. This concept is enhanced by gospel music such as, "this world is not my home, I'm just passing through," and "When we all get to heaven."

The "spiritual vision" model understands Jesus' words in John 14 as referring to a heavenly mansion that awaits every believer. We image Jesus working as a master carpenter, building our eternal home. What waits in heaven is no small flat, or even a modest house; Jesus is building each of us a mansion. We endure hardship and affliction during our days on earth, eagerly desiring to be in heaven instead. The more difficult life on earth becomes, the more we desire to be in heaven. People groups experiencing discrimination often look to this "spiritual vision" model for hope. When children of God feel disenfranchised from any earthly blessing, they place all their dreams in a future heaven. Long-term goals of making progress in this life are hopeless; it is the next life

---

[141] Three Views of the Millennium and Beyond, Darrell L. Bock, General Editor, Zondervan, Grand Rapids, Michigan, 1999, page 161

that captures our attention. For those adopting this model, separation from the world is a major theme.

I John 2:15

Do not love the world or the things in the world

The Scriptures teach Christians not to love the world. To what world is the Bible referring? In the Greek, there are two words for world. One refers to the physical world (Cosmos), and the other refers to the "age" in which we live, which is (Eion). The verse in I John is "eion." We are not to love the product (culture) of our sinful nature. The "age" is not the world that God created, but the conditions men have created. This verse teaches separation from the works of men not the physical world we live in. Another verse used to support the "spiritual vision" model is I John 2:17.

I John 2:17

And the world is passing away along with its desires, but whoever does the will of God abides forever.

Certainly if this world is passing away, we should not be working to make it a better place. If the world is ending soon, Christians should be working towards treasures in heaven and not work towards any material blessing on earth. Which Greek word is used? Again, it is "eion" meaning age. This verse says nothing about the physical world passing away. The age (world) of the old covenant is about to pass away. Those expecting our physical world to end cannot claim the Bible as their source.

The physical world is here to stay. God has plans for this world. There is no end to the world from the biblical view as some Christian writers have attempted to show. We should be expecting the current age (world) of sinful society to give way to a better world, a world expressing the Kingdom of God not the kingdoms of men. Those looking for scriptural support for their "spiritual vision" model cannot use this verse in I John to support their opinions.

In I Corinthians 7:31 Paul writes, *"The present form of this world is passing away."* Paul does use the word for the physical world (cosmos), yet it does not say the "cosmos is passing away but the "form" or "fashion" of this world is passing away. The

Greek word is "schema" meaning signifying. It is that which comprises the manner of life, and the actions of humanity in general. It is talking about the actions and manners of men, and says nothing about the created world.

In his book <u>Three Views on the Millennium and Beyond</u> Craig A. Blaising states...

> "The spiritual vision model of eternity emphasizes biblical texts promising that believers will see God or receive full knowledge in the future state of blessing. It notes that Paul speaks of the Christian life in terms of its heavenly orientation, and adds to this the biblical description of heaven as the dwelling place of God, as the present enthroned position of Christ, and as the destiny of the believing dead prior to their resurrection. In the history of the Church, many Christian theologians have claimed that the final state of the resurrected will be in heaven."[142]

Will the final state of the resurrected be in heaven? This is the core of the argument. Where will we spend eternal life? Will the resurrection of the dead change the believer's location? Wright comments about the misconceptions people have about the afterlife. "It comes as something of a shock, in fact, when people are told what is the fact the case: that there is very little in the Bible about "going to heaven when you die" and not a lot about a postmortem hell either."[143] Part of the problem may lie in that the gospel of Matthew translates the kingdom of God as the kingdom of Heaven. From this, we may assume that the kingdom of heaven is a way of speaking of heaven, and this is where we go once we die. Wright continues, "But the language of heaven in the New Testament

---

[142] Craig A. Blaising, Kenneth L. Gentry, Robert B. Strimple, Three Views on the Millennium and Beyond, Zondervan, Grand Rapids, Michigan, 1999, page 161

[143] N. T. Wright, Surprised By Hope, Harper One, New York, New York, 2008, Page18

doesn't work that way. "God's kingdom" in the preaching of Jesus refers not to postmortem destiny, not to our escape from this world into another one, but to God's sovereign rule coming "on earth as it is in heaven."[144]Before further comments on the "new creation" model let us examine some similarities between Greek philosophy and the "spiritual vision" view.

Both Greek philosophy and those advocating a spiritual vision model stress a clear contrast between spirit and physical matter. Since God is Spirit, then the world of the spirit is of a higher order than a material world. Since the spirit world is greater than the created world, our future as Christians will exist in a non-earthly spiritual existence. Salvation is freedom from the material world. The destiny of the saved is to engage in "spiritual worship" for all of eternity.

The spiritual vision model gained strength in the third century and was the dominant view until post-reformation times. This was also the period that amillennialism became a part of our Christian heritage. Amillennialism teaches God's kingdom is entirely spiritual in nature and not manifested through physical or created matter, hence there is no premillennial or postmillennial kingdom on earth. The "spiritual vision" model of eternal life and amillennial eschatology grew together and became an integrated system of belief. An interested note is that while amillennialism strengthens the "spiritual vision" model (and vice versa), today many dispensational Evangelicals maintain this view as their expression of eternal life.

Dispensationalists bring the two models together in their teachings of two different groups of God's people with separate destinies. The church has a heavenly destiny (spiritual vision model) and the Jews have an earthly destiny (new creation model).

The hope of reaching heaven after a long struggle on earth has given Christians hope and assurance for centuries. It makes earthly difficulties easier to endure. For this, we can be thankful. Those who spend their life in prison for the sake of the gospel, those who

---

[144] Ibid (NT Wright-same page as previous quote)

are tortured and are outcasts can look with eager anticipation to heaven, and a better life. Yet, the questions remains, will Christians spend all of eternity in heaven?

The New Creation Model

The thought of living forever in a state of "bodily" existence may seem odd to modern Christians. Nevertheless, it is the historic view of the church. The resurrection of the dead was "basic doctrine" in the first century. Accepting Jesus as the Son of God was the way to insure we would live forever. The "new creation" model of eternal life patterns itself after the resurrection of Jesus Christ. He was the first-fruit of those who are "*in Christ*" and they will follow in his example at his coming (I Corinthians 15:23). The resurrection elevates physical existence. Spiritual realities come first, the new birth, justification and regeneration. Our resurrection bodies follow the reality we experience in the Spirit. Living in a physical body that is free from corruption and sin is the biblical hope of Christians.

The New Creation model views our physical body as finally and completely free from sin and its effects. We are not spiritual entities floating through heaven as a puff of smoke for all eternity. We will live as God originally created us, in a human body. The resurrection of Jesus is the believer's pattern. Like his body, so shall ours be. It will be both similar but also slightly different from the body we now have. Jesus ate a fish dinner (similar) but also walked through walls (dissimilar). Philippians 3:21 in speaking about Jesus says he "*will transform our lowly bodies to be like his glorious body.*"

We will not be floating around forever in some bodiless form singing endless praise songs, but assigned tasks of dominion. Some will rule over cities, and this sounds more like earth than heaven. We will not cease to worship but worship matures by the removal of mental and emotional oppression from sin. The future will bring us closer to our environment not distance us from it. Even creation itself is suffering from man's sin. We see this in Paul's letter to the Romans.

Romans 8:18-23 brings together the concept that physical creation is a recipient of grace, and it is linked to the resurrection of the sons of God. The physical creation finds a new beginning, and now it is the proper home for God's transformed people.

The prayer of Jesus that *"Your kingdom come, Your will be done, On earth as it is in heaven* (Matt.6:10)" is not a wishful dream, but is exactly what God has planned. This earth will not be vaporized; it will not be destroyed in any manner. God has created this earth as the special dwelling place for His people, for all of eternity.

I Corinthians 15:12-14,

Now if Christ is proclaimed as raised from the dead, how can some of you say that there is no resurrection of the dead? But if there is no resurrection of the dead, then not even Christ has been raised. And if Christ has not been raised, then our preaching is in vain and your faith is in vain.

20-26

But in fact Christ has been raised from the dead, the firstfruits of those who have fallen asleep. For as by a man came death, by a man has come also the resurrection of the dead. For as in Adam all die, so also in Christ shall all be made alive. But each in his own order: Christ the firstfruits, then at his coming those who belong to Christ. Then comes the end, when he delivers the kingdom to God the Father after destroying every rule and every authority and power. For he must reign until he has put all his enemies under his feet. The last enemy to be destroyed is death.

God raised Jesus from the dead as the "first-fruits" for all those who are "in Christ." The "new creation" model rejects the division between the "spiritual" aspects of salvation and the "physical" aspects of salvation that the "spiritual vision" model dictates.

Wright;

"While eternal life is essentially continuous with present existence, it is not simply an unending extension of present conditions. To be sure, there will be significant differences in the quality of eternal life. Those who share that life will be immortal, having been freed through resurrection or translation. Sin will not exist. The saints will be confirmed and glorified in holy character by the Spirit of God. As such, they will enjoy communion with God as well as with one another in the new creation. This is the "spirituality" of eternal life in the new creation model-not the absence of materiality but the full effects of the Holy Spirit's indwelling the resurrected physical bodies of the redeemed."[145]

The revelation of God's Kingdom on earth and our understanding of eternal grow out of biblical revelation; they are linked. Victorious eschatology teaches the Messianic Kingdom of Christ advances until all areas of life are under His Lordship. When all nations are discipled and all the enemies of Christ are under His footstool, He will return in triumphant glory. Is that the end of God's Kingdom on earth? The majority of kingdom passages speak of God's Kingdom "having no end" (Daniel 2:44; Daniel 7:14, 27; Isaiah 9:7; Luke 1:31-33). As we study these two models of eternal life, we will then be able to integrate our view of "heaven" and "eternal life" with our view of the Kingdom of God.

There are areas of agreement to which both models adhere. Those in Christ who physically die are ushered immediately into heaven. This is primarily a spiritual existence. While it may be hundreds or thousands of years before the general resurrection, it is only a fraction of time compared to eternity. At the final resurrection, Jesus brings the saints from his abode in the heavens to earth. Heaven is not the place to be when Jesus and the throne of God re-locate to earth.

Eternal life (salvation) is first a "spiritual" experience. We must be "born again" (John 3:3) in order to enter the kingdom.

---

[145] Craig Blaising, Kenneth L. Gentry, Robert B. Strimple, Three Views on the Millennium and Beyond, Zondervan, Grand Rapids, Michigan, 1999, page 162-163

The "new creation" model sees the "spirituality" of salvation not ending in some unearthly, bodiless form in heaven, but in a resurrected body living out eternity on the earth.

Although the 16th century Reformation stressed the biblical doctrines of salvation, it provided a foundation for the "new creation" model.

> "The Reformation precipitated a revolution in Christian culture. Although the Reformers themselves did not directly challenge the "spiritual vision" model, they did unleash powerful currents of thought that led to both to the reemergence of new creation eschatology and the reconsideration of millennialism...most important, the Reformation emphasized the authority of the Bible's literal sense in theological expression... the Reformation triggered a more acute sense of the historical nature of human life...this sense of history and the prospect of future earthly conditions different from the past came to dominate the modern mind. Most important, however, the Reformation and post-Reformation sense of historical identity was defined in relationship to biblical history."[146]

There is sufficient biblical evidence that the "new creation" model of eternal life is an accurate interpretation. This model supports the advancing and eternal Kingdom of God. Christians will live on the earth in a resurrected body and live in a world set free from its corruption.

Where will Christians spend eternity? Will it be in Heaven? Yes! Will it be on earth? Yes! The New Creation understanding of eternal life is a blending of these two realties. We will be on earth, and realize the fullness of heaven at the same time. At last, the prayer of Jesus is true; that earth would experience the will of

---

[146] Ibid page 174-175

God just as heaven does. Heaven on earth, this is our hope; this is our destiny.

Study Questions

1. Before reading this chapter, did you have a "spiritual vision" or a "new creation" understanding of eternal life?

2. Explain what role the Protestant Reformation had in establishing the "new creation" model of eternal life.

3. Explain this sentence of the author, "The revelation of God's Kingdom on earth and our understanding of eternal life are hermeneutically linked."

4. What major biblical event does the "new creation" model build its argument?

5. Do you think "Greek philosophy" has influenced the Christian's view of eternal life?

Chapter 24

Dating the Book of Revelation

What is the meaning of Revelation? Our first step begins with determining the date of authorship. In the majority of New Testament books the message is clear regardless of when it was wrote. If Paul wrote Galatians in 58 A.D. or 68 A.D. it changes little in how we interpret it. Throughout church history, the book of Revelation has been one of the most hotly contested and confusing books of the Bible. There are numerous interpretations. There are various methods used to unlock the language and meaning of John's images and word pictures. Our first key of interpretation is to establish the date Revelation. The exact date is not vital, but what is imperative is whether John wrote Revelation before Jerusalem was destroyed or after. We know that Roman armies under Titus destroyed Jerusalem and burnt the temple in late summer of 70 A.D. This fact of history establishes the boundaries of our search.

Many contemporary evangelicals have accepted a date of 95 A.D. without ever asking why. Many accept the late date not because it is warranted, but because it fits into a futurist framework. If the bulk of Revelation (after chapter 3) is prophetic insight into our future, then the date matters little. Since many Evangelicals are influenced by dispensational eschatology (which interprets Revelation as prophecy for the future), the important aspect of dating has been overlooked. We just assume the prophecy is for the future, and begin studying from that point.

Partial-preterists begin their studies in Revelation by first examining the date. Our examination must include both internal and external evidence. Exegesis begins once a date is established. Serious Bible students should carefully study the arguments for a late or early date. In order for a preterist interpretation to be considered, a date before the fall of Jerusalem must be reasonable affirmed.If an early date before August 70 A.D. is not reasonable, then, the preterist interpretation must be ruled out.

What are the arguments for an early date? Since works advocating a late date are plentiful, only key points advocating an early date are included.

1. John's Opening Remarks

Revelation 1:1

The revelation of Jesus Christ, which God gave Him to show to His bond-servants, the things which must soon take place; and He sent and communicated it by His angel to His bond-servant John.

The book of Revelation provides us a revelation of God's Son, Jesus Christ. Too much modern religious literature stresses antichrist (never mentioned in the book of Revelation) rather than Jesus Christ. John presents Jesus not as a suffering savior, but as the Christ who rules creation.

John's first sentence states the events spoken about will *"soon take place."* The book of Revelation is not prophecies about the distant future but historical events in the first century. Our problem with John is that he wrote not as a historian (because for John the events were future), but in the mode of an Old Testament prophet. We are shown great images and pictures that for modern readers are extremely difficult to understand. What source did John use to describe his visions? He relied heavily on passages in the Old Testament. To the extent that we are familiar with Old Testament imagery, discerning the book of Revelation is somewhat easier. John also wrote in a common first century style called apocalyptic, which is very different from anything we have in the twenty first century.

A basic principle of interpretation is to carefully read the text and allow the words themselves to lead us. John says these events were to occur *"soon."* Why is it then that many today ignore this statement and immediately look for application generations in the future? The Scripture has greater authority than my pre-conceived doctrines. We must begin where the text takes us; look for first century relevance. Is this one verse our only clue? No, it is not. In case we overlooked His first statement about timing, John reminds us again in verse three.

Revelation 1:3

Blessed is the one who reads aloud the words of this prophecy, and blessed are those who hear, and who keep what is written in it, for the time is near.

Did John desire these first century believers to respond to his book? Yes, they were to "heed" them! Christians of the early church cannot "heed" prophecies that will be fulfilled over two-thousand years in the future. We speculate about the meaning of John's words but early Christians were to obey them.John says, *"For the time is near."* What time? The events described are about ready to become a reality. Twice in the opening chapter, John states clearly that the events spoken of are for the near future not the distance one.

Not only did John give us the key in his opening remarks, he also closes the book by repeating it.

Revelation 22:10

And he said to me, 'Do not seal up the words of the prophecy of this book, for the time is near.

At the end of John's writing, he was *"not"* to seal it. Why not seal the book, because *"the time is near."*The time for the fulfillment of the prophecy has now come. The events of the "great tribulation" are almost here. The old covenant will pass away soon.

Daniel 12:4

But you, Daniel, shut up the words and seal the book, until the time of the end. Many shall run to and fro, and knowledge shall increase.

Daniel 12:9

He said, "Go your way, Daniel, for the words are shut up and sealed until the time of the end.

Daniel's instruction is to seal the book until the *"time of the end."* Is this the end of the world, the conclusion of God's dealings with humanity? The end of the age we live in? I do not think so.

Daniel's prophetic revelations concern the Messiah (the son of man) receiving His authority to rule and reign. We know from the New Testament that Jesus' death and resurrection lead to his ascension. Jesus presently has *"all power and authority"* (Matthew 28:18, Daniel 7:13, Romans 14:9, Ephesians 1:20-22, Colossians 1:16-18, Philippians 2:7-11, Acts 2:29-36). Paul while writing to the believers in Corinth makes an interesting statement about the end of the age.

I Corinthians 10:11

Now these things happened to them as an example, but they were written down for our instruction, on whom the end of the ages has come.

Paul lived in a time called the end of the ages. This goes along with other New Testament references claiming that the first century was the *"last days,"* or *"last times,"* or as John in his epistle calls it, the *"last hour."*

Daniel was to seal up the book until the time of the Messiah. The age of the temple, the age of the Mosaic covenant, the age of Israel, was coming to its end. The book remained sealed for nearly five hundred years. Finally, John the Baptist walks out of the desert and proclaims, *"The kingdom of God is at hand."* As Daniel was told to *"seal"* his visions, John was told, *"do not seal"* the book. The reason should be obvious; the time for fulfilling John's vision was near. It was not 400 years, or 2,000 years in the future, but no more than five years. John wrote the book of Revelation before 70 A.D. and the events concerning the destruction of Jerusalem and the temple were only a few years in the future. There was no need to *"seal"* them up waiting for a distant future fulfillment.

2. The Temple is Standing

Revelation 11:1-2

Then I was given a measuring rod like a staff, and I was told, "Rise and measure the temple of God and the altar and those who worship there, ² but do not measure the court outside the temple;

*leave that out, for it is given over to the nations, and they will
trample the holy city for forty-two months.*

John's instructions are to *"measure the temple."* The crucial
question arising from this text is, "what temple?" If this refers to
the second temple (destroyed in 70 A.D.), then question over the
date is over; it had to be written before the temple was destroyed.
What other temple could he have in mind? Believers are called to
be a *"temple"* of the Holy Spirit, and there is a "heavenly temple"
(Hebrews 8:1-6). Was John referring to something other than a
physical temple? The language used by John leads us to affirm it
was the physical temple standing in Jerusalem. First, John states
that the outer court of the temple is *"to the nations."* This
reference cannot apply to the church being the temple or of a
heavenly temple. Secondly, the location of the temple is in the
"holy city." The holy city is Jerusalem (Isaiah 52:1, Matthew
27:52-53). We must remember that John was seeing this by vision
and was not literally in Jerusalem to measure the temple. This
does not take away the truth that it was the actual temple standing
in Jerusalem at the time of John's writing.

3. The Seven Kings

Revelation 17:10
*They are also seven kings, five of whom have fallen, one is, the
other has not yet come, and when he does come he must remain
only a little while.*

John writes that there are *"seven kings"*. Who are these kings?
If we accept them as Roman leaders, we can create a list of kings.
The historical list of Roman emperors is as follows.

1. Julius Caesar 49- 44 BC
2. Augustus 31 BC-14 AD
3. Tiberius 14-37 AD
4. Gaius (known as Caligula) 37-41 AD
5. Claudius 41-54 AD
6. Nero 54-68 AD
7. Galba 68-69 AD

Nero Caesar died in June of 68 A.D., and it fits that He is the *"one is,"* meaning Nero reigned while John wrote the book of Revelation. Five other kings preceded Nero, just as John wrote. These five kings *"had fallen"* (no longer in power) when John wrote. Who is the seventh king? According to verse 10, the final leader would *"remain a little while."* John's prophecy was accurate; Galba only ruled 8 months (from June 68-January 69).

The dating of Revelation is vital to its interpretation. I strongly affirm a date before 70 A.D., because of the internal and external evidence. For those wanting a scholarly and lengthy book on evidence for an early date, see the book, <u>Before Jerusalem Fell-Dating the Book of Revelation</u> by Kenneth L. Gentry, Jr.

Study Questions

1. Discuss the importance of dating Revelation in regards to its interpretation.

2. Explain why the list of seven kings supports an early date.

3. Why was Daniel told to "seal" his prophecy and John was told not to "seal" his book?

4. Should John's opening remarks about the timing issues be taken seriously? Why do many overlook these verses on the time issues?

5. If the book of Revelation is a prophecy about our future, how could the readers of the first century understand the message?

Chapter 25

The Two Witnesses

Revelation 11:1-3

Then I was given a measuring rod like a staff, and I was told, "Rise and measure the temple of God and the altar and those who worship there, but do not measure the court outside the temple; leave that out, for it is given over to the nations, and they will trample the holy city for forty-two months. And I will grant authority to my two witnesses, and they will prophesy for 1,260 days, clothed in sackcloth.

Who are the two witnesses described by John? When I conduct seminars on the kingdom of God and take questions, the identification of these two witnesses' ranks among the top three questions.[147] It seems everyone has an opinion. From Christians of many years to the new believer, this passage fascinates us all. How do we begin unraveling a complex passage like Revelation 11? Since many authors start with a futurist orientation, our focus is the plausibility of a first century interpretation.

John is to measure the temple. I believe this is the second temple standing in Jerusalem, it stood there until late summer of 70 A.D. This provides a period in which to base the rest of the events. In the final verse of the chapter, it says, *"Then God's temple in heaven was opened* (Rev. 11:19)," and this is after the first temple is measured and the two witnesses have come and gone. With this in mind, it seems best to see the first temple as the physical temple in Jerusalem and the second temple as the spiritual temple of God, which comes to its fullness once the first is destroyed. The author

---

[147] The other two questions are, "Why have I not heard this before," and "If these things are in history (Great Tribulation, apostasy, antichrist, Etc.) then what is left for us? The last is almost comical if not for its sad commentary to the degree dispensational thinking that has affected so many in Evangelical churches.

of Hebrews, after quoting Jeremiah about the coming of a new covenant says, *"In speaking of a new covenant, he makes the first one obsolete. And what is becoming obsolete and growing old is ready to vanish away* (Heb. 8:13). Notice it says that the old (old covenant and its temple worship) is growing old and about to vanish away. The early Christians reading the book of Hebrews were being encouraged that the "Day" is about here, only a few more years and the old will be obsolete.

The outer court of the temple is not measured. Why? Because it is given to the nations (gentiles) to *"trample the holy city for forty-two months* (Rev. 11:2). For three and a half years, Jerusalem is trampled, Rome literally destroying the city. It is during this time (Jesus calls it the Great Tribulation) that the two witnesses walk the streets of Jerusalem. They prophecy for 1260 days (a 360 day year times 3.5 is 42 months). David S. Clark writes on the timing of the two witnesses and the events during the three and half years. "Here is so plainly the destruction of Jerusalem that it could hardly be put in plainer words. It seems evident that there is no getting away from the fact that here we are dealing with the fall of Jerusalem in the year 70."[148]

The temple is the actual physical temple standing in Jerusalem when John writes. The period is three and half years leading up to the burning of the temple and the complete destruction of the city. If this is the case, do we find two people in history that lived in Jerusalem matching John's description? Before venturing into the identification of these witnesses, we need to take in account their activities. First, the witnesses echo from are Zechariah 4 that speaks of two olive trees and lamp stands. The old covenant version refers to Zerubbabel (king) and Joshua (priest). These two witnesses represent the royal house and the priesthood.

---

[148] David S. Clark, The Message from Patmos, Baker Book House, Grand Rapids, Michigan, 1989, page 74

Zechariah 4:6

Then he said to me, "This is the word of the LORD to Zerubbabel: Not by might, nor by power, but by my Spirit, says the LORD of hosts.

The seven lamps in verse two connect to the olive trees, "from which flow an unceasing supply of oil, symbolizing the Holy Spirit's filling and empowering work in the leaders of His covenant people."[149] The power of the Holy Spirit is imperative in our ministry. This is the clear implications of the two "*sons of oil*" or anointed ones.

Second, the witnesses' ministry lasts 1260 days, which is the same period as the forty-two months. Jesus called these the "*days of vengeance* (Luke 21:22)."This period of three and a half years is a literal number I believe, but the symbolic meaning of a broken seven needs consideration. Seven is symbolic of completeness or fullness. Three and a half being a broken seven may represent a breach of covenant whereby judgment is forthcoming. Israel rejected the Messiah Yahweh sent. Now after 40 years of grace, the city and the temple are set for destruction. James was correct when he wrote, "*The judge is standing at the door* (James 5:9)."

Third, these witnesses move in supernatural power. Fire flows from their mouths. They shut up the sky and stopped it from raining. The word of God is like fire, coming from the prophets of God. The word burns away what is unclean and brings judgment upon evil.

Fourth, the witnesses die and then experience resurrection. The story line now gets even more difficult to understand. They die by the hand of the "*the beast*." The beast is likely a reference to Rome in general, and Nero specifically. They lie in the streets for three and a half days (interesting number) and then experience a resurrection to life and ascend to heaven. If we interpret the witnesses as real individuals who lived in Jerusalem, then is this coming back from the dead real as well? On the other hand, does

---

[149] David Chilton, Days of Vengeance, Dominion Press, Ft. Worth, Texas, 1987,page 276

their resurrection symbolize Jesus' death and resurrection? Herein lies the problem; we have no record of any resurrections of individuals during this period of history. However, we do have a historic record of one witness who cried out during the three and half years of judgment.This may not be the "witnesses" spoken of by the book of Revelation, but is a historic record that reveals a similar pattern.

Josephus writes about a man, Jesus son of Ananus, who for a total of seven years and five month walked the streets of Jerusalem crying out a warning. He began four years before the war and continued throughout the 42 months of the war. This was his cry, "A voice from the east, a voice from the west, a voice from the four winds, a voice against Jerusalem and the holy house, a voice against the bridegrooms and the brides, and a voice against this whole people." [150] Josephus records his death but not any resurrection.

Over the years, many have stated their preference for the identity of the two witnesses. These include the law and prophets, Jesus and John, Enoch and Elijah, and numerous others. The degree of symbolic language used in this passage should keep us from being overly dogmatic in our interpretation. What seems clear is that it refers to a time in history. We should no longer be looking for possible "witnesses" in our day.

Study Questions

1. Why do you think many Christians today are fascinated with knowing who these "two witnesses" are?

2. Explain how the book of Zechariah is important in understanding the two witnesses.

3. Why is it difficult to be sure who these two witnesses are?

4. Discuss your conclusions about these two witnesses.

---

[150] Josephus, The Works of Josephus, Translated by William Whiston, Hendrickson Publishers, Peabody, MA., 1987, page 742

Chapter 26

The Work of the Kingdom

It may be advantageous in a 100-meter race to start at the 50-meter line. Winning is certain with this strategy, but races are not conducted this way. Likewise, biblical eschatology begins, not in Revelation but in the book of Genesis. Creating our views of the end times solely on the book of Revelation is likely to result in a distorted view of things. Our first step begins in Genesis.

Biblical exegesis works best when it builds progressively through God's word. By the time we get the last book, we will be lost unless we have a solid knowledge of the Old Testament Scriptures. By building our eschatology from Genesis, we hope to avoid missing key ingredients of the overall biblical message. A key missing ingredient found early in Genesis is the cultural mandate. The church is here to win souls and transform culture. With this in mind, the rest of Scripture makes more sense.

The church is not going anywhere. The church is not leaving planet earth. God has not revealed any plan that takes all believers to heaven at once. The church is on the earth for a purpose; we are here to experience Christ's kingdom and work towards its growth. We must put away living only for the present, and build upon spiritual and institutional structures that will endure for generations. The church will be on the earth for a very long time.

For years, Christian parents ignored their pastors teaching on the soon coming of Jesus and directed their children towards university education or some type of life preparation. Even though the pastors sermon on Matthew 24 told the congregation they are going up soon (no longer than five-ten years is the standard), many evangelical parents set that aside when wanting a better life for their children. If Jesus really were coming soon, would any serious minded young person spend six years to get a Masters degree in engineering? How about a Ph. D. in history? Of course not! Would any sensible young person begin a long apprenticeship as a master electrician? Yet these careers and thousands of others are vital for kingdom advancement. Most careers take a number of years for preparation. Yet many young evangelicals are choosing a short-term strategy.Better to work at the corner fast food chain, attend as many revival services as possible and wait for the world to end. The problem is that in ten years you are almost 30, married with two kids and still working for minimum wage. Our eschatology matters.

Genesis 1:3-5

Let there be light, and there was light. And God saw that the light was good. And God separated the light from the darkness. God called the light Day, and the darkness he called Night. And there was evening and there was morning, the first day.

In Genesis, we learn that God is the creator. This God, being the creator of all things, is the one and true God. As God brought forth Israel as a covenant nation, the truth that their God is the creator has far-reaching implications. If the God of Israel is the God of creation, then all other gods are false. The God of Israel is the God of the entire world. The mission of making Israel a covenant people was in preparation for Messiah's arrival, when all people are included. The kingdom of God reaches across all barriers and unites a redeemed people with their God and creator.

God is the creator. He created with purpose. Our existence and universe are not by accident. The narrative in Genesis quickly gets to the main point; God created the earth (and maybe even the entire universe) so that his special creation of human beings may have charge over it. The human race is specifically designed to inhabit the earth. In addition, God's created world is designed for us. We are earthlings-and this is vital in knowing the purpose of God's kingdom. The concept that "this world is not my home, I'm just passing through" is poor theology and distorts eschatology. God has no plans to destroy his creation again (Genesis 8:21). We are on a path towards renewing of all creation until the knowledge of God covers the earth.

Ask Christians about their plans for eternity and heaven will be the overwhelming choice. Christians have adopted a view that our physical bodies have little value and we as a "soul" will spend eternity, as a puff of smoke in the presence of God. Now even as a puff of smoke in God's presence is a good thing, nevertheless, it fails to see the reason for the creation of the earth. It was the Greeks, not the Jews who believed humans are only immortal souls and go into the next life as bodiless spirits. This Old Testament people believed in the resurrection of the dead. For most of Christian history, we believed in the resurrection of the dead. Resurrection means bodies, physical beings that work, eat, and have full use of their senses of touch, taste, smell, hearing and sight. We are created for this world, any time away from it is temporary.

If God wanted a new type of being to live with him in heaven (different from angels), He could have just created a space in heaven for us, no need for a physical creation. The earth is for humans to live in, to create, to exercise dominion and do what is necessary to fill the earth with the knowledge of God.

Rest assured, if you die before the sun sets, and you are confessing Jesus as the Son of God and believe God raised him from the dead; your immediate place is with the Lord in heaven. I just believe that is not the end of the story.

Made in His Image

Genesis 1:26-28

"Then God said, "Let us make man in our image, after our likeness. And let them have dominion over the fish of the sea and over the birds of the heavens and over the livestock and over all the earth and over every creeping thing that creeps on the earth. So God created man in his own image, in the image of God he created him; male and female he created them. And God blessed them. And God said to them, 'Be fruitful and multiply and fill the earth and subdue it and have dominion over the fish of the sea and over the birds of the heavens and over every living thing that moves on the earth."

The details of creation are crucial for eschatology. Because we are made in the image of God, this truth is foundational to our mandate. What is our mandate? It is a call to exercise dominion over the earth. This ability to rule derives from God. We are in his image. We are to be God's image bearers. Author Gabe Lyons on Genesis 1:26-28.

"Knowing God's image exists in every human being explains why all of us-not just Christians-know how to love and be generous, creative, kind, and caring. As people naturally seek to know where they have come from and what they were made to enjoy, the good design of creation explains a lot. For one thing, creation shows us how things ought to be. Our fascination with beauty, hunger for relationships, bent towards goodness and justice, and longing for connection with a transcendent God are all clues about our origins. Consider the innocence, idealism, and bigger-than-life dreams that come so easily to children. These ideas are hard-wired into every individual made in God's image."[151]

The Kingdom and Culture

This living as image bearers leads us to culture. Culture includes the work of our hands and minds. We create culture for good or bad. Reflecting God's image is what drives us to pursue something greater. We want to explore the world we live in. We want to create something never seen before.

The connection between kingdom and culture is key for Christians committed to a transformational gospel. Some (mostly dispensationalists) claim culture is beyond the responsibility of the church; Christians should be winning the lost not attempting any cultural changes. Leithart explores the theological ramifications of the kingdom and culture.

"Thus, the kingdom of God is indirectly, but inevitably related to human culture. It is in the kingdom of God that men are redirected to the fulfillment of the original mandate for human history: to know God and to share in His rule over the earth. The kingdom is not Christian civilization. Without the kingdom of

---

[151] Gabe Lyons, The Next Christians, Doubleday, New York, 2010, p. 52

God, there would be no hope of Christian civilization. We might say that while the kingdom is not Christian civilization, one of the achievements of the kingdom is to produce Christian civilization, that is, an historical social order that reflects and ushers in the eternal and eschatological order of God's heavenly city."[152]

In practical terms, what does it mean for God's glory to cover the earth? What does it means for international relationships? What does it mean for the domestic economic plans of a nation? What does it mean for social and welfare programs? What does it mean for business, education, transportation, the arts, entertainment, the use of natural resources and scientific research? This is just the start. I am concerned that our religious ideas and rhetoric is far greater than our knowledge about what this all means. We have a lot to explore, learn, and pass on to the next generation.

The truth is that few Christians even ask these questions; nevertheless arrive at the answers. When I ask these types of questions of Christian leaders, I often get the standard answer, "God will work those things out." God has done his part already. He gave us His Word and His Holy Spirit, and He expects His people to move with intelligence, wisdom, and compassion. He expects us to use all of the spiritual resources He has given us. Without getting into lots of theological terms, too many Christians who understand the present day Kingdom and work for its advancement in the earth, still think like dispensationalists when it comes to the practical outworking of the Kingdom. We still want God to show up and make everything right. This is not Kingdom thinking, this is escapism thinking. It is time for a change!

Many Christian leaders in 5-fold ministry feel inadequate when discussing anything outside of their expertise. Our training is not as scientists, engineers, educators or business people so we keep everything in religious and spiritual expressions. Our training is in spiritual realities and biblical knowledge. As a 5-fold minister

---

[152] Peter J. Leithart, The Kingdom of God, Biblical Theology Article from www.beginingwithmoses.org

trained in the Bible, ministry and theology, I know very little about the arts and entertainment, medical research, transportation systems and thousands of other areas; and that is ok.pastor's and those in the ministry of the word of God, must have as a goal, to raise people up who will enter these fields as a kingdom ministry. Pastors are best when they stick to theology, biblical preaching and shepherding. By their teaching, they should be inspiring people to achieve great things in their field of calling.

As a young pastor, I made the mistake of evaluating spirituality with people's interest. I can spend the entire evening and the next day talking about God, the Bible and the church. When I was around believers who were not interested in talking about "spiritual" stuff all the time, I saw it as a lack of commitment to the faith. Now I realize it had little to do with 'spirituality' but with their calling in life. Being a Christian does not mean we all have the same passions and dreams. Some people love to talk business by the hours, some educational strategies, some solving mathematical and engineering problems; others imagine what future transportation systems may look like. God calls people into different fields and puts desires in their heart for their chosen fields. My calling is full time church leadership, so if I did not find myself drawn to the "spiritual topics" something would be wrong. Finding the pearl of great price creates a love for God and creates the right balance in our life. Too many pastors and church leaders keep the saints so busy attending church services, there is little time to pursue their calling. There must be a balance.

Seeking first the kingdom of God cannot be a shallow life of Bible quoting. God wants us to be good husbands, wives, parents, bosses, friends, pastors and employees. People need to invest in their life and calling. We need to be prepared, work hard and then allow God to exalt us at the proper time.

Christians must embrace the concept of transforming culture. The root of transformation and influence is the family. John Barber; "God does not expect the culture to orient to the family. God expects the family to orient the culture to Christ. In the new Christian activism, the family will be seen as a catalyst for change in an immoral world. Families act as God's principle instruments for subduing the earth in righteousness as parents raise up and disciple their children. By obeying the cultural mandate, Godly families help to transform every sphere of society and culture. [153] Those who have children; this is where it all begins. This is the work we must do. This is our challenge and joyful commission from God.

What is Filioque?

Our discussion now takes us back into history to see how one word helps in understanding our work in the kingdom. Let me quote theologian Millard J. Erickson for some history, "During the medieval period there was little emphasis on the Holy Spirit. In part, this was due to relative disinterest in the experiential aspect of the Christian life, which is, of course, the special domain of the Holy Spirit. The one major issue that did arise within this period concerned the insertion of the word *filioque* into the creeds"[154] One of the great weaknesses of Pentecostal/charismatic churches is their failure to educate their congregations on basic church history (or individual believers taking the initiative themselves). The Azusa street revival of 1906 was not the start of church history. We know little about the events and developments of 1900 years of church life, and we know far less about creeds. Somehow, we have mistakenly believed that Christian creeds and Spirit-filled Christianity have little in common. This needs to change.

Filioque is Latin for "and the Son." It was included into the creeds and created quite a stir. The result was the largest church split ever occurring, the split between western and eastern Christianity. The meaning of "filioque" is that the Holy Spirit proceeds from the Father "*and from the Son*." Churches in the east found this word not to their liking and the controversy grew. The east maintained that the Father was the 'sole rule' and any

---

[153] John Barber, Earth Restored, Christian focus Publications, United Kingdom, 2002, page 90

[154] Millard J. Erickson, Christian Theology, Baker Books, Grand Rapids, Michigan, page 868

language that elevated the Son into a place of authority and rule equal to the Father was unscriptural. For the eastern leaders Father God was the sole root and cause of deity. The western fathers insisted that "filioque" was vital to stop the advances of Arianism. This was not the only doctrinal issue between east and west but it was a significant one.

Most Evangelical's find their historical roots in the protestant reformation that continued to endorse the inclusive of "filioque" as an important doctrinal position. The truth that Jesus is part of the "sending" process is Scriptural.

John 14:16-17

And I will ask the Father, and he will give you another Helper, to be with you forever, [17] even the Spirit of truth, whom the world cannot receive, because it neither sees him nor knows him. You know him, for he dwells with you and will be in you.

John 15:26

But when the Helper comes, whom I will send to you from the Father, the Spirit of truth, who proceeds from the Father, he will bear witness about me.

John 14:26

These things I have spoken to you while abiding with you. But the Helper, the Holy Spirit, whom the Father will send in My name, He will teach you all things, and bring to your remembrance all that I said to you.

Jesus states that the Father will send the Spirit, and later He says, "*I will send*" the Spirit. Then in another verse He says that the Spirit "*whom the Father will send in My name.*" This should not confuse us; we see this type of language in dealing with other areas where there is an involvement in different members of the Trinity. The Bible states that Jesus is seated on David's throne, His Fathers throne and on His throne. Which throne is Jesus seated? He is seated on all of them because they are the same throne, just different expressions connecting us to different aspects of His reign. Likewise, both the Father and Jesus are involved in sending the Spirit.

I believe it is vital that we see the Spirit proceeding from the Son. Since Jesus Christ has already resurrected and has ascended into the place of a King, the Spirit is now working to subdue all things to Christ. Jesus is the God-man. Through the resurrection, God lifts up the natural and physical elements of life and assigns them a place in the Kingdom. Whereas Eastern Christianity grew more mystical and "other worldly," western Christianity gives "physicality" a prominent role in the growth of the Kingdom.

The principle of "filioque" (from the Son) gives the ascended Christ the power, dominion, and the Kingdom. It assures us that the Kingdom of God will touch not just the mystical or spiritual elements in this world but the Kingdom will touch all areas of life.

Because of the word "filioque", Christianity is a faith for this world not just the next. We believe in changing cultures because of "filioque." We believe in education because of "filioque." We believe in good government because of "filioque." We believe in business because of "filioque." We believe in Christian institutions because of "filioque." The result is that we believe that our life "in the flesh" (physical, not our carnal nature) can be used to glorify God and advance His Kingdom.

The work of the kingdom is vast. Its scope is beyond what anyone has even thought or dreamed. God is looking for those who can step beyond the norm and create, build and bring into society new methods, inventions, and theologies, all for the betterment of society.

Yet, we must keep in mind it begins with making disciples one by one, house by house, city by city and finally the nations. Let us not trap new believers into a religious mindset where everyone has the single calling of evangelism. The work of the kingdom is advancing culture in every area of life.

Study Questions

1. Explain the meaning of the word, "filioque" and its historical importance?

2. How can the church build institutional structures that will last generations?

3. What is the role of the Christian family in long-term cultural transformation?

4. What is the relationship between creation and eschatology?

5. What are the theological and practical implications of Eastern Christianity being more mystical and 'other worldly' than most protestant churches?

Chapter 27

Glorious Kingdom

We have covered the kingdom of God and eschatology from numerous passages. We have read quotes from some of the best biblical scholars. We have entered theological debate and attempted to discern the Bible from good exegesis. We have stood on the shoulders of Isaiah, Daniel, Jeremiah, Jesus and Paul and saw the kingdom through their words. We now understand the importance of a kingdom centered eschatology. We now know that our view of the future effects decisions we make today. Eschatology must be applied. It must work in our real lives. We must live what we embrace. We must walk what we talk.

A final Scripture comes from the book of Hebrews.

Hebrews 12:18-24

For you have not come to what may be touched, a blazing fire and darkness and gloom and a tempest [19]and the sound of a trumpet and a voice whose words made the hearers beg that no further messages be spoken to them. [20]For they could not endure the order that was given, "If even a beast touches the mountain, it shall be stoned." [21]Indeed, so terrifying was the sight that Moses said, "I tremble with fear." [22]But you have come to Mount Zion and to the city of the living God, the heavenly Jerusalem, and to innumerable angels in festal gathering, [23]and to the assembly of the firstborn who are enrolled in heaven, and to God, the judge of all, and to the spirits of the righteous made perfect, [24]and to Jesus, the mediator of a new covenant, and to the sprinkled blood that speaks a better word than the blood of Abel.

The old covenant is gone; the new has come. We now live in Zion; the city of our great king. We now live in the heavenly city; the New Jerusalem. Old Jerusalem has gone and the new creation is here. Most of all, we have come to God and his Son, Jesus. This is the kingdom.

If we only learn information about eschatology then we miss the point. The message must change our hearts. The message must change and renew our minds. The kingdom is more than a list of wonderful events in the future. The kingdom is a lifestyle. It must be lived every day.

The kingdom of Christ is here! The kingdom of Christ is advancing. We live in a glorious kingdom.

Comprehensive Study Questions

1. When did the kingdom of God come to earth? Use at least five Scriptures in building your argument.

2. What are the results of dispensational eschatology over the last 100 years?

3. What term did the biblical writers use to speak of the ending of the old covenant and its temple worship? Give three or more Scriptures and discuss their meaning.

4. What does the Bible teach concerning the growth of the kingdom of God over time? Should we expect the church to gain members and increase our influence in the earth or will the church fail to disciple the nations and fall into apostasy?

5. What is your view of the nature of eternal life?

6. Explain the partial preterist view of the "coming" of Jesus in 70 A.D.?

7. What does the Bible teach about the antichrist?

8. Do we as Christians have a part of the Abrahamic and Davidic covenant? Provide Scripture for each and explain.

9. Why is it that many believers today have not heard of the victorious kingdom message?

10. What have you learned in this class and how will it help you in making life decisions?

Appendix 1

Definitions

Eschatology

Our definition of Eschatology comes from the Dictionary of Theological Terms. The Greek word "eschatos," is the foundation of the word eschatology. It means the last of an age. In theological studies, the doctrine of last things is part of systematic theology. Eschatology sets forth the truth that the history of the individual, of the race, and of the world will reach its appointed consummation. Individual eschatology covers the subjects of physical death, the immortality of the soul and the individual state. General eschatology covers the subjects of the second coming of Christ; the millennium, the resurrection of the dead and heaven and hell.[155]

Premillennialism

Premillennialism is the belief that the second coming of Jesus occurs before the 1,000-year millennial kingdom. Historic premillennial eschatology holds to a single coming of Christ, followed by the millennial kingdom.

Dispensational-Premillennialism

Dispensational-Premillennialism teaches Jesus comes in the clouds to receive Christians and takes them back to heaven. After the rapture, a period of seven years of tribulation takes place on the earth. After the seven years, the second coming of Jesus happens, returning to earth with the saints to set up the millennial kingdom that is to last 1,000 years. Key ingredients of this eschatology are the separation of Israel and the church, with different purposes. The millennium kingdom is primarily a Jewish kingdom where

---

[155] Alan Cairns, Dictionary of theological Terms, Ambassador Emerald International, Belfast/Greenville, 2002, page 148

Old Testament conditions return. A rebuilt temple is required and this includes animal sacrifices.

Amillennialism

Amillennial eschatology believes there is no clear biblical teaching concerning any millennium kingdom on the earth. There is NO millennium kingdom. The kingdom is the reign of God in heaven, not on the earth. Amillennialism teaches a single second coming of Christ, followed by the resurrection of the dead and the final judgment.

Postmillennialism

Postmillennial eschatology believes the Bible teaches the second coming of Christ occurs after the millennial kingdom, not before like Premillennialism. Postmillennial eschatology teaches Jesus established the kingdom of God during his first coming and it continues to grow throughout history. When the nations are discipled, the enemies of Christ defeated, and the knowledge of the glory of God covers the earth, then the second coming of Christ occurs. The resurrection of the dead and final judgment follows the Second Coming.

Older postmillennial scholars believed there would be a thousand years of peace and blessing before the Second Coming. Now, the vast majority of postmillennial scholars see the messianic kingdom beginning with the incarnation of Christ and ending with his Second Coming.

Partial-Preterism

Partial-Preterism is not a complete eschatological position. It is way of interpreting certain passages of Scripture dealing with eschatological themes. Preterism means "past fulfillment." Partial-Preterism interprets "part" of the biblical passages dealing with eschatology as having already been fulfilled, primarily in the first century. These would include the circumstances of the last days and the great tribulation. Most partial-preterism holds to a future coming of Christ, the resurrection of the dead and final judgment. Most postmillennialists and those advocating victorious eschatology use partial-preterism as a tool of interpreting prophecy.

Full-Preterism

Full-Preterism is the belief that all prophesies concerning the second coming of Christ and surrounding eschatological events, including the resurrection of the dead and final judgment were fulfilled in the events of 70 A.D. There is nothing in Scripture that predicts any event past the first century.

Appendix 2

The Christ Event

Seven Steps of the Kingdom

There are seven major eschatological significant events enacted by Jesus that results in the full expression of the kingdom on earth. Once all seven were completed in history, the age of the old passes away and the age to come arrives.

1. Birth of Jesus

The birth of Jesus is the most important birth in human history. None can compare. His birth stands alone as the miracle of God to save the world. Jesus' birth, as humble as it was, is the beginning step in the coming of the God's kingdom in the first century. His birth was eschatological in that it was the beginning of the age to come. It was the start of God's redemptive plan to renew all creation.

If God's kingdom is the center of his redemptive plan, then the birth of Jesus is the genesis of everything. Everything in life experienced the effect of Jesus' birth. He changed history. He changed the world.

2. Life and Teachings of Jesus

We cannot skip over the life of Jesus. Evangelicals must plead guilty for the last few decades of almost ignoring the life and teaching of Jesus in favor of his death. The past tendency for mainline Protestants to use the gospels to preach a "social gospel" was more than enough to push evangelicals away from the life of Jesus to almost inclusive focusing on his death.

The four gospels present the story of Jesus. We have the unusual circumstance of having four different accounts of a single story. Instead of despairing over the extra work needed to form a "synoptic" gospel, we should delight in the slight differences, as this is how God chose to tell his story.From the opening pages and continuing to the end, one central message emerges, the kingdom of God. The message of the kingdom may be the reason we see a decline of preaching from the gospels.We are not sure what to make of this "kingdom of God." How should we preach it? Did it arrive with Jesus and then disappear? Is it here now? If the kingdom arrived with the announcement of John the Baptist; then why then is it also in future tenses? It is easier to preach out of Ephesians; at least we think.

Seeing the shape of the New Testament depends greatly on understanding the kingdom of God. Our exegesis must not be lazy here lest we end up with some strange views. Many of us were taught God's kingdom was primarily a future event. We called it the millennial kingdom. Therefore, since this kingdom language is mostly for the future and has little bearing on the Christian life, it is better to stick with Paul and the rest of the New Testament.

The gospels are important. They tell us about Jesus and his message. The problem for some of us is that we have neglected the message of Jesus and only focused on his life, mainly his death. The death of Jesus on the cross is of the upmost importance, yet if separated from his message, we lose the impact of what God did for us through Jesus. Yes, we have the forgiveness of sins by the death of Jesus. It does not stop there. Because of the work on the cross, we have access to his kingdom. We now live in a new age. We live in the time where all things spoken of in the past are now coming true.

Is the kingdom of God a realm or a reign? Discussions on these questions continue because of its importance in understanding the basic nature of the kingdom. Is the kingdom like entering a room or is it a subject bowing to a king? If it is a room, then all within the "realm" are in the kingdom, regardless of their salvation status. On the other hand, if the kingdom of God is a reign over the lives of believers, then it is correct to see the church as the full expression of God's kingdom on earth. Yet, is not the kingdom larger than the church?

This argument pits realm verse reign as opposing Scriptural definitions and this is the problem. The Bible does not give us an exact definition of the kingdom; except maybe in Romans 14:1, "For the kingdom of God is not a matter of eating and drinking but of righteousness and peace and joy in the Holy Spirit," and this is not an inclusive statement. Instead of seeing the kingdom as either a realm to enter or a reign to submit to, we need to conclude the Scripture portrays the kingdom as both.

3. The Death of Jesus on the Cross

The cross is the payment for entrance into the kingdom. Without Jesus' sacrifice on the cross, we are still in our sins and without hope. The criticism that preaching the kingdom diminishes the cross is a position without biblical support. The cross and the kingdom are part of one gospel; the good news that the Messiah and his kingdom have come. The cross is the path Jesus suffered to insure God's promise for his people and the earth.

When Jesus offered the kingdom to the first century Israel, would Jesus have avoided the cross if they had accepted? First, Israel as a nation rejected Jesus and his kingdom, so any other scenario is only speculation. Secondly, the question assumes a pathway to the kingdom not found in the writings of the New Testament authors. The path to the kingdom is the cross. Without the cross, there is no kingdom.

Upon arriving in Jerusalem, Jesus desires to keep the Old Testament feast of Passover by hosting the meal. The meal in itself was a familiar event for the disciples, rooted deep into Jewish culture and faith. It was a yearly reminder of how Yahweh delivered his people from the slavery of Egypt. In the prepared room, Jesus and his chosen participants followed the standard sequence of the Passover meal. Four glasses of wine and unleavened bread were the centerpiece of the meal.

Christians often overlook the context of Old Testament expectations. The standard line that "Jesus died for my sins so I may go to heaven" would be foreign to first century believers. Salvation so that we can live in heaven was not the message of the early believers; it was about God's kingdom is here, Jesus is Lord, and one day we will rise from the dead. When Jesus took the final

Passover meal with his disciples, it was sign of his coming death and more.

When we partake of the Lord's Supper, we are directed back to the Passover Jesus held before his death. What is the purpose of this Passover meal? Bitre sees the Passover as an eschatological sign. "Clearly, if the Last Supper was in fact an eschatological meal in which Jesus reconfigured the Passover sacrifice around the offering of his own body and blood-especially if he did so in the presence of the Twelve disciples, representing the twelve tribes of Israel (Mark 14:17, Luke 22:28-30)-the implications of such an act would have been very clear. By means of this prophetic sign, Jesus was inaugurating an eschatological Passover that would do everything the first Passover had done, but which all those since the Exile had failed to do: atone for the sins of Israel, set in motion a New Exodus, and bring about the end of the Exile.[156]

Those living in the times of Jesus would have concluded, rightfully so, that a New Exodus, the end of the Jewish Exile and talk of a sacrificial death, all pointed towards the inaugurating of Yahweh's kingdom (the kingdom of God). The point Jesus makes, is that his death is the entry point for all their expectations. The disciples were confused when Jesus brought up the subject of his death (how can their Messianic king die), so this use of the Passover meal, may have brought some clarification to the conflicted followers of Jesus.

Could it be that all their hopes lie, not in protecting Jesus and keeping him alive, but in a path leading to his death? Can death bring about life? Can the end of their dreams of a restored Israel bring about hope for the entire world?

The cross is central to our Christian faith. The cross leads us to the kingdom. Even though we preach the kingdom, it is through the cross and being "born again (John 3:3)" that we enter the kingdom.

---

[156] Brant Pitre, Jesus, The Tribulation, and the end of Exile, Baker Academic, Grand Rapids, Michigan, 2005, page 448

4. The Resurrection of Jesus

With the resurrection of Jesus, we have God's verification that the Messiah's vicarious death is accepted. The cross was successful in paying the full penalty for sin. Jesus once for all paid the penalty for sin; therefore, any type of "sin offering" is an abomination to God. The resurrection is the first step in the exaltation of Jesus, which empowers him to reign in the kingdom. Because of the resurrection, Jesus sits on David's throne in heaven.

5. The Ascension of Jesus

When Jesus ascended into heaven He enters as the "God-man." Divinity and humanity merged in one body, Jesus the Christ. At the ascension, Jesus received all power, glory and the kingdom. The ascension is a major eschatological shift.

6. The Power of Pentecost

Pentecost is important for its eschatological significance. The kingdom of God comes not by human power or might but by the Spirit. The arrival of the Spirit on the day of Pentecost marks the beginning of the gospel's proclamation regarding the fullness of power. The fullness of power is now in the people by means of the Spirit. Pentecost is about the kingdom of God.

7. The Spiritual Coming of Jesus in 70 A.D.

When Jerusalem burned along with its temple, we must remember this event fulfills the wrath of God Jesus prophesied to the Jewish leaders. It is not just a random war brought about by the Roman lust for power. God uses Rome as his weapon of judgment upon fruitless Israel. It is significant as it is the last eschatological event establishing the kingdom of God on earth. There is nothing more to wait for. God's kingdom is on the earth; and its continuous growth over the generations is certain.

Appendix 3

Why I am Not a Full-Preterist

I have been hesitant to enter the debate between partial and full preterists for good reasons. First, combined together, both positions are a small minority compared with dispensational eschatology. My primary concern is for those remaining within the grasp of dispensationalism and the escapist's mentality, which has brought great harm to the church. I have written on God's victorious kingdom in relation to partial-preterism. The next 20-30 years may see some coming together from both preterists groups, or we may not. Certainly, studies must continue and the areas of difference intensely examined. Theology is a process that takes time. Let us not react in haste, let the debate continue. As partial and full preterists in non-Charismatic groups call each other heretics and worse, I would like to hope that within the Pentecostal/charismatic church we could find a better path to resolve differences. We want truth. Let us work together and show that the Holy Spirit does make a difference.

With this said some aspects of full-preterism are not acceptable and therefore a caution sign needs to be constructed.

1. No Messianic Kingdom

According to full-preterists, we are left without Scripture to advise or lead us in the present state. All promises were fulfilled in 70 A.D.   Therefore, the promise of a glorious reign of Christ (which in my view is the present kingdom of God) is over, ending with the destruction of Jerusalem.   Since I am committed to kingdom-centered eschatology, I cannot accept the great kingdom of Christ is only 40 years in length. According to full preterists, all the promises of God's kingdom are fulfilled by 70 A.D. We do not live in the age of the messianic kingdom but in some unknown uncharted age that never ends. We have no promise that the world will get better or even worse, we have no direction from the

Scripture about anything happening now or in our future. This is unacceptable and counters a host of Scriptures.

2. No End to Sin and Death

The sin that cost Jesus his life continues forever. Although defeated in principle in the cross, its power continues. Since everything is fulfilled, no event in the future can change the present status of sin in the world. Sickness, disease and sorrows of all types continue indefinitely. The veil between heaven and earth may be thin but will always remain.

3. No Resurrection of the Dead

The full-preterists position is that a spiritual resurrection occurs at each believer's death. There is not a final general resurrection of the dead in the future.

4. No Holy Spirit

According to a leading full-preterist, Ed Stevens˙, the ministry of the Holy Spirit ended in 70 A.D. There are evangelicals with cessationists' views (that the supernatural gifts and ministries ceased after the apostolic era) but Stevens goes further, much further. The Holy Spirit no longer abides in Christians. This should cause all believers and especially those of charismatic persuasion to examine seriously the results of full-preterist logic. True, Stevens does not speak for all full-preterists, but he is a leading advocate and therefore his views must be considered.

Stevens, "Christ Has Returned – He is here now to stay – He will never leave again. We will live in His presence forever. Jesus the High Priest has returned out of the Holy of Holies (heaven) to manifest the fact that Final Atonement has been made. How many times does Christ need to make atonement and come back out of heaven to proclaim it? The idea of multiple comings just does not fit the picture here (Hebrews 9). Now we have a better indwelling than what the transition period saints had. They had the miraculous indwelling and empowering of the Holy Spirit. We have Christ

Himself dwelling with us and in us."[157] According to Stevens the indwelling and empowering of the Holy Spirit was only for the transition period (from Pentecost to 70 A.D). In my mind, this follows the logical assumptions of full-preterism to an extreme position.

157 Ed Stevens, Doctrinal Implications of Preterist Eschatology, http://www.preterist.org/articles-ol...plications.htm

Appendix 4

Israel and the Land

The subject of Israel and the promise of the land stir emotions in many Christians. Teachings concerning the restoration of the Jews to their land in the "last days" have resulted in millions of dollars given to relocate Jews back to Israel. Is this a worthy project? Is this fulfillment of biblical prophecy? Our point here is simple; to offer an alternate.

Genesis 12:1-3

Now the LORD said to Abram, "Go from your country and your kindred and your father's house to the land that I will show you. ² And I will make of you a great nation, and I will bless you and make your name great, so that you will be a blessing. ³ I will bless those who bless you, and him who dishonors you I will curse, and in you all the families of the earth shall be blessed

From our previous study of Abraham, it is now necessary to take up the question of the land. Abraham received a promise of land and this becomes part of the Abrahamic covenant. Should Christians support Jews returning to Israel? Is the promise of land spoken of to Abraham still unfulfilled? Many think so, yet a Scripture found in Joshua points in a different direction.

Joshua 21:43-45

Thus the LORD gave to Israel all the land that he swore to give to their fathers. And they took possession of it, and they settled there. And the LORD gave them rest on every side just as he had sworn to their fathers. Not one of all their enemies had withstood them, for the LORD had given all their enemies into their hands. Not one word of all the good promises that the LORD had made to the house of Israel had failed; all came to pass.

The Bible states Israel possessed all the land. Everything promised came true. This may be one of the most overlooked passages in the Scripture. The promise to Abraham concerning the land is fulfilled. It is God who determines when a prophecy is completed or not, not our theology or our system of eschatology.

Yet the meaning goes deeper because God's intentions are beyond blessing a small piece of land, but it includes the entire earth. The word came to Abraham that every family in the earth would benefit from his promise and covenant. We have already seen from our study in the book of Galatians how the New Testament brings gentiles into the promises of the Old Testament. Paul in Romans 4 expands the "land issue" beyond the original promise to Abraham.

Romans 4:13

For the promise to Abraham and his offspring that he would be heir of the world did not come through the law but through the righteousness of faith.

God's intention has always been greater than the physical space taken up by Israel. In Christ all the promises of Abraham are true. Through Christ, we are heirs to the entire world.

Numbers 14:2

But indeed, as I live, all the earth will be filled with the glory of the Lord.

The plan of God is to fill the earth with his glory. This takes place not beyond time but within time and history. It is progressive; it grows from generation to generation. Matthew 28 commands us to make disciples of all nations. This is beyond preaching the gospel in each nation; it means a culture of obeying biblical principles. We are instructed to bring the nations to a place of submission to all that Christ taught. It begins with evangelism, but winning the lost is only the start. The promise began with Abraham and a small part of land; it ends with the entire world.

Bibliography

Oswald T. Allis, Prophecy and the Church, Phillipsburg, Presbyterian and Reformed, 1972

Alan Cairns, Dictionary of Theological Terms, Belfast/ Greenville, Ambassador Emerald International, 2002

Grady Brown, That All May be Fulfilled, Bryan, Daysprings Publishing, 2006,

L.S. Chafer, Dispensationalism, Dallas, Dallas Seminary Press, 1936

David Chilton, Paradise Restored, Tyler, Reconstruction Press, 1985

John J. Collins, The Apocalyptic Imagination, Grand Rapids, William B. Eerdmans, 1988,

Gary DeMar, Francis X. Gumerlock, The Early Church and the end of the World, Powder Springs, American Vision, 2006

Gary DeMar, Last Day Madness, Atlanta, American Vision, 1997

Millard J. Erickson, Christian Theology, Grand Rapids, Baker Books, 1983

Gordon D. Fee, Douglas Stuart, How to Read the Bible for All its Worth, Grand Rapids, Zondervan, 2003

Wayne Grudem, Systematic Theology, Leicester, InterVarsity Press, 1994

Gabe Lyons, The Next Christians, New York, Doubleday, 2010

Richard Kyle, The Last Days Are Here Again, Grand Rapids, Baker Books, 1998

Michael W. Holmes, ed., The Apostolic Fathers: Greek Texts and English Translations, rev. ed., Grand Rapids, Baker Books, 1992

Peter J. Leithart, Deep Exegesis, Waco, Baylor University Press, 2009

Peter J. Leithart, From Behind the Veil, Monroe, Athanasius Press, 2009

Charles Caldwell Ryrie, Dispensationalism Today, Chicago, Moody Press, 1965

Charles C. Ryrie, The Basis of the Premillennial Faith, Loizeaux Brothers

Keith A. Mathison, Postmillennialism an Eschatology of Hope, Phillipsburg, P&R Publishing, 1999

Keith A. Mathison, From Age to Age, Phillipsburg, P&R Publishing, 2009

Dave Macpherson, The Incredible Cover-Up, Plainfield, Logos International, 1975

Milton S. Terry, Biblical Hermeneutics, Grand Rapids, Academie Books Zondervan Publishing House

John Noe, Beyond the End Times, Bradford, Preterists Resources, 1999

Vern S. Poythress, God-Centered Biblical Interpretation, Phillipsburg, P&P Publishing, 1999

Andrew Sandlin, A Postmillennial Primer, Chalcedon Foundation, 1997 C. Jonathan Seraiah, The End of All Things: A Defense of the Future, Moscow, Canon Press, 1999

J. Stuart Russell, The Parousia, Grand Rapids, Baker Books, 1999

J. Rodman Williams, Renewal Theology, Grand Rapids, Zondervan Publishing House, 199

N.T. Wright, Jesus and The Victory of God, Minneapolis, Fortress Press, 1996

C. Michael Patton, Case Studies In Inerrancy, http://www.reclaimingthemind.org/blog, 2010

About the Author

Stan Newton – A graduate of Moody Bible Institute and has received his Doctorate of Ministry from Vision International University. He served as a pastor for over 20 years in the United States before relocating to Europe. Along with his wife Virginia, they founded Kingdom Missions and now live in Bulgaria where they continue their calling to teach and demonstrate the kingdom of God. They have two married sons and four grandchildren. You may contact them by mail or e-mail.

Kingdom Missions
PO Box 731988
Puyallup, WA. 98373
svnewton@hotmail.com

Lightning Source UK Ltd.
Milton Keynes UK
UKOW06f1142010416

271309UK00010B/162/P

9 781615 290475